D0266539

MY STIR-FRIED LIFE

Selected works by Ken Hom

Truffles (with Pierre-Jean Pébeyre) (Serindia Contemporary, 2014)
**Winner Gourmand World Cookbook Award 2015 for Best Mushrooms (USA)

Exploring China: A Culinary Adventure (with Ching He Huang) (BBC Books, 2012)
**Winner Gourmand World Cookbook Award 2013 for Culinary Travel
**Shortlisted for The Guild of Food Writers Awards 2013 for both the Food
Broadcast of the Year Award and the Award for Work on Food and Travel

Complete Chinese Cookbook (BBC Books, 2011)

Ken Hom's Chinese Cookery: 25th anniversary edition (BBC Books, 2009)

Ken Hom's Quick Wok (Headline Books, 2001)
**Cookbook of the Year from Food & Wine magazine, USA

Ken Hom's Foolproof Chinese Cookery (BBC Books, 2000)

Easy Family Dishes: A Memoir with Recipes (BBC Books, 1998)
**Winner of the Andre Simon Memorial Book of Year 1998
**Winner Gourmand World Cookbook Awards Best in the World in Year 1998
in the category Best Chinese Cuisine Book

Ken Hom's Hot Wok (BBC Books, 1996)

Ken Hom's Illustrated Chinese Cookery (BBC Books, 1993)

The Taste of China (Pavilion Books, 1990)
**Shortlisted for Andre Simon Memorial Book of Year 1990

Ken Hom's East Meets West Cuisine (Macmillan, 1987)
**Shortlisted for Andre Simon Memorial Book of Year 1987

Ken Hom's Chinese Cookery (BBC Books, 1984)

Ken Hom's Encyclopaedia of Chinese Cookery Techniques (Ebury Press, 1984)

KEN HOM
MY STIR-FRIED LIFE

with

JAMES STEEN

The Robson Press

First published in Great Britain in 2016 by
The Robson Press (an imprint of Biteback Publishing Ltd)
Westminster Tower
3 Albert Embankment
London SEI 7SP
Copyright © Promo Group 2016

The Promo Group Ltd has asserted its right under the Copyright, Designs and
Patents Act 1988 to be identified as the copyright holder of this work.

ISBN 978-1-84954-978-3

10 9 8 7 6 5 4 3 2 1

A CIP catalogue record for this book is available from the British Library.

Cover image © Christian Develter www.christiandevelter.com

Set in Dante and BentonSans by Adrian McLaughlin
Icons made by Freepik from www.flaticon.com

Printed and bound in Great Britain by
CPI Group (UK) Ltd, Croydon CR0 4YY

MIX
Paper from
responsible sources
FSC
www.fsc.org   FSC® C020471

This book is dedicated with love and affection to
all the people of the United Kingdom who embraced me
and took me into their homes and especially their kitchens.
Thank you from the bottom of my heart!

Contents

Introduction

A COUPLE OF WEEKS ago I was in Bangkok, and in Departures at the airport. At check-in, there was a woman and her daughter in the same queue, and close enough for me to hear them as they chatted. The daughter said, 'Mum, look. It's the Dalai Lama.'

I turned and realised the daughter was nodding towards me. Well, if I were to be mistaken for anyone, I figured, let it be the highest-ranking monk of Tibetan Buddhism. I could not stop myself from smiling.

It was the third time, of which I am aware, that I had been confused for His Holiness. The first time was in a restaurant in London. The second occasion, coincidentally, was also at an airport, but in Arrivals; at a baggage carousel. 'Excuse me, are you the Dalai Lama?' a lady had asked me, as I tried to spy my suitcase amid the circling luggage. (Yes, just the type of place you'd expect to see the spiritual leader.)

At Bangkok's airport there was a twist. The daughter had pointed me out, but then the mother looked me up and down before she tutted and said, 'It's not the Dalai Lama, darling. It's only a cook.'

I *am* only a cook. I am only a cook and feel as if I am the luckiest person in the whole wide world. I have lived well. I have cooked almost incessantly and to my heart's content, and have eaten everything I have been offered, including insects and reptiles galore, although I also have cravings for fish and chips in Britain. The tastes of life from all corners of the globe I have relished. Marvellous experiences have been there for the taking, and I have taken them. I have wonderful friends and family. I am not an unhappy person.

As you read on, you will see that this is a story about food and its ability to inspire. It is the story of how food shaped my life, beginning as a child fed by a mother who had little but sacrificed all that she had. I was a minute speck in a tiny corner of Chicago, and part of the minority that kept themselves to themselves in Chinatown. Head down, button up. I did not set goals. That has never been my way. Instead, I relied on the virtuous belief, instilled in me by my mother and my Chinese-American relatives, that if I was good, then good things might happen to me. They did and they have. Thank God.

Of course, bad things have happened too. My father passed away before I had reached my first birthday. Often, however, I have felt that he is watching over me. That sense of reassurance was more frequent when I was young and craved fatherly guidance but lacked wisdom. Even though I grew up in an impoverished style, I do not regard the early years of my life as an enduring struggle. I was neither the wayward teenager nor the angry young man.

My formative years were spent as a wide-eyed pupil, not necessarily at school but learning from my mentors, who included my uncle Paul. He gave me a job in the kitchen of his restaurant when I was eleven. Through him I learnt, and throughout my life I have never stopped learning or wanting to learn. Curiosity, politeness and a decent meal have taken me onwards and, with the help of British Airways, upwards.

—

MY life has been one great, big stir-fry. In California, I taught cookery at my home to an audience hungry to learn about Chinese food and its folklore. In Hong Kong, I realised my dreams and for the first time felt accepted. I came to London for a ten-minute audition for a BBC series about Chinese food and cookery, the first of its kind.

It brought success I never dreamt I would have. Eight million woks have been sold, all with my name on them. I have been the author of thirty-five books (thirty-six now), many of them bestsellers. I have cooked for prime ministers and presidents, as well as a few of my childhood heroes.

Every day I reflect on my existence, and am grateful for what I have been given, and for what I have achieved, as well as travelling the world and meeting people who share my passion for food, cooking and life (even if they are not quite sure who I am).

Chi fan le mei. This is a Chinese greeting, and perfect for an introduction. The phrase is often heard when one person meets another. Translated literally, it means: *Have you eaten yet?* The phrase is the closest you can get to the Westerners' greeting: *How are you?* So even if food is not always in the mouths of the Chinese, it is often on their lips, in the form of words. *Chi fan le mei*. I certainly do hope that you have eaten, but either way you are about to get hungry.

1

Eating

THE KEY TURNING in the lock, and then the slam as the door closed. Two sounds I dreaded. They were followed by that high-pitched yell – 'I'm here!' – and next came the swish of her slippers as she walked towards the kitchen. I figured the cleaner had arrived again. I figured right, and her name was Mrs Kelly.

I was staying in a basement flat in Lincoln Street, just a minute's stroll from Sloane Square, Chelsea. My home was in California, where I had my own cookery school, but this was the summer of 1984 and I was here, in London, to film my first series for BBC Television.

This was a big deal. We were venturing into unknown television territory, and success was by no means guaranteed. The British were not well accustomed to shows about food and cookery, and this was to be the first of its kind devoted to Chinese food and cookery. As the presenter, and someone who had not previously appeared on television,

I was a little nervous and apprehensive. Therefore, I was determined to ensure the dishes were just right.

In Chelsea, I spent hours in the kitchen of the apartment, testing the food that I intended to cook the following day in the studio. There were stir-fried dishes of shellfish, as well as cashew chicken, sweet and sour pork and the majestic Peking duck, with its skin roasted brown and as crisp as parchment. I was content in that kitchen, darting about – stir-frying and steaming, creating and crafting, tasting and … and smiling. This contentment was interrupted twice a week by the key in the lock, the slam of the door – 'I'm here!' – followed by those banana-yellow slippers as they swished towards me.

When Mrs Kelly reached the entrance of the kitchen, I always knew what was to come. She'd grimace, tilt her scrunched-up nose to the ceiling, inhale – with considerable dramatic effect – and then say loudly, 'What's that muck I smell?'

What's that muck I smell? That was my food. Chinese food.

After two months of filming, the series was in the can and only a couple of months away from being broadcast. I thought, *Oh God, Mrs Kelly could have a point. What if this series bombs? I mean, maybe it's not going to fly … Maybe fifty people will watch it … And they'll switch it off after ten minutes. And sure, Mrs Kelly will not be one of them.*

Part of me wanted to lie in a dark room with a cold washcloth on my face. Instead, I hatched a plan to escape. I had to get out of London town, and out of the country. My plan coincided with the dollar being at a record high. So a few friends came over from California, and we set off on what would be a fantastic European road trip, gourmet style. Oh, there was a whole bunch of us: Ron Batori, Ted Lyman, Terri McGinnis and Susie Maurer.

The journey would turn out to be the trip of a lifetime, and took us through the cities and countryside of France, motoring in a rental car, stopping to eat amazing food and sip, and sip again, exceptional wines in Michelin-starred restaurants. Often these places had rooms, so we could simply haul ourselves from table to bed without exerting too much energy. We'd settle for two-star restaurants, but they were mostly three. And we reckoned they were virtually free because the healthy American buck could buy us so many French francs. None of us was rich but, for a brief period, we lived as if we owned the world. Or France, at the very least.

This was a mouth-watering adventure, through country lanes and over rickety hump-backed bridges, passing brightly speckled fields of lavender and forests of buried truffle treasures; all of it purely in the pursuit of exceptional gastronomy. And driving in the opposite direction to Mrs Kelly. As we hurtled along, we sang to the radio, every music station blasting out Stevie Wonder's hit of the summer, 'I Just Called to Say I Love You'...

——

WE were joined by a French friend, Yves Vidonne, who worked for the grand chef Joël Robuchon, and who would later become highly successful in the world of pâtisserie. Yves, in turn, invited his father to join us on the trip. Monsieur Vidonne knew all the best restaurants, and if we knew his first name we never used it. He was always Monsieur Vidonne.

At the first restaurant, we sat at a large, round table and, as the sommelier poured champagne into exquisite crystal flutes, Yves's father produced a small gold pill box from the inside pocket of his navy blazer. This box he carefully opened as if it were the world's most delicate object, and then he counted out the contents – little grey pills – onto the tablecloth. He passed around the pills, one for each of us, saying in whispered French, 'Take it. This pill means you can eat all you like, but will never gain weight.'

As he whispered, he patted his stomach; the wizard casting a magic spell. Monsieur Vidonne was quite heavy, by the way, but we were in awe of him. We all popped the pills and then spent the next few hours cheerfully tucking into six courses from heaven. Not one of us asked about the pills. We were too respectful to question the master. He assured us they were not illegal and, I assure you, they were not. Subsequently, at each fantastic restaurant M. Vidonne performed the same routine – pill box, grey pills, pat stomach, whisper, whisper, pass around, swallow, eat six courses (minimum).

This patriarch of the Vidonne clan possessed immense knowledge about food and wine and steered us towards the finest places of indulgence. He took us, for instance, to Georges Blanc's restaurant in Vonnas, an hour north of Lyon, the belly of France. There, we dined on house specialities such as *crêpes vonnassienne* – a generous spoonful of caviar is spread between two thin slices of salmon, and fried for merely a matter of seconds upon a fluffy crêpe made from potato purée. We ate Bresse chicken, that small, world-renowned bird, roasted to perfection and served with foie gras. From the incredible cellar – it contains 135,000 bottles of wine – we chose, among others, a spectacular bottle, or probably two, of Moulin-à-Vent from the 1964 vintage; purple, concentrated and suitably opulent for us, the young group from California who were feeling wealthy.

We went to Paul Bocuse's restaurant Auberge du Pont, just a couple of miles outside Lyon, and on the banks of the Saône. I must tell you that I may have been small but in those days I had an enormous appetite. I think I began with *Soupe aux truffes noires* (black truffle soup beneath a lid of golden, flaky pastry), which Bocuse created in the mid-'70s especially for the new President, Giscard d'Estaing. Then I ate a divine salad of lobster.

Now, I had also ordered *Volaille de Bresse truffée en vessie*. This is a famous Bocuse dish, which I had heard about. A whole Bresse chicken is poached in a pig's bladder, which swells into a big ball as it cooks. This bird-in-a-ball is carried to the table, and next comes the real theatre of it all: the bladder is burst by a waiter with a steady hand, and the chicken is carved and served on the plate, coated in a creamy sauce made more indulgent by the addition of small slices of black truffle.

On our visit, the waiter carried the chicken dish on a silver platter, and then burst the bladder in front of me. My senses were aroused. However, he gave me only a slice or two of the breast meat before taking the bird on the chopping board back to the kitchen. That was not supposed to happen. He was meant to give me the whole chicken. I felt cheated, so beckoned another waiter and said, 'I've only been served a bit of the chicken. I'm paying for a whole chicken – where's the rest of it, please?'

They quickly brought me the rest of the bird, and I ate every last succulent morsel on the plate. Later on we discovered that the restaurant was popular with Japanese tourists, who often ordered this *en vessie* dish but did not eat the whole chicken. The waiter thought I was Japanese.

In Les Baux-de-Provence, less than an hour's drive from Marseille, we lunched in style at Baumanière. The restaurant overlooks vineyards and rolling fields that inspired Van Gogh and Cezanne, although Terri lost her umbrella there. We bundled up masses of wild lavender to take home, optimists that we were. The flowers' scent was so overpowering that we almost choked. Five miles down the road, coughing and sneezing, we stopped to toss away the purple bundles.

The escapade went on, taking us from Arles to Moustiers, where we had a great meal at La Bastide, and then for a couple of nights in Eugenie-les-Bains, and Les Prés d'Eugénie, the restaurant of Michel Guérard, one of the founders of nouvelle cuisine. Every detail was perfect, and afterwards Susie said of the chef-patron, 'Did you see how Michel came through the dining room, made eye contact with everyone and made them feel very special and loved, but never slowed down one notch?' I nodded. One day in the future I would cook with the great Michel at Château d'Yquem.

We, too, did not slow down. As the villagers slept, we danced like tipsy angels in the narrow streets; I tried to be Fred Astaire to Susie's Ginger Rogers, and it was magical.

We drove to Château Raymond-Lafon, producer of the fine Sauternes, where we were entertained by cellar master Pierre Meslier from Château d'Yquem. Susie bought a magnum and carried it home like a baby, and we consumed it that *réveillon*. From there, we travelled to La Rochelle, and then, en route to Paris, we were hungry for more, so stopped at a few châteaux on the Loire, to dine beside the river.

In the French capital, we went to Yves's home, and to his kitchen and then his fridge, which he opened to reveal a few shelves of chilled champagne, Cristal no less. Corks popped, the party continued. We danced and sang and toasted life and living it to the full. Then we went for dinner at Taillevent, where Claude Deligne ruled the kitchen. The following lunchtime was spent at Joël Robuchon's restaurant Jamin, which had just won its third Michelin star.

I love cooking because I love eating. When the passion of eating is strong enough, you will want to cook.

RON had noted the name of Monsieur Vidonne's pills. About a decade later, he said to me in his soft Californian lilt, 'You remember the grey pills...'

I said, 'The grey pills that Yves's father passed around the tables in France?'

He said, 'That's them.'

'What about them, Ron?'

'I've found out what they were.'

'What were they?'

'Ken, those pills were laxatives.'

He said, in a sombre way, that it accounted for the moment when he felt stomach cramp on the streets of Paris, following lunch and a grey pill at Chez L'Ami Louis. He had made a dash to a public toilet ... but did not have a coin to pay for his entry. 'I would've paid a king's ransom to get into one,' said Ron.

As for grumbling Mrs Kelly, she was a fastidious, brilliant cleaner but she would have made a lousy controller of BBC Two. *Ken Hom's Chinese Cookery* began in October 1984, eight thirty-minute episodes running over eight weeks. It was a phenomenal hit. It launched my career and, ultimately, would lead to my mini industry in woks.

Yesterday I was back in London, which I adore with all my heart, and a young lady came up to me in the street to say, 'My earliest memories are watching my dad learn to cook with a Ken Hom wok.'

I was flattered. 'Those may be your earliest memories,' I said. 'Mine go back a little further.'

—

FOOD tells us who we are and where we come from. Food made my earliest memories, and not just food but the sheer excitement of being with others to share the enjoyment of eating.

Even though we were poor, we still managed to eat well. There were banquets – yes, there were banquets in Chicago's Chinatown – with dishes of plump pigeons, which my uncles, on my mother's side, would cook with great skill.

There were gelatinous soups of shark fin, as well as tureens of bird's nest soup, said to be good for one's complexion. The nests are made from the regurgitated spittle of a certain type of swift from the East Asian tropics. Sold dried and then soaked before use, the nest is bland, soft, crunchy jelly that relies on the broth for its flavour, and is an expensive and acquired taste. (Soups are rarely served as a separate course in China, except at the banquets. They are used to signal the end of a course, and to cleanse the palate in preparation for the next one.)

For adults only there were platters of expensive slices of abalone (enormous clam-like seafood). There were mountains of pink, plump prawns, as well as whole, steamed fish, usually pike, which was caught fresh from nearby lakes. Pike is bony and therefore not to everyone's taste, but hey, the Chinese don't mind bones. After birthdays and banquets, the dishes, plates, bowls and platters were returned to the kitchen, spotless: the Chinese always box up the leftovers to take them home. What feasts! Nevertheless, as a kid I was so skinny. I mean, really super-skinny, just like so many of the post-war kids.

Mum and I lived in a block of apartments on Wentworth Avenue. The block had previously been an office building, and you still knew it. The front doors of the apartments were an ever-present legacy of the office days: they were wooden frames surrounding two sheets of mottled glass. So when you entered the building you felt like you had walked onto the set of a Humphrey Bogart movie. The doors' top part of glass had been covered with squares of chipboard, the cheapest way of stopping anyone peering in. You know what; even with the board on the glass it still felt like a Bogey set.

Behind our mottled-glass door, we lived in a two-room flat. The place was small. I had the bedroom. Mum slept on the sofa in the kitchen-cum-living room. For company, she had a fridge, a stove, a sink and a pair of heavy, old-fashioned radiators.

The communal loo was down the hallway, although the residents on the opposite side of the hall had their own private bathrooms because the apartments were larger. Every month my mother paid the grand sum of $40 in rent. That was about a fifth of her salary, so it wasn't a bad deal.

Uncle Winston lived across the hall from us and was skilled at making Chinese sausages, which, when fried, despatched the sweetest smell from the wok and throughout the block. The craving was instant. You just wanted to be there, in that kitchen, so that you could have just one, gigantic bite. Sometimes I was. Uncle Winston also had a bathtub. Like, *he had a bathtub*! Every Sunday I got to cross the hall, knock on his chipboard, mottled-glass door, and scrub clean and relax in a bath. That was a weekly luxury. (The extravagance of warm water was not wasted on me: I swim most days now, although I only learnt to swim in later life.) Unlike us, Uncle Winston also had a television, and would invite us in to watch it.

Downstairs, beneath our apartment, there was a bad Chinese restaurant. If you came out of our apartment block and took a left, you'd be on Cermak Road, and would pass the billiards and pool hall and the fire station. One Saturday, my mother was just about to cook lunch when we heard shouting outside our front door. 'Quick! Get out! Get out!' A fire had broken out in the bad Chinese restaurant downstairs, and the building was being evacuated. It was pretty scary, with thick smoke billowing.

The bad news was that lunch was delayed. The good news was that the firehouse was right across the street from us. The firemen just strolled casually over with their hoses. In the history of Chicago's blazes, it must have been the fastest-ever extinguished.

Every day the fire engines' sirens screamed. And they made me want to scream. The worst season for sirens was summer, because we were so poor we couldn't afford air conditioning. This meant that all the windows were open, and the siren volume was unbearable. Wax earplugs were an unknown luxury back then, though they would have been ineffective against those sirens.

If you came out of the apartment block and took a right, you were a minute's stroll from the heart of Chinatown, passing the KK coffee shop where my mother would send me to buy a takeaway if she felt flush on a Saturday and didn't want to cook. I'd stand at the counter. 'Ngoh yiu chow mein, m'goih.' 'Stir-fry noodles, please.' Hand over a dollar, and then take them back to my mother.

On the corner was – to me at that time – the largest grocery store in the world, called Sun Ching Lung. It was an old-fashioned shop, and I would wander the aisles, staring up at the shelves, which reached to the high ceiling and were crammed with foodstuffs and other products from China. Don't get me wrong; I don't want to make the store seem organised. It was a total mess. Typical Chinese. The shelf-stacking system wasn't really a stacking system.

But – oh, the thrill when something arrived from Hong Kong!

There would be a knock on the door of our apartment, and my mother would answer. I can picture the excited faces and voices, as one of our friends broke the news of a delivery at the grocery store. 'Fai di *bei ngoh yat loh Heung Gong lai ge sun sin ma tai.'* 'Quick! Fresh water chestnuts from Hong Kong.' A whole barrel. Swiftly, my mother would wrap up warm – you wrapped up warm most days in Chicago – grab her purse and scurry off to the grocery store. We all adored water chestnuts: white, crunchy, walnut-sized bulbs which, in China, are eaten as a snack, having first been boiled in their skins, or peeled and simmered in sugar, or as an ingredient in cooked dishes, especially in southern China. Mum's purse was not always necessary. Often she needed only to glimpse at the Chinese food; merely to gaze at it.

She was not alone. Our neighbours and friends also busied themselves by chattering about the delivery at the grocery store. No matter what had been delivered, the messenger always told the listener (in Cantonese), 'You've got to see it!' There were two compelling reasons for having to see the new delivery. First, it was about the food, and the Chinese want to see anything to do with food. Second, it connected us in Chicago to those in China: it was like a long-lost friend reappearing on the doorstep, and saying, 'Remember me?' Or even, *'Gei m'gei dak ngoh ah?'*

People hung out at the grocery store. They did. This store was *the place to be*. Some went to the store to collect letters that had been sent from relatives in China who had only the grocery store address. When you were growing up, *you* may have had a community centre. *We* had the grocery store.

If you haven't been to Chinatown in Chicago, then I can tell you it was like Chinatown in San Francisco, but smaller. And if you haven't been to San Francisco, then take my word for it – the large grocery store is a common feature in Chinatowns. Above the store is usually where you will find what we call the Six Companies: they are the big names that would run Chinatown.

CHINATOWN in Chicago covered, say, four or five blocks. Beyond that, there were the Italians. Then there were the Projects, where the black people lived. Many of my classmates and teachers were black, including Miss Luckett. She was a large woman with formidable presence and the sort of powerful voice that could silence a class of children and make them listen, which is precisely what she did on that January day in 1961 when John F. Kennedy was inaugurated as President. 'This is going to be very good for all of us,' she said. And she was right.

In fact, Kennedy led a passionate campaign for civil rights and against racial prejudice, and it made him so much of a hero of the minority races that, if you visited any one of the homes in any one of America's Chinatowns, you were certain to see a photo of the man, framed out of respect, and hanging with pride on the wall.

I call Kennedy a *man*. He was like a god to the Chinese-Americans, well beyond the 'promising' and 'charismatic' descriptions that others gave him. When Kennedy came to Chicago, I went downtown to see him and his cavalcade progressing slowly along the tree-lined avenues, the President in the backseat of a long, gleaming black limo, waving at the cheering crowds and smiling his nothin'-can-go-wrong-when-I'm-in-charge smile.

My friends and I were especially impressed and inspired by the news of Kennedy sending in US troops to allow a black student to walk into the University of Alabama when the governor of the state had barred him from entering the building. How can it be right, said Kennedy, that there are Americans who would fight for the country and who would pay their taxes, and yet they cannot even get into school in the same country as the rest of us? On a wall in our apartment I saw Kennedy's photo many times every day and I did not mind one bit that he shared our home and our lives.

On 22 November '63, I was fourteen and in my typing class – typing was a standard part of the curriculum – but the tapping halted as the door opened and a teacher, ashen faced and in shock, came into the room and broke it to us hurriedly: 'I have some horrible news. The President has been shot.' I was stunned by disbelief.

America toppled into an abyss of shock and deep grief. Kennedy was the great hope for us; for those who were not the big, white middle class. As Chinese-Americans, we were a small minority and therefore on the periphery of the civil rights movement, but still, we were motivated by JFK's pledges and grit. He was there to bring change. His assassination came with the force of a powerful blow to the body.

By then I had been working for about three years. Since the age of eleven, after school and at weekends, I had a part-time job in a restaurant kitchen. The job was the result of unusual circumstances, centring on my spectacularly unsuccessful efforts to become a criminal.

2

The Tea Ritual

MY LAWLESS PERIOD was not as long lived as, say, Chicago mobster Al Capone, and it evolved shortly after I learnt how to take a bus downtown. Not *take a bus* in the criminal sense, as in take a bus and not give it back to the bus company, but *take* a bus, as in board the vehicle, pay a few cents for a ticket, take a seat and feel grown up, chewing gum to feel even more grown up.

Downtown, I would wander around the shops, mesmerised by what they had to offer. I didn't have anything and the shops seemed to have everything. It didn't seem right. So one day, I thought, OK, maybe one of the shops can give me something for nothing. (Was there a little socialist at the heart of this little communist?)

Now, dear reader, you will never have shoplifted; you won't appreciate how it works. Let me explain. I took one thing and got away with it. That produced an overwhelming rush of adrenalin and a sense of being unconquerable and uncatchable. Then I swiped another thing. That, too, went into my pocket without a heavy hand coming down on my shoulder. Well, pretty soon I was just helping myself to shopping. Pretty soon after that, I was caught. Probably because I was about ten years old.

The policeman who caught me then took me to the station. When I was put in a cell and the door closed behind me, I was confident I would never again steal. However, what ensued – and it involved a true punishment, beyond a police caution – ensured I would never steal. It went like this... My mother was telephoned by the police and she came to collect me, accompanied by my uncle Paul, who was lending support and playing the role of interpreter because Mum did not speak English. Once we were out of the police station, my mother meted out a reprimand which was so severe it remains the fiercest retribution I have ever received – though it did not include a slap or a smack, or even one single raised voice. Quite the contrary.

Instead, my mother did not speak to me. I would get home from school and await her return. 'Hello, Mum.' She did not speak. 'Would you like tea, Mum?' Silence. 'Is there anything I can do?' No response. It was as if I had begun a period of penance, but with no end in sight. It went on and on. Each evening my mother would cook a meal, which she served to me. We ate in silence, and afterwards she would sit in the corner of the room and weep. We're talking real tears for the son who had shamed her.

This ritual – silence, cook, eat, weep, more silence, sleep – continued. It lasted for two whole weeks. If my mother felt humiliated at the beginning, by the end of the fortnight I felt suitably mortified and disgraced by my behaviour. I was far worse than merely a ten-year-old fool. I had dishonoured the family name.

Eventually, there was finality in the form of an act of penance. It would bring closure and, in typically Chinese fashion, it required food and a gathering. Specifically, a crowd of family members and friends came through the chipboarded, mottled-glass door to gather in our apartment. Even the neighbours were there, squeezed into our home and looking on with serious expressions, but in reality they were excitedly awaiting the drama that was about to unfold. I made a pot of tea, carried it to my mother and then knelt before her. With my head bowed, I whispered, 'Mother, I have made tea for you. Please take the tea, and forgive me.'

Of course, you have never stolen anything. But if you had, and then had to offer tea to your mother and kneel and ask for forgiveness – in front of family, friends and a few nosy neighbours – you too wouldn't be in any kind of a hurry to head downtown and steal again, believe you me. After that fiasco when I was ten, I never stole anything ever again. Well, maybe a bar of soap at a hotel, but certainly nothing that would have given my mother nights of sleeplessness or bring shame to our family name.

———

THIS is probably an ideal point at which to take a pause and tell you about my name. My birth name was Wing Fei in Cantonese (Rong Hui in Mandarin). It translates as *glorious son*. To Mum, I was always Fei, and not Ken. Maybe I was not so glorious after the shoplifting episode, but ever after I tried my best to live up to the name. Kenneth was a popular name at the time, and one that was given to many Chinese boys. To Westerners, I was Ken or Kenny.

I was born in Tuscon, Arizona, on 3 May 1949. At the time of my birth, the final days of the big band era, Harry S. Truman was America's

President and *The Barkleys of Broadway* was the hot movie. TV was progressing from black and white: RCA was perfecting a system of broadcasting in colour. That same year, in October, Mao Tse-tung established the People's Republic of China. Britain, meanwhile, was under Clement Attlee's Labour government, rationing of clothes had just ended, and George Orwell was soon to see the publication of *Nineteen Eighty-Four*.

I was Tuesday's child, which, according to the rhyme, means I am 'full of grace'. Born a day earlier, goes the rhyme, and I would have been fair of face. If I had arrived on the Wednesday I would have been full of woe. So you can't complain, can you?

I was the first and, as it turned out, the only child of my parents. Shortly after Christmas of that year, when I was eight months old, my father died. His death may have coincided with the traveller being born in me. You see, soon after his death we uprooted and moved from Tucson. I did not return to Arizona for twenty years, and then went to visit my father's grave, to pay my respects and take a photograph of his gravestone, a snapshot to treasure.

Why did we move? I think there were problems with my father's family in Arizona. Initially, we went to live in San Diego, California, staying with one of my mother's oldest friends, another Chinese woman. We had relatives in Chicago who offered my mother a job and so, in 1955, it was time for another upheaval. Chicago, Illinois, was our next stop, and would remain my mother's home until her death. The city is 'Hog butcher for the world ... stacker of wheat', though I would be raised on my mother's traditional Chinese cookery.

I was five years old and yet to live in an environment where English was spoken: Cantonese was the only language I heard. My mother, throughout her life, never learnt to speak much English, but she knew how to say 'dollar', 'money' and 'no'. So my mother would never adopt another language, and she would never take another husband. The subject of her remarrying was never raised.

For the first year, we lived with my aunt Jean – a relative of my mum – and my uncle Yook Lam, and their children in Chinatown. It was cramped. My mother went to work with many other Chinese people at my uncle's factory, which produced Chinese food in tins. These tins were shipped off to the army and other destinations. Yook Lam's food business, quite bizarrely, was called the Great China Beauty Company.

During school holidays, my mother would head off, as usual, at 7 a.m., and leave lunch for me to have later in the day. Sometimes it was a mixture of sticky rice and chopped pork in a bain marie, which she put on top of a radiator: the apartment was filled with enticing smells as the heat of the radiator slowly warmed the food.

———

MY uncle Paul was among the throng of observers who packed themselves into our little apartment on that evening, to witness my performance of the embarrassing tea-bearing rites. I was not related to Paul Lee, but to Chinese children close family friends are also known as uncles and aunts.

He was, however, a relative of Uncle Yook Lam, and he was many things to me. He was inspirational mentor to me, the fatherless child in the wild jungle of an American city. He was a surrogate father, too. And Uncle Paul was also about to become my employer. He owned the restaurant King Wah, the kitchen of which would become my workplace.

I poured the tea for my mother, and she accepted it and then drank. There was an audible sigh of relief from the mass of witnesses, and then

Uncle Paul spoke to my mother. 'I'll give him a job. I'll do something for him, and keep an eye on him. He's got plenty of energy. He can use it by working for me in the restaurant.' I looked at my uncle as he talked, unaware of precisely how much energy I would need for the job.

'He'll be able to make some money so that he can buy whatever he wants.' The implication being, he can *buy* rather than *steal*. And not really whatever I wanted, but mostly whatever my mother wanted, as he knew I would hand over the wages to her. I do not remember if I accepted the job, or if my mother accepted on my behalf.

But that was it. As I turned eleven, I began my first job and, as for the shoplifting, it was never mentioned again. My mother and I did not have the sort of relationship in which we reflected on the low points of our lives. We did not analyse or dissect human nature, be it our own or that of others. Crucially, there was a lesson to learn – don't steal – and I'd learnt it. She did her bit as the caring mother. I did my bit as the obedient Chinese son.

Then she cooked for the audience – family and curious neighbours – and our apartment was filled with the delicious aromas of Chinese food, stirred and fried and served from the wok.

I loved the smells of my mother's cooking, though I am reminded of an episode many years later, when a company came to me with an idea for a business venture. They said, 'Our idea is an aerosol spray can. But not just any aerosol spray can.'

Me: 'OK. What type of aerosol spray can?'

Company with idea: 'You spray it in the kitchen and it makes the room smell of cooking odours.'

Me (incredulous): 'Makes the kitchen smell of cooking odours?'

Company with idea (insistent): 'Yes.'

Me: 'That's insane. Most people hate cooking smells in their kitchen.'

Company with idea: 'Do they?'

Me: 'Yes. They want a spray that gets *rid of* cooking smells.'

I never found out what happened to their spray.

3

Never Play with Chopsticks

THERE ARE TWO recurring dreams in my life. One is a nightmare, the other is extremely pleasant. Both centre on food.

The nightmare is infrequent, thankfully, as I like late nights followed by plenty of undisturbed sleep. This bad dream places me in the kitchen of a restaurant just as the guests are about to arrive. The guests are not the bad bit. The bad bit is that my *mise en place* is not ready and this predicament has left me in a hot-sweat panic. I know, I know, worse things happen at sea. But please bear with me; this is chef stuff.

As we all know, in order to reduce the possibility of failure, you must prepare well in advance. The home cook will appreciate the anxiety of my dream. When you're cooking Sunday lunch for friends, you want to have the vegetables peeled and the dessert in the fridge by the time the doorbell rings. Who wants to end up struggling with a kitchen catastrophe?

My nightmare, however, is propelled by fear rather than experiences from my past. I have done events for thousands of people and have never been unready. In real life I am organised, prepared to the point of obsession. In the dream, however, I don't have my stuff together and awake in a fluster, feeling like the actor who's about to go on stage but doesn't know his lines. Indeed, it's making me feel anxious just reflecting on it, so I'm going to put the nightmare to one side and let me take you to the pleasant dream.

This dream is also about food, and goes like this … I am eating something – anything – and it is delicious. The dream is so powerful, colourful and real to life that upon awaking I feel full up and completely satisfied. Last night I had such a dream. I was eating a plate of sashimi and particularly recall salivating over the raw slices of abalone and tuna. It was the kind of delicate, ocean dish you'd see in Japan. But then it vanished. I said, 'Hey! Who took my plate away? I hadn't finished.' There I was, moaning about my food being snatched away, when I woke up, slightly irritated to have lost the food – but still, I was full, appetite sated.

You know, and just to digress for a moment, I never had abalone as a child because it was always so expensive, although it was talked about as a great delicacy, perhaps in the same way you may have heard about caviar or foie gras but never got to try it during childhood. The first time I had abalone was as an adult in Hong Kong. The Japanese like it fresh, raw and sliced. The Chinese dry it and then cook it until tender and serve it in a light oyster sauce. In Chinese restaurants, one dish of abalone could cost hundreds of pounds, though it is indeed the stuff of dreams when perfectly cooked.

Throughout my life I have had this eating dream (though sashimi did not feature in the ones of my childhood, which were less ambitious). Sometimes I wonder if the root of these dreams lies in poverty; as a kid, I was often hungry. There was food, but usually not enough of it. My dreams, therefore, fed me. They were a sort of method of survival via subliminal nurturing. In an unconscious state, I was experiencing a joy I didn't get enough of while conscious.

Or maybe I just wanted to eat and eat and eat.

BEFORE I began working in the kitchen for Uncle Paul, I knew his restaurant. Everyone knew King Wah.

The Chinese restaurants were closed on Monday nights and King Wah was no exception. But on Monday nights it was filled with my uncles and their friends, who gathered for a weekly feast and a catch-up. They worked in the restaurants of Chinatown and had the night off. Their wives stayed at home.

My mother, husbandless, was the only woman at these lively meals. I was her companion. We were the odd ones out, but extremely well cared for and well fed by a roomful of male chefs, who cooked the dishes before we all served ourselves.

When the crowd of us sat down at the long table, the critiques began. Often dishes were criticised because we happened to be in America rather than China, home to the best produce. 'This doesn't taste like it used to,' they'd say, a reference to how it tasted in China. 'You can't get the ingredients.' Meaning the best ingredients were only available in China. I was fascinated as they spoke of dishes they had eaten in China, such as drunken shrimp: the shrimp (or prawns as the British call them) are immersed in rice wine before being poached. There was self-criticism, too. 'Oh, I cooked this for a second too long,' one of them might say.

There is a great deal of superstition in Chinese food culture, as was apparent on those Monday nights. For example, in Cantonese, the word 'yu' means both fish and prosperity – it follows that serving a whole fish should bring ample luck to those who are eating it. The platter is put on the table so that the head of the fish is pointed towards the guest of honour. I know this bit can bother Westerners who are unaware of the custom and hate to see the head of a fish.

Taking this further, if you have respect for someone else at the table, you grip the communal chopsticks, pick up the choicest part of the fish – the succulent cheek – and place it on your guest's plate. At those Monday night meals, the fish was brought to the table and then one of my uncles would take the cheek upon chopsticks and give it to my mother. 'Thank you,' she would say. In turn, she would lift the cheek with her chopsticks and put it into my bowl.

So much was conveyed by this almost-silent ritual involving food. It said, for instance, do not think only of yourself; that we should all look after each other; that food is about sharing; that my mother would be fed generously. There was another unspoken message: *We're looking after your mum, and you better look after your mum. Take care of her, and if you don't, we'll come and punish you.* So it was through food that I learnt how to be in life, and how not to be. In return for the fish cheek, I tried to acknowledge that I got the point, and had learnt the morality lesson.

The upper side of the fish is eaten before the entire bone is removed, and then the underside is enjoyed. The fish is never turned: to do so will bring bad luck. If there's a bone in your food, spit it out – in Chinese company, do not use your fingers to remove the bone from your mouth. Please.

There were other gastronomic customs that I learnt in those early times. Food, for example, is served to the side of the guest – never, ever reach across the table to grab a bowl. At a British table, if a child eats noisily there is likely to be a reprimand from the parents. 'Stop making that horrible noise. Eat nicely!' For the Chinese, meanwhile, eating nicely means making some noise. Actually, the louder the noise, the better the table manners. Eating noises mean that you are happy and enthusiastic about the food. From now on, I'd like to hear Western mums and dads telling their children, 'Hey, what's wrong with you! Why aren't you slurping? Start slurping and guzzling – just eat properly!'

In King Wah, I really mastered the chopsticks, having used them very awkwardly for the first few years of my life. You must master chopsticks when you are young because otherwise you don't get to eat. And you have to learn fast, especially when you are hungry, because you're up against the other chopsticks. So I suppose I learnt by osmosis, along with the many rules of Chinese eating etiquette.

In my early years, I learnt never to play with the chopsticks, because to do so is disrespectful of the food and of others at the table. I tried not to drop chopsticks on the floor – this brings bad luck. They should be put down – and never crossed – at the side of the bowl. Also, they should never be stuck into the rice in your bowl, which is only ever done when we are respecting the dead at funerals.

I was told not to use my fingers when eating, nor to be so rude as to leave a single, little grain of rice in my bowl. Now, that wasn't a problem for me because, as you know, I was *always* hungry.

Food is medicine. I was not given syrups, pharmaceutical powders or pills from the chemist. Depending on my ailment, my mother plied me with any combination of bok choy, bitter melon (my favourite), Chinese broccoli, cabbages, various meats or sauces, and exotic herbs and roots. I absorbed the Chinese attitude towards not eating too much meat because *fan* foods (grains) and *cai* (vegetables) are the foundation of good and wholesome diets.

Numbers are symbolic. The words 'four' and 'death' are written in the same way, so four of anything is to be avoided. Colours, too, carry messages. Orange is like gold, the symbol of wealth, while red denotes a happy, good-luck colour. Wander through the streets of any Chinatown in the world, and you will see that the signage for restaurants and shops are ablaze with oranges and reds. Strangely, the colour code changes for correspondence, which must never be written in red, the colour of blood. For Westerners, it is also poor form to write in red ink, but I am told that is because the colour is reserved for showing accounts are 'in the red'. To write in red is impolite.

In the West, black is the colour of death. In China, it is white which symbolises the end of a life. Mourners wear black to British funerals. Mourners wear white to Chinese funerals. If you want to win friends in Britain, send white flowers – symbolising peace, serenity and happiness. If you want to lose friends in China, send white flowers – it's like death just pitched up on your doorstep.

———

WHEN I began school at the age of six, I didn't know how to hold a fork. Chopsticks, yes, I was an expert. In the school cafeteria, I jabbed the fork into the food – and, I should add, this was food that was new and different to me. There was strange food, with so much meat, and there were dishes such as macaroni and cheese. I remember it was at school that I first came across potato. But I don't remember very much because my mum did not give me money for the cafeteria.

Instead, I stayed in the classroom during lunch breaks and my meal was the contents of a thermos flask, given to me by my mother each morning. It might be minced pork meat with preserved vegetables. Or perhaps it was my favourite – peas and Hong Kong sausage, which my mother had cooked in sticky rice. It made me feel warm and really stuck to my ribs.

I needed something to make me feel warm. I never hated Chicago. I just did not like the wintry weather. In the '50s and '60s, schools were not heated like they are these days. They had mile-wide hallways and corridors with wooden floors and didn't stand a chance against Chicago's notorious wind factor.

—

In the winter months we had soup most days, served at the same time as a couple of other dishes. (Drinks, by the way, such as water, wine and tea are rarely served at a family meal.) Sweetcorn has always been one my favourites, and I liked the American staples of corn on the cob and mashed potatoes.

My mother's sweetcorn soup with crabmeat was always a treat. To make enough to feed four (we both had seconds), she used 450g (1 lb) of sweetcorn on the cob, washing the cobs and then removing the kernels with a knife or cleaver. However, 275g (10 oz) of canned or frozen sweetcorn can be used. Mix an egg white with a teaspoon of sesame oil and set aside.

In a large pan, bring 1.2 litres (2 pints) of chicken stock to the boil. Simmer for 15 minutes, before adding 1 tablespoon each of Shaoxing rice wine (or dry sherry) and light soy sauce, 2 teaspoons of finely chopped fresh ginger, a teaspoon of salt and the same of sugar, ¼ teaspoon of freshly ground white pepper. And add a mixture of 2 teaspoons of cornflour blended with 2 teaspoons of water.

Bring the soup back to the boil and then lower the heat to a simmer.

Add 225g (8 oz) of freshly cooked crabmeat or frozen crabmeat. In a steady stream, slowly pour in the egg-white mixture, stirring all the time.

Ladle the soup into a large tureen, garnish with finely chopped spring onions and serve immediately. 🥢

—

MY mother bought vegetables in season, as they are the cheapest. Come the summer months, we gorged on the abundance of available vegetables. We disagreed on sweet potato: she loved it, I hated it. Cabbage remains one of my favourites. In Yangzhou, there is a saying: 'If you do not eat vegetables for three days, your eyes will catch fire.' We ate vegetables so often I never got to challenge that adage.

Often, we had fish and seafood because it was inexpensive. The fish was steamed by my mother in a wok to become a simple but particularly good dish. Chunky halibut, for instance, steamed with ginger and spring onions, made a substantial meal and I could fill up on it. I was encouraged also to fill up on rice. In China, when you eat a lot of rice you are known as 'a rice barrel'. However, I remained a beanpole, and my mother took me to the doctor to have me tested for tapeworm. I never told the doctor about my eating dreams. My relatives, meanwhile, were constantly amused by my rice consumption, and poked fun of me, 'Oh, you're a rice barrel.'

—

THERE were others who made fun of me, though with no affection. The other kids at school ridiculed me because I didn't speak English.

Although the school was close to Chinatown, there weren't that many Chinese-Americans. Chinatown wasn't that big at the time, and certainly not large enough to produce enough kids to make an impact on the school's population. I learnt very quickly to speak English. It was about survival. The alternative was to be traumatised. I saw some kids who came from China and, sure enough, they would withdraw into themselves.

At the age of ten, I moved up to junior high, which was in a bad, mostly black neighbourhood. My friends and I had to be careful, watching out for gangs of young thugs who would try to rob us or beat us up if we didn't hand over whatever we had, be it candy or cash.

However, I was never prejudiced. I never once felt racist or uttered a racist comment. That is because my mother had frequently said to me, 'You know, there are bad black people and there are nice black people.' Pause. 'Just as there are bad Chinese and good Chinese.' And she'd add, 'I know, so believe me. You must judge people on how they are.'

I'd moan to her that I was eating strange food when all the other kids ate bologna sandwiches. 'I am American,' I'd tell her.

'You're American?' she replied one day, in a mocking tone of surprise. 'Just take a look in the mirror.'

In order to deal with the bullies who taunted my appearance and Chinese-ness, I mastered a put-down, of which I was extremely proud. 'Well,' I'd say, looking the bully straight in the eye, 'at least our food is better than yours.' I don't remember knocking out anyone with this line, but who could argue with it?

My classmates were fascinated by my thermos flasks of Chinese food, and when I let them try a bit, they fell in love with the stuff. Some days I traded my food for theirs, and so I got to enjoy rich bologna, sandwiched between thick slices of ethnic rye or pumpernickel – proper bread!

4

Cracking Conch, Peeling Prawns

UNCLE PAUL TAUGHT me how to cook. More than that, he taught me how to love food, though that sounds a peculiar statement. Also, he instilled in me a strong work ethic and an astute sense of business.

Uncle Paul was small, skinny as a rail, impeccably dressed and dapper, charming and intelligent. Somehow he managed to have three wives. He was also incredibly demanding, and I admired him for believing that nothing was ever good enough for him or, rather, that perfection was achievable. He was a shrewd entrepreneur who had opened the restaurant a few years earlier. Later on, he would go on to own a steel mill, and set up a film production company in Taiwan.

Whatever he did had to be the best. King Wah should be the best restaurant in Chinatown, he had decided, and it was. He was passionate about food and passionate about making money. The two combined, and drove him to triumph in this venture. The restaurant had a motto, which was printed on the menus: *Good enough for a king.* The place was unlike other Chinese restaurants, in that it was extremely clean, free of clutter and modern. My uncle was fastidious about cleanliness and unbelievably organised, which is also a rare quality in the Chinese. 'You can't achieve anything unless you're organised,' he used to tell me. He was right.

The whole room could be quickly transformed – and often was – for Chinese banquets, at which about 150 guests would be served ten to fifteen courses. Banquet dishes always included a fish for luck, and the last course was noodles, symbolising longevity.

The restaurant had a few booths, as well as tables and chairs, and a miniature bar at the back of the dining room. Sometimes my tiny aunt May sat at a table close to the door, standing to greet customers when they came in. She was so minute that when she stood up there wasn't much difference in her height. I would join her in the afternoons, when there was not much to do in between lunch and dinner service. This gave me a break from the kitchen. Plus, the dining room was air conditioned: this comfort was bragged about on the signage outside, and it was a treat on those hot summer days when the temperature outdoors was in the nineties (and the kitchen heat was ten degrees hotter). The next time you go into a sauna or steam room, please do me a favour and think, *OK, so now I know how hot it was in the kitchen at King Wah.*

Uncle Paul employed a cleaner, a tall black man called Roy. Sometimes when I arrived for work Roy was standing upright against his broom. He was asleep. I was fascinated by Roy's ability to nod off when vertical. Uncle Paul, meanwhile, was not proud; he was not above the chore of cleaning, grabbing a mop and bucket and washing the kitchen floor so that it was spotless.

The Chinese-Americans of my childhood, by the way, were hard workers. Yet we knew we were, and we acted like, the minority race within Chicago. We just buttoned up, kept our heads down and our eyes and ears open. Early on, it became apparent that if I did not want to live like this, I would have to study hard. Studying would take me to a better place. Even if it was not apparent, I was advised to study hard because my mother was making so many sacrifices for me.

On Saturday nights, the bookkeeper Shirley Fong came to go through the accounts in the building's basement, where Uncle Paul had an office. I would take her a tray of supper. I figured her job wasn't too difficult as Uncle Paul kept faultless records. I was not privy to the books, of course, but I saw the receipts and guessed they were making piles of money.

Although I was given drab chores, my eyes were opened to the joys of restaurants, places of warmth, wonderful aromas and bright colours. My uncle served not only foods that were familiar to me because my mother prepared them at home, but also 'Chinese' foods that were new to me.

Uncle Paul was a gourmet, and he delighted in the cooking as much as the eating. He was, for instance, adept at making rice noodles. When I arrived at 6.30 in the morning he would be in the kitchen already, making large sheets of *fen* (rice noodles) from rice flour, wheat starch and water. The sheets were later steamed and, when cooked, cut into noodles ready to be eaten and usually served with a sauce.

Vividly, I recall those times when Uncle Paul came back into the kitchen and donned an apron to make pressed duck. This is a Cantonese speciality which is said to have originated in northern China. During the Ming Dynasty, the Emperor and his court fled the invading Manchu, taking dishes such as this one to the south and introducing it to the Cantonese. (Traditionally, a duck was boned and literally flattened and then cured with various spices before cooking.)

Fortunately, much of the preparation can be done ahead of time, and it makes a superb main course for a dinner party or special family meal. The bird is braised and then boned, steamed and then, finally, it is fried. Uncle Paul also liked to stuff the duck with a filling of taro root purée before it was steamed and then fried. Let me tell you – it was out of this world. (Taro is a starchy root-like vegetable. In some parts of China, at the Lantern Festival – an extension of the New Year celebration – taro is softly boiled and eaten under the lantern lights.)

Pressed duck is an unusual and delicious dish, unlike any duck you have ever had. It is simple to make, and your family and friends will applaud you for making it. Let me take you through the method, if you have time.

First, get yourself a duck. One that weighs about 1.6–1.8 kg (3½–4 lb), which is large enough to serve four people. It can be fresh or frozen, preferably Cherry Valley. If frozen, please ensure the bird is properly thawed before cooking, of course. Am I sounding preachy?

Put the duck on a chopping board in front of you and, with a heavy, sharp knife, cut it in half, lengthways. Using kitchen paper, pat both halves dry.

Next, make the sauce by combining all the ingredients in a large pot. Those ingredients are chicken stock (900 ml), dark soy sauce (900 ml), light soy sauce (400 ml), Shaoxing rice wine or dry sherry (400 ml), caster sugar (110g), 5 whole pieces of star anise, 3 pieces of Chinese cinnamon bark or cinnamon sticks. Bring the mixture to a boil. Add the duck halves and turn the heat down to a simmer. Cover the pot and turn your attention to something else for one hour.

When you return an hour later, your kitchen will be alive with the most wonderful smells, and the duck should be perfectly braised and tender.

Skim away the fat from the surface. Remove the duck and let it cool down. Once the sauce has cooled, remove any lingering surface fat and reserve. Take your cooled duck and carefully remove all the bones, keeping the meat and skin intact. Place the duck halves between two pieces of cling film and press the meat and skin together.

We're almost there, I promise.

Baste the duck halves with two beaten eggs and dust with cornflour (or potato flour or starch).

Set up a steamer, or put a rack into a wok or deep pan, and fill it with just a couple of inches of water. That's 5 cm deep for the metric generation. Bring the water to the boil over a high heat. Put the duck onto a heatproof plate and carefully lower it into the steamer or onto the rack. Reduce the heat to low. Cover the wok or pan tightly, and steam gently for 20 minutes. Allow the duck to cool thoroughly. The dish can be completed to this stage a day in advance.

When it is time to serve the duck, heat a wok or large frying pan over a high heat and, when it is hot, add a couple of pints (1.1 litres) of groundnut or vegetable oil. When the oil is so hot that it is slightly smoking, add the duck halves. Deep-fry them until they are crispy. Remove and drain them well on kitchen paper.

Heat up some of the reserved braising liquid and serve it as a fantastic sauce with the crispy, pressed duck. 🥣

MY first chore of the day was to peel the prawns; 200 pounds of them!

That's about fourteen stone, or ninety kilos; a little bit more than the weight of an adult red kangaroo. The task left my hands feeling extremely itchy.

On Thursdays, a massive burlap bag would arrive at the restaurant. Inside was 80 lb (36 kg) of sea conch. My job was to lug the bag to the outdoors part of the kitchen and then, using a hammer, crack open the conches by pounding them hard. Substantial force was required, and I broke three hammers during my time at King Wah.

I hope you've had breakfast before this next bit. I extracted the guts, which were super-smelly, resonant of something that had been dead for days, even though the conches were alive. Only the conches' 'feet' are edible, so I put these bits to one side and the rest I discarded. Once the job was done, the bag of conches was reduced to a large bowl of edible parts, and these were a costly delicacy. I gave the bowl to one of the chefs, who used a cleaver to finely slice the conch before quickly blanching it in boiling water or stir-frying it in a wok.

No self-respecting Chinese chef would be seen with a knife instead of a cleaver, which is used for all kinds of cutting, ranging from fine shredding to chopping up bones. Usually, a Chinese chef has three types of cleaver: lightweight, with a narrow blade, for cutting delicate foods including vegetables; medium-weight, for general cutting, chopping and crushing purposes; heavy, for heavy-duty chopping. (Of course, knives will do the job, but you would be surprised by how easy it is to use a cleaver. A medium-sized all-purpose, stainless steel cleaver is the best kind to have around.)

There were two fridges at King Wah: one for the ethnic Chinese; the other for the Westerners. That is because we had two menus and each fridge was filled with the appropriate ingredients for each menu. The Chinese fridge contained the stuff Westerners didn't eat – things like conch, snails and shark fin. This restaurant, which stayed in the same hands for half a century, was also one of the first in Chinatown to serve dim sum. This was made by a special chef – my uncle had brought him over from Hong Kong.

The dim sum was great, but for me it was also a pain, as it required lots of little plates and they all needed to be washed up. The washing up, incidentally, was overseen by a lady I called Auntie. She was tall and thin. I was her helper. We had only a minuscule part of the kitchen, and as I was minuscule, that was all right. The dishes were scraped and rinsed before being stacked in the dishwasher, and I timed myself, ever eager to improve my scrape–rinse–stack speed.

In the Westerners' fridge we stored the ingredients for dishes such as egg foo yung, as well as slabs of steak. Uncle Paul had a loyal Chinese clientele who came mostly on Sundays, when the Chinese take a day off work and therefore have the time to eat with their families. (Fortune cookies, by the way, were not invented in China 1,000 years ago, but in Los Angeles around about 1915 by a Chinese-American noodle maker called Jung, or by a baker in San Francisco thirty years earlier, or indeed – some claim – at a bakery in Japan. Whatever the origin, it's definitely not China and three billion cookies are made each year, mostly in the States. I can't recall which comedian said he cracked open his cookie to find the message: 'Help! I'm a prisoner in a Chinese bakery!')

The Westerners came for the takeaways (or 'takeouts' as the Americans say) of chop suey, sweet and sour pork – that was a big seller – or chow mein. To them, that was Chinese. Chop suey and chow mein sure sound Chinese but are as American as vichyssoise and cioppino, those equally exotic dishes invented in the States. America, after all, has a food culture founded by immigrants who have arrived with the recipes of their respective homelands. The Americans also liked sup gum (a stir-fry vegetable mixture), won ton soup, asparagus with beef, tomato beef (we had lots of beef dishes for the American clientele), egg flower soup, egg roll (extremely popular) and fried rice in all its permutations, with prawns or egg.

I appreciated the business sense of the 'two menus': serve the customers what they want to eat. My mother was immersed in Chinese culture and was unswayable. But as I grew up I became more aware of America in terms of social experiences, even if I remained heavily Chinese.

The Westerners comprised many black Americans and lots of Italians. Uncle Paul was one of those people who always had a few deals going on, and he knew who to look after. So a heap of politicians came in, and they got a free meal. Cops came, and they got a free meal. The Italian Mafia came in, and they got a free meal. We're talking about Chicago, remember. Giving a free meal to the cops and the Mob ensured your place was protected, that no harm would come to it. He did not give them money. Just free meals.

One of those meals was Hong Kong steak. (And I say meal because although served as a single dish on one plate it was a massive meal in itself.) Please don't beat yourself up if you've never heard of Hong Kong steak. It was incredibly popular with the big, broad and hefty Irish-American cops who ate bill-less in King Wah, but it was unknown outside Chicago's Chinatown. Which is because Hong Kong steak was one of Uncle Paul's inventions.

From the Westerners' fridge he took out a well-aged porterhouse steak, large enough to qualify for the rodeo if you added a tail and horns. (Often confused with the T-bone steak, the porterhouse looks similar, also has a T-bone, and is cut from the tenderloin, but the porterhouse is a much larger cut. On one side of the T is the fillet, on the other side is the sirloin. Or, as they would say in the States, it's the filet with a silent 't' and the strip loin.) My uncle seasoned the porterhouse with salt and pepper before grilling it to order. Once cooked, the plump, thick cut of meat received an Asian twist: a little splash of sesame oil, half a ladleful of oyster sauce. The steak rested and was then sliced – for appetising presentation and so that it could be easily picked up with chopsticks – and served hot on a bed of blanched bok choy (the Chinese cabbage also known as pak choy), along with the stripped T-bone. West meets East.

From my spot at the sink in the kitchen, I saw the returning plates and so could gauge the customers' level of affection for Hong Kong steak. The blue-uniformed cops – always with hats and truncheons on the seats beside them – seemed to have licked their plates clean and gnawed on the bones. But the Chinese tummies were too small for my uncle's creation. The Chinese cheerfully ordered Hong Kong steak and they certainly started to eat it, but seldom did they finish. The portion was too American in size. So their plates came back into the kitchen still with a few succulent pieces of steak upon them.

One day, early in my career at King Wah, a plate was plonked down beside me, ready to be cleaned and washed. Upon it, slices of beef were staring up at me. There were three of them, medium-rare tenderloin, perfectly browned around the edges, glistening, tempting and available as they sat beside the T-bone. My hunger combined with my curiosity. I grabbed a slice with my fingers and quickly popped it into my mouth, and then savoured that instant – you know it, don't you? – of the first and second chew when the meat's flavours hit my taste buds. Juicy, sensationally seasoned, and tender too. Within a few seconds I had gobbled down the other two slices. That was a new sensation for me. It was my first taste of beef, a meat that, no matter the cost of the cheapest cut, was still too expensive for my mother's food budget.

From then on, beef was a staple in my diet. For as long as the Chinese continued to order Hong Kong steak at King Wah.

5

Sticking to the Ribs

CHINESE KITCHENS ARE not noisy. Unlike Western kitchens, where the head chef barks the orders from the kitchen's pass, there is little shouting in the Chinese kitchen. All the prep is done well in advance and ready to go. Or it should be.

The customer's order comes in to the kitchen and goes first to the prep person. He looks at the order and puts the ingredients for that dish on a plate. Then he hands that plate to the chef at the smoking-hot wok. The chef throws the food into the wok and cooks. To the observer, the high speed of cooking is noticeable: the ingredients are tossed into the wok, and within seconds they are in a bowl or plate and all set to go to the table. Into the pan and then out.

Thinking further about this, for a chef to be good, he or she might have impeccable timing. Heat the wok, add the oil, sear the meat or fish for just a few seconds. Take it out. When this protein is removed from the wok, it is still cooking, so you have to take that into consideration. That period out of the wok is still part of the cooking process. In the same wok, cook the other ingredients. Plus, make the sauce in the same wok. Throw the meat or fish back into the wok – it will cook some more. Mix it up and put it on a plate when it is still so hot that it is continuing to cook, and by the time it arrives at the table, the dish is perfectly cooked.

The talent of the chef is to make sure the food is not undercooked or overcooked but just right. So there you have it – it's all about timing and ferocious heat.

Chinese dishes, remember, have never been codified like French cooking. There are no rule books, as there are for the classic cuisine of France. Instead, Chinese cooking is very personal, and in my uncle's restaurant each chef might make the same dish but he would make it differently to the others. For instance, one of the best head chefs made fried rice that always had a barbecue smokiness to its aroma and flavour, and was quite amazing. His sous chef, meanwhile, made fried rice with less barbecue smokiness.

I watched the head chef to see how he did it. His technique, quite simply, was to let the wok get as hot as possible before throwing in the rice. The result was a little more flavour, which I preferred. Just a few extra seconds of heat beneath that wok, but that slight difference produced a really fantastic result.

The Chinese person learns to cook from watching the cooks, just as I had done with the head chef and his fried rice. Observing in that way also enables you to realise that instinct is an essential quality if you want to be a good cook.

The briskness of cooking at King Wah appealed, of course, to customers who did not have much time to spare and were after a quick bite. In the winter months, there were plenty of solitary customers

who came through the door, icicles on their noses and the wind slam-
ming the door behind them. They were after a big, steaming-hot bowl
of happiness, something that would stick to their ribs.

—

No matter the speed of serving, much care went into the garnishes.
Simple ingredients were transformed into mini works of art, as is the
Chinese way, from the spring onion brushes to the tomato roses. They
are fun to make and easier to create than you would imagine – your
guests will be envious of your artistic skills. Years after Uncle Paul's,
I would show how to make these traditional garnishes on television,
in *Chinese Cookery*.

For the spring onion brush: Cut off the green part of the spring
onion and trim off the base of the bulb. This should leave you with a
7.5-cm (3-inch) white segment. Make a lengthways cut of about
2.5 cm (1 inch) long at one end of the spring onion. Roll the onion
90 degrees and cut again. Repeat this process at the other end. Soak
the spring onions in iced water. They will curl into 'flower brushes'. Pat
dry before use.

Fresh chilli flowers: Trim the top of the chilli but do not remove the
stem. Make 4 cuts lengthways from the stem of the chilli to the tip to
form 4 sections. Remove and discard any seeds. Soak the chillies in cold
water. They will 'flower' in the water. Pat dry before use.

Tomato roses: Use firm tomatoes. Using a very sharp knife, peel the
skin from the top in one piece, as if peeling an apple. Do not break
the strip. Roll the strip of tomato skin into a tight coil. 🥢

—

SPEAKING of walking into restaurants, I remember going to Australia in the early 1990s. For about three weeks, I travelled the continent and ate in sixty-three restaurants. I had to eat substantially and more frequently than anyone else on the planet, as I was in Australia to judge the Restaurant of the Year awards.

I was accompanied by an extremely tall blonde woman. She was striking and statuesque and looked like a beautiful Viking. She was the PR person, escorting me from table to table – and picking up all the bills.

One time we walked into a Chinese restaurant and I ordered eight dishes. I wanted to sample all of them. I will never forget the look of alarm on the waiters' faces when the beautiful Viking – and not I – asked for, 'the bill, please'. Then, when she – not I – handed over a credit card, their jaws were on the ground. I tell you, when the Viking and I walked out of that restaurant, a regiment of Chinese waiters lined up to glare at me and, although they did not say it, their expressions were shouting, 'Hey, you little guy, you've got this big lady paying – you must be one helluva stud.'

—

I worked for Uncle Paul for four and a half years on weekends and school holidays. I can't say I really enjoyed all of it, even if I was learning as I went. It was a bit Dickensian – the young boy toiling for poor wages – even if the story was set in Chicago rather than Victorian London. My friends were out playing ball while I was working.

My uncle paid me 75 cents an hour. After two years he gave me a raise, which I desperately wanted. My mother was unaware of the hike in my pay, so I would steam open the envelope, remove the money that amounted to the raise, and then re-seal the envelope. This I handed to my mother. She took the lion's share. Secretly, I retained the pay increase. One day, my mother confronted Uncle Paul. 'Ken's been working so hard and you never give him an increase.'

Uncle Paul, taken aback, responded sharply, 'I have.' Yet again, he was right. Uncle Paul was never wrong. I'd been rumbled.

———

THE nearest school to Chinatown was called Tilden, and I was destined to go there after Haines, my junior high school. It was renowned as the place where young tough guys went before moving into jail. I mean, it was a dangerous school where kids didn't have time to study because they were too busy having fights and gang battles.

Uncle Paul, forever the fixer, came to my rescue and sorted out the potential problem over my schooling. He happened to employ a chef who, when he wasn't a chef, helped his wife run a launderette. Let's call it the *laundry*, as that's what we called it. (The Chinese in Chicago tended to be in the restaurant business or the laundry business, or both.) This laundry was in Chicago's North Side, deemed to be a 'safe', white neighbourhood. The kind of place where I wouldn't get the living daylights kicked out of me.

The plan was simple: all we had to do was tell the school authorities I had moved to the address of the laundry, and it would mean I could go to the nice school. In modern-day parlance, I'd be in the school's 'catchment area', though to me catchment involved a group of thugs chasing after me and then circling me.

Anyway, we followed the plan and lied our socks off. I got into

Amundsen High School. It was scrupulously clean and attended by students who had no desire to stab one another. So my life was spared.

There was a downside. If the lie had not been a lie, and I had genuinely lived at the laundry, I could have walked to school in a couple of minutes. But because we'd all lied and in reality I lived near Chinatown, it took me about an hour and a half to get there every day.

In the winter months, when the roads were clogged with snow, slush and ice, the walk took two or three hours. It was vile and ridiculous. Each year it was taking me the equivalent of three months to walk to and from school. All the other kids actually lived nearby, and they'd go skipping into the classroom. I'd trudge up to the school gates, shivering, exhausted and bedraggled. Forget about the North Side; this was like the North Pole. Sometimes I just didn't go to school. I mean, *would you*?

So yes, there were mornings when I would get up at the same time as my mum, and I'd watch her put on her coat, and I'd get mine too. Then, I'd say, 'Look at the snow. It's gonna take me hours to walk to school.' She would nod, and make noises of sympathy. Then I'd hear the door close behind her. At that point, I'd remove my coat, climb back into bed and go back to sleep. Don't act surprised. I told you, I like my sleep.

There was an upside to the Herculean treks. I was introduced to the north of Chicago, and that was like a whole new world to me. Until then, I knew only Chinatown and Downtown. In the north there were new cultures. Like, I met Greek people!

I started to make lots of friends, and discovered places where young people went to dance. On West Lawrence Avenue, there was the Aragon. Built in the 1920s, it had been a ballroom where all the big bands played. In my time it became the Cheetah, a disco and a venue for 'monster rock' concerts – there were so many fights it was nicknamed the Aragon 'brawlroom'. But I went in the 1960s, an era when they would play and we would dance and boy, did I dance. My friends and I fancied ourselves as being black, as being cool.

At the Cheetah, I saw stars of Motown such as the Supremes and Stevie Wonder, as well as Neil Diamond and Eddie Floyd, riding high in the charts with 'Knock on Wood'. They weren't like concerts; there were no seats. If you wanted to watch the bands, you had to stand and watch. Come Friday and Saturday nights, we all swarmed to the Cheetah. It was really cool and, more importantly, we felt cool just being there.

James Brown came to town to perform at the Regal Theatre and, as we set off to see him, others in Chinatown warned us about going into the predominantly black South Side area. 'You won't come back alive. They'll kill you.' Instead, the young black people thought it was fantastic that we were fans of James Brown, dancing in the aisle to his music. The tickets cost $5, but he played for four hours: we got our money's worth.

One of my friends in Chinatown had a car, so we would drive up to the Cheetah, cruising along, and we'd try to pick up girls – we liked the Italians. We'd ask them to dance and they might say yes. But you know, it was odd for us. We weren't black and we weren't white, and our eyes were slanted. We looked remarkably different to everyone else. Some of the girls were interested in us, but some of them were not. They didn't see too many Asian people at that time, especially in Chicago.

If you wanted to see something Asian and exotic, you went to Chinatown, such was the level of segregation in Chicago at that time. Similarly, my friends and I found it weird to see mostly white people. But this area was ethnically mixed as well, and there was a substantial number of Greeks around North Side. There were also many Poles and, from my experience, they could have benefited from one of my mum's chats about racism. (There were many Chinese, however, who hated the Japanese for the atrocities of the Second World War. 'Two was not enough for them,' they would say; a reference to the atom bombs that were dropped on Japan.)

At the age of sixteen, I started dabbling in shares on the stock market. That sounds a bold and adult remark. A bit arrogant, perhaps. Truth is, I was too young to trade. So my mother signed the paperwork and I traded under her name. No kidding.

By this stage, I was beginning to make money. By now I had quit King Wah. Uncle Paul was working me too hard, and I did not have weekends off to spend clubbing with my friends. After leaving the restaurant, I worked at a supermarket and then as an office assistant. I had saved up, had a decent stash, and became what is now known as a day trader. Admittedly, I was probably the only day trader who traded under his mum's name. For a few weeks, I viewed myself potentially as a sharp-suited, financial demon making millions from buying and selling on Wall Street. Without the suit. But you know, I was never that good at trading, and finance did not interest me. The excitement faded as I realised that a comfortable living was all that I wanted. Also, let's not forget that I was supposed to be a student but was working harder at making money than at studying.

The best purchases were the ones that improved my mother's life. I could give her cash and buy her things for the home. I bought her an air conditioner and a sofa.

And I bought a television for my mother, which meant less-frequent visits to Uncle Winston's across the hallway. Watching American television, I identified totally with the happy, prosperous, American and *white* family scenes it portrayed. My Chinese boyhood friends, I know, shared my sense of being 'American'; our folk heroes were the Lone Ranger and Superman. We knew we were not quite the same as our Irish, Polish, German and black schoolmates, but this did not make us doubt our own place in America.

My childhood in Chicago had in fact been a rather sheltered one, but there was no question in my mind that I was growing up 'American'. However, this sense of belonging, even if I were a cultural hybrid, was weakened, undermined and assaulted as I had made the transition into adolescence.

It was as a teenager that I first began to realise what it meant to be an ethnic-racial minority and an Asian male in America. At that stage, when I expected to move out into the mainstream of society, I was brought up short by situations and challenges I had earlier escaped, or unconsciously ignored. In the first place, it was then that I met with or finally recognised racial prejudice. Strange stares as if I had just landed from Mars, or comments that I should return to China.

In retrospect, I now realise that racism, anti-Asian prejudice, had been all around me as a child, but in my innocence and in my identification with America, it had not affected me.

I don't understand now how I could have sat through all those movies and television programmes I enjoyed as a child, watching in isolation, with their depiction of supposedly typical, and certainly stereotypical, Chinese and other Asians: Hop Sing, the excitable but always faithful cook in the popular TV series *Bonanza*; the egregious *Charlie Chan* films with their inscrutable, clever detective, speaking in a refined pidgin English and his 'Number One Son', so faithful and so uncomprehending. And these, I think, were the *good* images of Chinese manhood!

Stereotyping of all Asians – indeed, all non-Caucasian men – had a cruel impact on my image of my developing manhood. Whatever the stereotypical Asian image in films and on TV was, it was not a sexually powerful or attractive one. To the pubescent Asian male, trying to figure out his identity, trying to come to terms with his growing sexual imperatives, this only added to the confusion.

Even if my father had been alive, would that have helped? If John Wayne symbolises the epitome of American manhood – and Madison Avenue makes money out of it, to this day – consider the situation of the Asian male confronting such an ideal. A 'man' is supposed to be tall; I, typically Asian, am relatively short: five feet, seven inches. Hair symbolises masculine virility. I, again typically, have a relatively hairless body. No hairy (manly!) chest, no impressive beard or flowing musta-chios for me.

When a little peach fuzz struggled through above my upper lip, my horrified mother plucked it with her fingernails – to the Chinese, hair-lessness is a sign of male comeliness.

However, when I was older and wanted to be allowed into bars, I was shooed away at the door because I looked so young. I did not have ID (as I had no intention of learning to drive, so was without a licence). The only way around this, I figured, was to grow a moustache. This would make me look my age. It worked. I kept the moustache until I was thirty-five years old, at which point I shaved it off, confident that the facial hair was no longer a necessity to get past the doormen at bars and clubs.

The hair on my head would have to wait longer before it was removed. Men who are going bald have a choice: keep it long or cut it short. However, there was a moment when I tried other options, having seen snippets of myself – and my hair – on television. These snippets brought the striking realisation that I was losing my hair and it was not a good look.

I tried a hair restorer which claimed to rejuvenate hair growth. In my case, this claim was unsubstantiated. Next, I read up on hair transplants, but most of them were dreadful and I dropped the idea because it was simply too absurd. There was, of course, the option of wearing a tou-pee. Again, this seemed ridiculous.

The solution, I concluded, was to divest my head of all its hair, every last wave and wisp. I shaved it. Surprisingly, people said, 'You look great.' They could have been lying, but the general consensus is that I look younger, and nowadays people don't even remember me with hair. One time, someone said to me in astonishment, 'I saw an old photo of you – I didn't even know that you used to have hair.' I figured that during introductions at social events I could adopt that as a funny punchline to put everybody at ease: 'I don't know if you remember, but I used to have hair.' It gets a laugh, by and large.

6

Going West

THE GOLDEN NOON sun was so powerfully bright that I needed a blindfold. I was happy with shades. Beneath my feet, the powdery sand was so hot it was taking me towards extreme levels of pain. Boy, it felt good. My skin was being scorched by the rays. I did not mind one bit. Excessive heat was a pleasurable sensation.

Before me, the beach and the glittering expanse of the Pacific, and a few storm petrels hovering over the waves, ready to swoop under the water to pick up a lunch of tiny fish. Behind me, a forest of towering redwoods, 1,000 years old. Even further behind me, by about 2,000 miles, was Chicago, shivering like Niflheim – the kingdom of ice in Norse mythology – in the state of Illinois.

I had dreamt of California. Now I was here.

A few things had caused my migration across the States. First, I had been invited to Arizona, to attend the wedding of my late father's niece, and this would place me about a twelve-hour drive from California. Second, I reckoned I could take the opportunity of heading to California after the wedding and staying there for the summer. Third, my friend Jeffrey Moy, who owned an antiques store in Chicago's Chinatown, said that if I could get myself to San Francisco then he had friends in the city and they'd put me up until I found a home of my own.

So I went to the wedding, and then to San Francisco. Smitten! I thought, *Wow this is not Chicago.* I was right; it was San Francisco. But I mean it was *so extraordinarily cool.* Everybody had long hair, smoked dope, and went to rock concerts at the Fillmore.

In those days, it was easy to find work in the States. You'd simply say that you'd done this and that, smile, and you'd get a job. I wandered into an office, smiled, and got a job in the mail room and running errands for the staff. I was there through the summer, and concluded: this is where I want to be. California, that is, not the office.

During those summer months I had made friends in Berkeley – only forty minutes by train from San Fran – and the camaraderie strengthened my resolve to move there permanently. Plus, I had money saved – a nice kitty – so I could do it. I was twenty years old and told myself, this is where I've got to be.

I returned briefly to Chicago, gathered my bits and pieces, and took a Greyhound back to the west. It was December '69 and Chicago was under a blanket of deep snow and the city's temperature was down to minus ten. As I headed along Route 66, my mother's farewell words echoed in my mind. 'I know you have to do this,' she had said to me. 'It's hard. But I understand.'

The legion of uncles in my life had also shared their concerns: 'Don't forget your mother.'

To each of them, I had responded with the assurance, 'Don't worry. I won't.' I did not, as you will see.

———

JUST as others, a century earlier, had rushed to California in search of gold, I prayed and hoped for a destiny of promise and excitement. I moved into an apartment, and my flatmate, Len Lesachander, found me a part-time job as teacher at a pre-school nursery, where he also worked. This gave me a bit of breathing space, and soon I was enrolled at the local college, called Merritt, in Oakland. Also, I applied for a place at the University of California, to study History of Art.

The college played its own role in America's history of civil rights because, pre-dating my arrival by only a few years, two of the students were Huey Newton and Bobby Seale. In 1966, they founded the Black Panther Party, the revolutionary organisation that fought, and fought hard, for the constitutional rights of black people. This band of activists wanted the basics – decent housing, education, jobs and an end to the police brutality of black people. They also had a reputation for violence, and there were members who carried guns and, from time to time, shot people.

The Black Panthers had an established, faithful core at Merritt, and I remember glancing down the hallway to see Huey Newton walking in my direction. He was there to deliver a rousing speech to the many black students at Merritt.

I am not a violent person and do not condone violence. But I admired the stance of the Black Panther Party. These young people had devoted themselves to a struggle for their rights, trying to do something different, and most of the students were caught up in the movement. Meanwhile,

I became involved in the Asian-American community centre. Before going to California, I wasn't political, but now I was immersed in the prospect of change.

We were all strongly opposed to the war in Vietnam. A month before I arrived in California, the news had broken of the My Lai Massacre, in which hundreds of unarmed civilians in South Vietnam were slaughtered by US soldiers; the women raped and their bodies mutilated. News of America's napalm bombings ignited yet more fury back home in the States.

The war was a bloodbath, and Berkeley was a centre of anti-war protests and demonstrations. We all hated the war, and the US had no business being there. I participated in many marches. My Chinese friends and I felt that we were also victims because of our Asian appearance. They were killing gooks – which meant us.

These were exciting times, full of firsts for me. For the first time, I was living in a climate that I just adored. There were no winters. Every day I awoke to another day of sunshine. Winter in Chicago and it would be dark at three o'clock in the afternoon. We could wear our hair long, submerge ourselves in free love and dance away to the Beach Boys, Cream, Janice Joplin, Jimi Hendrix and the Stones' 'Gimme Shelter'. I was thinking, *I'm part of this!* In Chicago, I had never felt as if I belonged. Chicago now seemed stale.

All over the States, young people packed their duffel bags with beloved tie-dyed jeans (adorned with flower power patches) and cherished vinyl records, and flocked to California to become students. The peace sign was the familiar greeting in this comfort zone state. People didn't care if I was Chinese, which was another new experience for me. For the first time, I was in a place where I didn't feel excluded. In Chicago, there was something of an apartheid system: blacks stayed with the blacks; whites with the whites; races didn't mix. San Francisco, meanwhile, boasted the country's largest Chinatown.

When I moved to Berkeley, the place was buzzing with Asian activists. I made even more friends, and joined the Workers' Viewpoint, a Maoist group. For the first time, we were reading news stories and seeing films about what was happening in China during what was the height of the Cultural Revolution. We considered the revolution to be a great event. How foolish we were. Overthrowing society meant throwing out the bureaucrats and revolting against authority. How fantastic was that? Let's throw out all the rascals.

What particularly disappointed us, and brought us back to reality, was what was happening in Cambodia. When we found out about the mass genocide under Pol Pot's murderous regime – at least two million civilian deaths, it is believed – we became seriously disillusioned.

———

I began to cook again. After leaving my job with Uncle Paul, I had not cooked often. My mother made the meals at home, or I'd eat in restaurants. In California, the interest in me as a Chinese-American extended to an interest in Chinese food. My flatmate, who was a little older than me, enjoyed cooking and had a large circle of friends. It was not unusual for him to say, 'There's a crowd coming tonight. Your turn to cook.'

My cooking also benefited from this period of discovery: I started to explore non-Chinese cuisines. I bought Julia Child's books on French food and read every single word. I worked my way through her book *Mastering the Art of French Cooking*, cooking every recipe. Like many people of my generation, I learnt how to cook French food from Julia's book. As the title promised, it did enable me to master the art.

I appreciated the audience of hungry students who pitched up to be fed, and they were appreciative of my food.

Through cooking, my own social circle developed and grew. All cooks know that food creates smiles and friendship. I found myself thinking increasingly about the dishes I'd serve when it was my turn to feed the famished.

I was one of the millions of poor Americans entitled to 'food stamps', the government programme introduced to help the malnourished through the Great Depression and then reintroduced by President Kennedy. The stamps meant cheaper meals, and I was using them to buy food for my dinner parties – probably not their intended purpose.

I studied History of Art at the University of California, in Berkeley, and was fascinated by the great moments of European history. In order to illustrate what they were teaching, the lecturers used photographs on slides, which were beamed onto a large white screen. Video and DVDs had yet to come along. They were photos of art and monuments and sculptures, on display in large European cities.

Now, after about eighteen months of the course, I was sitting in class one day, observing the screen and listening to the lecturer, when suddenly I had an idea. After class, I approached one of the tutors and said, 'I'm planning on going to Europe. Would you like me to take photos? You could use them as slides.' I tossed in the names of a few works of art notably found in Europe and worthy of a slide shot.

The teacher said, 'Sure, we'll pay you for them.'

Within a matter of seconds, I transformed myself from mere student at Berkeley to business partner of Berkeley. For about $150, I bought myself a Europass, a ticket around Europe that was popular with American students at the time. Off I went, to travel and stay in the cheapest hostels. In fact, in Amsterdam I slept on park benches and hung out with hippies, puffing on exotic, conical, hand-rolled joints. As part of the trip to Europe, I visited Italy and France, where I ate oysters for the first time.

When the three months were up, I returned to California … only to arrange a student grant that would enable me to live and study in France. So, in 1973 and at the age of twenty-four, I began a twelve-month escape.

In France, I missed little about America but pined for Chinese food. The cravings were strong. However, at that time Chinese food and ingredients were unavailable in Aix-en-Provence, in the south of France. I wrote to my mother, asking her to send a box of goodies, the sooner the better.

I was delighted when the box arrived, crammed with delicious ingredients. There were Chinese spices and bright, golden-yellow lily buds, or golden needles, which I could use for *muxi* or moo shu pork, a stir-fried dish. There were black beans: small black soya beans which have been cooked and fermented with salt and spices, and impart their own special richness to steamed, braised and stir-fried dishes. The bounty included Chinese dried mushrooms, which I soaked in water for about twenty minutes before straining and using, keeping the water as a vegetarian stock for soup.

I had some English and French friends who were also students in Aix, and invited them for dinner. 'My God,' they said, as they inhaled the wonderful smells coming from the tiny cooker. They had never eaten Chinese food. They came back for more, again and again.

My financial wizardry came into play once more when I Channel-hopped and visited Bristol University to see my friend Carol Mason, who was studying for a doctorate. When I told Carol about my photos of European artworks, she whisked me to the Art Department to meet a lecturer. He flicked through my vast collection of colour photos, soon to be slides at Berkeley, and said, 'This is exactly what we've been looking for. We'll buy them.'

My photographs would end up on white screens on both sides of the Atlantic, enabling students to see artwork they could only hope of seeing in real life and that I had seen up close, of course.

———

I returned to California, minus the funds to support myself. I was destitute. During my final months in France I had resorted to my credit card to finance my existence, and the extortionate interest rate on an ever-increasing debt was new to me. Students don't have cash; they're not supposed to have cash. Now I was no exception. I'd have to hustle. I needed to get some work.

Enter Ron Zuckerman. He was a dear friend with a loveable surname, and he happened to go out with Carol Mason, who had looked after me in Bristol. Ron was a teacher at a posh school and he had eaten my food. Apart from that, he knew the extremely wealthy wife of a congressman, and she happened to own a farm in California. Ron said, 'She's wondering whether you could come out to the farm for the weekend and give classes on Italian cooking.' I had eaten well in Italy, and was passionate about Italian cuisine. Who isn't?

'Ron, it sounds great. What's the fee?'

'Three hundred dollars.'

Imagine an oak treasure chest overflowing with shiny gold and silver coins, and diamond necklaces cascading down its sides. In my mind's eye, that's how I saw the $300. So I paused for a few seconds, as if I were mulling over the sum, and whether I could bring myself to work for such a paltry amount, and then I said to Ron, 'Please tell her yes, I'll do it.'

Apart from earning what, to me, was a fortune – and I was about to say *small fortune* but it was probably a large fortune – the weekend was a huge success. When I was packing up to head home, the congress-man's wife asked me, 'Do you know anything about Chinese cooking?'

'I could do it blindfolded,' I responded. She booked me for three more weekends. At these, I would show the 'pupils' how to cook Chinese food. Two final points: no, I didn't wear a blindfold; no, I did not guess this would lead to a career.

However, soon I was cooking private dinner parties in people's homes, many of the gigs coming by word of mouth. At Christmas, I would make coulibiac of salmon to sell. It was a very profitable and thriving business. Catering had become an extension of my cooking classes. So in the autumn of 1975, at the age of twenty-six, I had no problems when I asked my bank for a loan to buy a house in Berkeley, even though I was still a student. I liked my Chinese-American bank manager.

Duck in Two Courses à la Julia Child

This recipe is directly inspired by a traditional French custom of serv-ing two courses from one duck; something I learnt from reading Julia Child's book, *Mastering the Art of French Cooking*.

The origin of the custom is easy to imagine. It is based on the same necessities that lead one to substitute steaming for roasting a turkey: the breast cooks more quickly than the thigh. A boned duck breast may be grilled in less than 10 minutes but the rest of the duck takes closer to 45 minutes to cook.

So it makes sense to cut the duck into pieces before cooking and then to prepare at least two dishes, using different techniques. Most cooks understand that it is best to work with the cut-up duck.

For this dish, I separate the breasts from the rest of the duck. The boned and skinned breasts are then seasoned and marinated. After a quick sauté, the breasts are finished off in my Chinese vinegar and butter sauce. Remember that the Chinese vinegar is slightly sweet and will not offend the richness of the duck breast. I prefer my duck a bit pink, so you should let your own taste guide your timing – but be careful not to overcook.

The duck legs are marinated in a traditional Eastern mixture of soy sauce and Chinese Shaoxing rice wine, a flavouring that the robust character of the duck nicely absorbs during the roasting process. In effect, you and your guests will enjoy and complete the first duck course just in time to welcome the second course as it emerges piping hot from the oven.

Serves 4

1 x 1.8–2 kg (4–4½ lb) duck

2 teaspoons Chinese seasoned salt (see end of recipe)

For the marinade:

2 tablespoons light soy sauce

1 tablespoon Chinese Shaoxing rice wine

1 tablespoon dark soy sauce

1 cup basic chicken stock

1 teaspoon dark soy sauce

1 teaspoon Chinese dark vinegar

2 tablespoons butter

To obtain breast meat, cut through the length of the breast, slicing to the bone. With a boning knife, cut the meat away from the bone. Repeat the procedure for the other breast.

Cut the thighs from the carcass.

Skin the breasts and cut the skin into 2-inch pieces crosswise. Dust the breast meat with the Chinese seasoned salt. Mix the marinade ingredients in a heatproof casserole or baking dish and add the thighs, tossing to coat evenly. Marinate for 40 minutes.

Render the duck fat by cooking the skin pieces over low heat in a medium-sized frying pan for 20 minutes, or until the skin is crisp. Remove the skin (crackling) with a slotted spoon and reserve. Turn up the heat and sauté the breasts for 2 minutes on each side.

Remove the breasts from the pan and keep them warm. Drain off the fat and return the pan to the heat. Add the chicken stock and reduce to a quarter of a cup. Add the soy sauce, dark vinegar, and butter, and stir to combine thoroughly. Remove from the heat. Cut each breast crosswise into slices.

Cover a serving plate with a little sauce and fan the sliced breasts around it. Sprinkle with skin cracklings.

Preheat the oven to 200°C (400°F, gas mark 6). Bake the thigh pieces, uncovered, along with the marinade for 40 minutes.

To make Chinese seasoned salt:
2 tablespoons roasted Sichuan peppercorns, finely ground and sieved
3 tablespoons salt

Heat a wok or large frying pan until it is hot and add the ground peppercorns and salt. Stir-fry for 1 minute, remove and allow to cool. Then mix in a blender for 1 minute.

It is now ready to be used or can be saved for future use. 🥣

7

A Career

MY STUDIES HAD opened a vista to subjects that fascinated me, such as the French Revolution, or the development of Britain from a small island in the Atlantic to the ruler of an empire spread across the globe.

The curriculum focused on sculpture from the late Romanesque to early Gothic periods, and I had an excellent teacher. Born in Le Mans in 1908, Jean Bony had been appointed at Berkeley in 1962 and was an eminent professor of art and architectural historian of the medieval era.

As a young man, he had been a French teacher at Eton, before returning to his homeland at the outbreak of the Second World War to fight in the French infantry. He was captured and spent three years in an internment camp as a prisoner of war, though he never talked to me about either his past or food. However, his imprisonment did little to dampen his spirit, and his CV positively glittered with his impressive positions at places such as Yale and Cambridge.

Professor Bony was a small, wiry man who was extremely agile, and he was expressive and had real gravitas. He was also kind to me and gave some thought to my next step. It was 1976; I was in my mid-twenties and taking stock. I could not be a student all my life. That next step was a career. The professor was an acknowledged authority around the world and he happened to be well-connected at the Courtauld Institute of Art. Today, it can be found within Somerset House, on the Strand in London, beside Waterloo Bridge and the River Thames. Then, the institute was in Portman Square, a stroll from bustling Oxford Street in the West End.

It was founded in the 1930s by a triumvirate of art collectors, whose aim was to improve the understanding of the visual arts in Britain. 'Perhaps I could get you into their graduate school,' said Professor Bony. 'I will have a word with them, if you like. Ken, have a think about it.'

I had a think, and returned to my teacher to say, 'I have had a think. I am so grateful to you. But I just cannot see myself in a career of academia.' Even, I might have added, if it involved living in London, a city I adore and that I had visited for the first time five years earlier.

'What will you do?' he asked.

'I am going to be a teacher,' I said. 'But in cooking, not art.' I had totted up the pros and cons. Being a professor could not bring in a good living and, what's more, I knew how to cook. Enthused by the prospect, I made an impulsive decision to quit the course, leave university and throw myself into the art of cooking and the pleasure of teaching about it.

I was six months short of completing my four-year course, and if the cooking didn't work out I would have returned to my studies. However, there was a momentum building in my cooking career. I was running my own little private catering business and was now teaching not only Chinese but French cookery classes. I even had a special Christmas class, when I'd gone to Chinatown and bought pheasants and hung them, before cooking the birds with my students.

—

I know, I know, I know – it was a big risk. You don't need to tell me that. My mother was telling me that, everyone was telling me that. But you know what? I figured, *OK, if you don't take a chance, nothing ever happens.* I pressed on to build my business.

First, I had to spread the word. There was a newspaper that was distributed free and most readers avoided the news pages and flicked straight to the classified ads, to see where they could enrol for art or yoga classes – typical California zen-hippy stuff. I placed the ad for cookery classes. People came to the Ken Hom Cooking School.

Second, I visited my Chinese-American bank manager (who had loaned me the money to buy my house) and took out another loan to extend my house. The extension would provide me with an office and a kitchen that was open, casual and easygoing, and large enough for each of a dozen or so students to have work surfaces. I had a professional wok, a duck-roasting oven and plenty of space in which to hang equipment. There was also space on the wall to hang a framed photograph that I had cut from *Gourmet* magazine which always made me smile. The shot showed a Frenchman sniffing, through his long, white beard, an extremely large black winter truffle, one of my favourite foods. He was Alain Pébeyre, of the iconic Pébeyre truffle farming dynasty.

—

The kitchen is changing. Nowadays people seem to like a minimalist kitchen. They want to hide their oven, kettle, toaster, fridge, freezer, as well as their pots and pans, knives, whisks, mashers, tongs, forks, sporks and spoons (be they slotted, wooden or silver, or for the purpose of spaghetti, salt, melon, grapefruit, coffee or caviar). Not me. My kitchens aren't changing. I like everything on display, easy to see and easy to grab when needed.

In Berkeley, the kitchen walls at my home/cookery school were lined with shelves. Upon them were hundreds of bottled spices and dried ingredients (so many, I required an inventory). Chinese knives and cleavers were on a special wall-mounted rack, with the razor-sharp blades behind Plexiglass. The island in the middle housed a massive chopping board at one end and a pastry marble at the other. I bought a Hobart dishwasher which had a ninety-second cycle – one of my best-ever purchases.

OH, the twists and turns of life. One minute, I was being lined up for a lofty and intelligent career in the art world. The next, I was teaching hippies how to cook. Boy, it was a bargain for my pupils. I charged $10 a class so, when you think about it, they could just come and eat, if they wished, and it was still a fantastic deal because there was wine, too. But most of them wanted to learn how to cook, so I began each session with a masterclass and it ended with a mini feast.

I did not have a car and still don't drive. There are too many crazy Chinese drivers on the road, and the world is a better place without having one more. So I would load my bicycle with two empty baskets, cycle to the Bart Station, which is the local underground, and head for Chinatown, where the good-quality ingredients were cheaper than elsewhere. Then I would return home with two full baskets and do all the prep. Pay someone to prep for me? No way.

———

JEREMIAH Tower was one of the pioneers of what we know as California cuisine. He was born in Connecticut and then well schooled (he crossed the Atlantic to be a pupil at Parkside in Cobham, Surrey). It wasn't until the early '70s, when he was about thirty, that he began his career. This happened after he ate a fruit tart at Chez Panisse, Alice Waters's iconic restaurant. He was so taken by the taste of this solitary flan that decided he wanted to cook, and to cook in the kitchen of that particular restaurant.

He applied for a job, and when he went for the interview in the kitchen he was shown a pot of soup and asked how he would improve it. Casual and cool, but also skilful, he threw in wine, butter and plenty of herbs. It was fantastic. He got the job on the spot. Within a year, through talent, skill and hard work, Jeremiah had been made an equal partner in Alice's restaurant.

The partnership survived about six years, during which time Jeremiah's reputation flourished and the appropriately named chef became a tower, so to speak, within the area's gastronomic evolution: someone to look up to.

Things soured, fruit tart-style, at Chez Panisse and the partnership came to an end. Jeremiah went briefly to London, to work with the fine cook and great food writer Richard Olney, who was editing the Time Life cookery books. They had a serious budget, some of which was spent on cases of red Burgundy; all in the name of research, of course. Jeremiah returned to California and that is when I met him. We were introduced by Vernon Rollins, a wine merchant and a popular man with the Chez Panisse crowd.

8

The Call and the Calling

JEREMIAH PHONED ONE morning in '78 and said, 'The dean of the California Culinary Academy wants to see you. Go see him.' Jeremiah could be forceful.

The dean was Ron Batori, a young man who was in charge of this cookery school that taught and trained people to become professional chefs. About fifty students attended the Academy. I figured, *Why not?* I went to meet Ron. He was friendly and we took a stroll to a nearby bar. As we sat sharing a bottle of wine, Ron told me his story, which I found fascinating and which, if you don't mind, I'll share.

Born and raised in Oakland, California, Ron could not wait to leave home and the area. In fact, he went so far as to leave the country. He had gone to Britain to study at the London School of Economics. On graduating, he and a friend, Paul, decided to buy a boat. Their sole intention was to sail around the world. They set off from a harbour on the northeast coast of England and on day two they were about twenty knots south. This point marked the end of their round-the-world voyage.

Next, they sold the yacht and, with the money, moved from sailing into the hospitality industry, as you do. They opened a restaurant, the Tudor Rose, in the market town of Midhurst, in the county of West Sussex. There was a third partner in this venture, a man called Earhart, if I remember rightly.

Now, Ron had an interest in fine wines. It was a fast-developing passion, which had blossomed earlier when he lived in Paris for a year, before the boat episode. He was in the French capital to research the Yaoundé Convention, the first treaty between Europe, or the Common Market as it was called in those days, and former French West Africa.

As an LSE student, Ron met the presidents of many of the West African countries – Léon M'ba from Gabon, Léopold Senghor from Senegal, Félix Houphouët-Boigny from the Ivory Coast, Ahmed Sékou Touré from Guinea. Along with a few fellow students, Ron was seconded to help the dignitaries. They all dined down in the Quai d'Orsay area, and inevitably ate and drank like kings, or even presidents.

When they were not talking politics, the francophone Africans pondered the beautiful produce of the grape. Actually, they spent more time talking wine than politics. The seed, you might say, was planted: Ron was intrigued. He had seen the enjoyment that wine brings to a meal.

'And for that reason', he told me, 'I set my heart on having a fantastic wine list at the Tudor Rose.'

Ron went to Augustus Barnett and bought a dozen or so wines, at a discounted price because the high street wine merchant – or off licence or 'offie' – was eager to clear its shelves as it was going out of business.

The majority of British drinkers had yet to acquire a palate for wine and discover that there were good ones.

Ron seemed transfixed by the memories alone, and he told me, 'I had never seen a bottle of Mouton Rothschild before, or a Margaux '66 … I'd never seen them. I just looked at them and fondled them … And then I bought them.'

On the restaurant's second night of business, a Sunday, there was a grand total of four customers in the Tudor Rose. They included a certain Barry Phillips – distinguished by his long hair and velvet bow tie – and his wife Dot. Now, Barry owned the White Horse in Chilgrove, and he'd heard about this new place and come to check it out. They ordered steak and kidney pie, or whatever, and Barry took a look at the wine list and was astonished. In the quiet town of Midhurst he had unearthed some wondrous wines. There was the Mouton and there was the Margaux. When Ron came to the table to take the order, Barry said, 'I think you're interested in wine.'

And Ron said, 'I think I am too.'

Barry invited Ron to join the Four Walls Wine Club – there were only six members, they were all gentlemen and they swore a pledge: anything that was said within those four walls would never leave those four walls. They drank great wines. Ron was flabbergasted when Barry produced, let's say, a '47 La Tâche. As wine prices dwindled, Ron was becoming even more enthusiastic about wine. He would go to London's auction houses, buying up wines at a good price; wines which today would be worth a tidy sum, but then went into the tummies of the lucky guests at the Tudor Rose. And in those days he was buying them very, very cheap.

Ron also enjoyed reading the musings of wine connoisseur Harry Waugh, who travelled around the States, being fabulously entertained at every stop from Washington DC to California. Those who entertained him included a couple called Belle and Barney Rhodes. They featured prominently in Waugh's memoirs because, unsurprisingly, they often treated him in Napa.

I listened, captivated by Ron's excitement. Sure, I wondered where the story was heading, as you do now. So, anyway...

One day, Ron noticed an ad in the *San Francisco Chronicle*, looking for a European-trained wine instructor at something called the California Culinary Academy, a school for people who wanted to be professional chefs. He thought, *That's me. I'm tired of what I'm doing.*

The Academy had been started by Danielle Carlisle, a former Stanford biology research assistant ('I gave up mice for mousse') and there was a dean called Barry West, a Briton with City and Guilds qualifications. Ron applied for the wine instructor job and was accepted. As he told me, 'I thought to myself, I'll be running this place in six months.' Six months later, he was part owner. Ron and Barry bought out the man who originally had financed the school, who was an architect in Pittsburgh, Pennsylvania. Soon Barry left and Ron became the new dean. This gave him considerable influence within the school, of course. The Academy had started with about twenty students but, as mentioned, had grown to around fifty when I met Ron.

So in '78 – about a year after the Academy started – Ron got a phone call. 'Hello, my name is Belle. I'd like to be able to use your school for a cooking demonstration with Marc Meneau.' Monsieur Meneau being the chef-patron of L'Espérance, the three-star Michelin restaurant in Yonne in Burgundy.

Ron said, 'Belle, are you by any chance Belle Rhodes? A friend of Harry Waugh?'

'Yes.'

Then Ron said to Belle, sweetly, 'I've had dinner with you lots of times already. But in my imagination.' He explained to Belle how he had learnt of her unsurpassed entertaining from Harry Waugh's books. Belle arrived at the Academy the following day with a bottle of Heitz Martha's Vineyard and invited Ron to dinner – this time real rather than imaginary.

Come Thursday evening, the guests at that dinner table amounted to: Jeremiah Tower; Narsai David, who had a restaurant in Berkeley; the wine merchant Darrell Corti – he and Ron had gone to the same school but hadn't seen each other in many years; and a neurologist, Dr Stanley Short. It was a proper gathering of aficionados of wine and food – an extremely small community in those days. When it came to the farewells, Jeremiah said, 'Are you looking for a teacher?'

Ron: 'Yes.'

Jeremiah said, 'Well, I know the person. His name is Ken Hom.'

That's how I came to be sitting in a bar, sharing a bottle of wine with Ron and listening to his fascinating story.

'When can you start?' said Ron.

I told him, 'Any time you want.'

Ron flicked through a few documents, including the curriculum. He scribbled and muttered to himself. Then he looked up at me.

'How about this?' he said. 'We could have Chinese Cookery with Ken Hom.'

I ordered another bottle.

—

BARNEY and Belle Rhodes were the king and queen of Napa Valley. They had one of the ten best wine cellars in the world.

To be invited to their home was an honour and always an experience, and would undoubtedly feature astounding wines. Barney's palate was unbelievable. Belle was the great hostess; she looked like a former show girl, with her hair swept back, and was meticulous when it came to the art of entertaining at home.

Before arriving at their home, guests would receive a handwritten note from Belle: it was a short biography of each person who would be at the dinner. This meant you could identify common interests ahead of the gathering and would have no problems with conversation. If you and I had never met, I would already have a brief biography of you, and you would have a brief biography of me.

She wrote a separate page detailing the dishes that were to be served. The Rhodeses entertained on a grand scale and frequently. On each occasion she wrote these briefing notes for each guest.

9

The Academy

L ET'S BE CLEAR about this. In the 1970s, most people did not aspire to be chefs. Most people aspired not to be chefs.

The Academy was a pioneering set-up, appealing to the small number who wanted to learn how to cook well. There were college graduates, though many of the students were professionals, with a bit of cash, but not happy with their careers. There were, for instance, actors, teachers, policemen, plumbers; all of them having left their jobs, searching for a new path. That path was drawing them towards the restaurant profession, which was becoming something other than just a place for cooks who had not done well at school.

In the States, the only other similar organisations were the newly opened National Cooking Institute in Denver, and the Culinary Institute of America, based in Hyde Park, New York. As it turns out, Ron and his team – ambitious but admittedly quite new to the game – copied just about everything from the Culinary Institute. They even copied its application form and its curriculum. In fact, they wanted to be similarly named, but when Ron suggested the California Culinary Institute, there was a swift retreat and a re-think after stern objections from the established Culinary Institute of America.

However, the new school rapidly became acknowledged as a place worthy of learning the culinary arts. Every aspect of cooking was taught, with Ron giving lessons in wine and tasting, too. There were plenty of endorsements from respected figures in the business. On graduation days, for instance, students got to shake the hands of esteemed guests of honour such as M. F. K. Fisher and James Beard. Julia Child was there two or three times. On her first visit, she said to Ron, 'You know, the people who are here remind me of the kind of people who went into the peace corps during the Kennedy times. They're idealists.'

It was a sixteen-month course: four terms, each of four months. Eventually there were 200 students, all of whom wanted to be professional chefs rather than excellent home cooks. They were fitted out with toques – tall white hats – and aprons. From day one they were called 'chefs' by the teachers. This was controversial, and criticised by 'real' chefs, mostly Europeans, based in California and San Francisco. 'How dare they call themselves chefs! You're not a chef until you've spent six months peeling potatoes every day!' And so on.

But the Academy was marketed very much as a solid foundation of culinary learning. Upon leaving, you would be an excellent cook, and recognised as a chef. You would easily find a job in a professional kitchen or have the nous to set up your own restaurant or catering business.

Before enrolling on the course, students paid a fee of about $8,000. Not a small sum in those days; they were a committed band ready to invest in their futures. The hours were pretty intense. The first shift began at 7 a.m. and ended at 3 p.m. The second shift lasted from 3 p.m. to 9 p.m. There were four kitchens and a large dining room, where, on Friday nights, local residents came to enjoy the students' food at a buffet.

That buffet was much-adored and well-priced, which meant the locals got a cheap meal. Often, they were out to get the most for their money. The ladies found one way of achieving this: they arrived with large but empty handbags and at the buffet they filled the bags with cream-filled pastries. This infuriated Carl, the maître d', who liked to spot the pastry thieves, dash over and bump into them. 'Oops, I'm sorry,' he would say, apologetic but quietly confident that he had crushed the pastries in their handbags. 'Ken,' he said to me one evening after I spotted him bag crushing, 'if they're gonna steal pastries, I wanna make sure those pastries are all smashed up.'

——

THE teachers included experienced and highly skilled chefs, although the pastry chefs caused headaches for Ron and his team. There was a belief at the school that pastry chefs were either flirty or thirsty.

Pastry chefs are frequently regarded by the rest of the brigade as the eccentric characters. The pastry part of a professional kitchen is usually hidden away from the other sections, with no windows; so no natural light. Days without natural light might affect the mind. They are also exposed to liqueurs, so the booze is there if they want to indulge.

They could be boastful, and would stand in front of the class, reminding students, 'I made Elvis Presley's wedding cake,' or something similar.

There was one pastry chef-teacher, Denis Martig, who was Swiss. Come to think of it, he had made the wedding cake when Elvis Presley married Priscilla in 1967. Denis would cheerfully tell interested students

– or indeed anyone else who was interested – about the extravagant cake: six tiers of sponge, filled twice with apricot marmalade and kirsch-flavoured Bavarian cream; the layers were glazed with kirsch-flavoured fondant icing and decorated with royal icing and marzipan roses.

One of the pastry chefs made petits fours which had the most spectacular sheen to their surface. When asked by a student how he achieved the gleam, the chef said, 'That's my little secret.' This response startled Ron and the other bosses, who found it bizarre. The chef, after all, was being paid to share his secrets with the students, who were, let's face it, paying his salary.

He would arrive very early in the morning, so that he could create his petits fours without anyone spotting his glaze tricks. Then the students would arrive and finish off, though mystified about the secret. One day, Ron took him to one side. 'That gleam on the petits fours – how do you do it?'

The chef replied, 'My little secret.'

Ron tried to explain. 'These students are paying $8,000. You're supposed to tell them how to do it.' The chef wouldn't budge.

There were other anxieties for Ron. He became concerned about the ever-increasing pastry bills – not for butter, flour, cream and sugar. But for booze. Crème de menthe, sherry and Grand Marnier were legitimate ingredients for cakes and desserts, but not in the swimming-pool quantities that were being shipped into the Academy. There were a couple of chefs who walked with the sort of wobble you would only want to see on an underdone crème brûlée or, indeed, a perfect British jelly. There was gossip that the drink, inevitably, led to passes from the chefs to the pupils.

—

MY role was to teach Chinese cuisine in five days, the length of time the students spent with me while they were on the course. I put together a curriculum, which I love to do, selecting certain dishes that would illustrate the simplicity and complexities of Chinese cooking. Into the curriculum, I weaved the history of the food – why we cook the way we cook – and would try to make it relevant for chefs. In other words, I was conscious that people would say, 'I'm not here to study Chinese,' but I wanted them to discover the skills and applications that would help with other cuisines.

Nevertheless, they were mostly fascinated by Chinese cookery, with its big wok and cleaver, and they were raring to go.

Many of them had never seen a wok, and I would take them through the process of seasoning the utensil. All woks (except non-stick or stainless steel) need to be seasoned. Many also need to be scoured first to remove the machine oil that is applied to the surface by the manufacturer to protect it in transit. This is the only time you will scour your wok, unless you let it rust.

Rub it with kitchen paper and water to remove as much of the machine oil as possible. Use a plastic cleaning pad or a coarse cloth, not a metal scourer.

Dry the wok and place it over a low heat. Add two dessertspoons of vegetable or sunflower oil. Use kitchen paper to rub the oil over the inside of the wok, coating the entire surface. Gently heat the wok thoroughly for 10 or 15 minutes – it will smoke – and then wipe it clean it with kitchen paper. Repeat the process until the kitchen paper is clean.

Your wok, meanwhile, will darken. This is a good sign. The darker the wok, the more prolific the cook. 🥣

I had about thirty-five students, half of them women. Shortly after I began my classes, I went one day to Chinatown and bought a chicken. The chicken was alive and when the students came into the room, the bird was flapping and squawking. I proceeded to despatch it. Many people are squeamish about such things but the fact is that the animal's life must be sacrificed in order to prolong ours. Plus, I thought my students were serious about cooking. Ron had assured me that was the case.

Swiftly, I cut the chicken's throat to let it bleed. 'Now,' I said to the class, 'you have to collect the blood in a bowl – and put salt in the bowl so that the blood will coagulate.' As I collected the blood in the bowl I gave a clue as to what would come next: 'Once I've done this, I'm going to show you how we're going to use every part of the bird.'

Wanting to check that my students were paying attention, I glanced around the room. There was a mass of faces, ashen and grimacing. Then the room started to empty, as the students made a dash for what the Americans call the bathroom, though I can assure you they were not going to have a bath. Most of those who hurried off to throw up were men, not women. They just couldn't take it.

From a seat in the corner, Ron Batori had been observing his new teacher. When the class finished, and it may have ended a little earlier than planned, he came up to me and said, 'That was fantastic. But please don't ever do that slaughter stuff again.'

I said, 'Slaughter stuff? I thought they were serious about food.'

Deadpan, Ron replied, 'Not *that* serious.'

Ron became a dear friend, and at weekends he'd host parties at his house, which was up in the Delta and built in 1863 during the Civil War period. Jeremiah and I would cook; Ron was generous with the wine cellar. Darrell Corti, the wine merchant, would also arrive with a few drinkable gems.

I am not sure if it was the episode of the despatched chicken that did it, but at some point Ron suggested it might be best if my cookery classes took place at my home. My classes were increasingly popular, and there was space to accommodate more students in the kitchen of my house in Berkeley. I agreed to the suggestion.

I'd drive Ron's colleagues crazy by charging for every cost. I charged for aluminium foil, for cling film and even sent in bills to cover part of my water bill – the students, I figured, used bucketloads by flushing the toilet and there was a drought in California. One of my invoices for reimbursement read: 'Cost to replace Eau Sauvage stolen from bathroom by student.' Another invoice read: 'Cost to replace chair broken by large female student.'

Begrudgingly at times, the Academy coughed up, knowing that my classes were drawing in large crowds and fees. Why, the students awarded me a nickname: Hollywood Hom, deriving, I imagine, from the fact that I dressed well, perhaps with a bit of style. There was also comedy and drama during the classes.

———

BY now I was good friends with Jeremiah Tower. One night he cooked a spectacular feast at his home: pig, and it was every part of the pig except the oink. My idea of heaven. And I remember taking Jeremiah on a guided tour of Chinatown, pointing out the best places to buy certain foods and ingredients.

I knew, however, that Jeremiah was having a difficult time, financially. So I said, 'Why don't you come and give cookery classes at my place? Just pay your expenses, and you can keep the profits.' He was happy with that, and his classes filled up immediately, as he was a bit of a legend.

He was also good to have around if I was organising an event. 'Let's get George Linton along to the party,' he would say of the renowned wine collector. 'George will bring some nice bottles.'

Jeremiah was keen to introduce me to James Beard, a deity of the national food scene. Known as 'the Dean of American Cookery', James was a writer, teacher, author of cookbooks and a champion of local produce. His childhood summer holidays were spent on the beaches of Oregon, where he would fish, make a fire and use it to cook his catch from the sea. In the mid-1940s he appeared in his own segment for what would be America's first cookery show. A decade later he established the James Beard Cooking School in New York (Madhur Jaffrey was among the people who taught there). His legacy is an eponymous foundation which, every year, presents the James Beard Awards, the Oscars of American gastronomy.

I liked James. I met him several times, including on a couple of occasions in New York, where he died in 1985. He was also extremely kind about my first book, writing a supportive review for one of the New York papers.

10

Dining with Danny and James

JAMES BEARD WAS a large man with a huge reputation. Gossip was a big part of his life. James had an opinion about everybody, whether they were in the James Beard circle or out of the James Beard circle. (Most people, I would learn, had their circles. Usually, you were in either one entourage or another. I wasn't really in anyone's entourage. This was partly because my career was international. I wasn't Californian or American, and was destined to spend a lot of time in Asia and Europe, keeping me away from the cliques. But everyone was respectful to me.)

I'd like to take you back to the 1920s, when James was a young man. He had finished college and his dream was to become an actor. He toured with a theatrical troupe and then travelled abroad, studying voice and theatre but not achieving any real success. He returned to America, still determined to become well known on the stage or in the movies. Well, he was making barely any money from acting and – by now in his mid-thirties – he figured he better earn some money to see him through his periods as a 'resting' actor. So he set up a little catering business and, sure enough, he had found his vocation.

Should you ever wish to prove the point that you can take the man out of acting but never the actor out of the man ... I give you James Beard. He loved, loved, loved to be the centre of attention. And he regaled us with long stories with all the booming power and projection of a seasoned thespian centre stage at the Old Vic.

Even heart problems had seemingly been unable to silence him. Once you were friendly enough with James, he would raise the subject of surgery and say, 'Hey, take a look at this...' Then he would unbutton his shirt to reveal his broad, bare chest and the horrendous long, deep scars of heart surgery. In those days, they had yet to perfect tidy surgery so, take my word for it, the great Beard's chest was a far from pleasant sight. It was like, *too much information, James.*

———

MY friend Ron Batori once gave me an incredibly useful piece of advice about lunch or dinner parties. 'Never', said Ron, 'invite two stars on the same night.' This does not apply merely to Hollywood stars. If you know one person who loves to be the focal point, then it is foolish to invite another friend who also craves all eyes upon him or her.

I will always be grateful for Ron's advice, but regrettably he gave me the tip after I had invited James Beard to dinner on the same night as Danny Kaye. Too late, in other words. Now, Danny, of course, was indeed a Hollywood star. He could sing and dance, was funny, and was a big hit in the '40s and '50s, in films such as *Up in Arms*, *The Secret Life of Walter Mitty* and *Hans Christian Andersen*. When his movie career faded, he moved into television, presenting his own show. All around the world, Danny was adored.

The 402-room Stanford Court Hotel – where the cable cars intersect on Nob Hill, in San Francisco – hosted events with chefs from all over America, drawing in a crowd of connoisseurs and gourmets. I happened to be friends with the hotel's managing partner and president, Jim Nassikas, one of the best hoteliers that ever lived (his style and innovations were copied all over the world). One day, Jim phoned to say he was coming over to mine, 'and I've got someone I want you to meet'. Shortly afterwards, he pulled up outside the house with Danny Kaye. That initial meeting was memorable because there were French friends staying with me and, although Danny did not speak the language particularly well, he managed to greet them in rusty French, saying: 'What I do not understand about French – why is the woman's vagina masculine – *le*? And why are the male genitals feminine – *la*?' Danny sure knew how to break the ice.

Danny was a keen cook and crazy about Chinese food, and that is why Jim had figured we should meet. We exchanged phone numbers and subsequently I invited him over for that dinner when Danny and James Beard were both in town, for an event at Stanford Court. The minute they were both in the house, I knew I had messed up. Each one of them was accustomed to being the sun, with everything spinning around them. Once you have two suns it gets to be a problem, and I had two suns in my house.

I was not quite sure where to sit them at the table, and each was vying for attention. If one of them told a story about so and so, the other had to tell a funnier, longer story about so and so. Not really a dinner, but more like being a spectator at a grand slam tennis match, one second looking to the right (Danny), the next second turning to the left (James). Retaliation by anecdote. No one else at the table dared say a word. James, remember, had always yearned to be a movie star, which just added to the slightly tense air of competition between the two men.

I kept in touch with Danny, and a couple of times when I was in Los Angeles (where I was a consultant for a restaurant) he invited me for dinner at his home in Beverly Hills. Here, he was the Sun King, in his mid-sixties. The house was the largest I had ever set foot in. The walls were lined with scores of framed photographs of … the ever-smiling Danny. There was Danny with royalty, Danny with other movie stars and Danny with world leaders. I was amazed by the variety of people he had met. On one wall, I spotted a photograph of Danny with the Duke of Edinburgh, who was dressed in uniform. We stood and looked at the photo and Danny said the shot was taken just as he was about to have lunch with Prince Philip. 'I told him, "Before we eat, take off that silly jacket with all the medals. You're not going to be comfortable at the table…"'

There were two kitchens next to each other: one was a Western kitchen, should Danny fancy cooking French or Italian cuisine; the other was a Chinese kitchen, fitted with three powerful gas rings specially designed for woks. Each of the kitchens was spotless, kitted out with professional equipment, and large enough to cater for an eighty-cover restaurant. This man was taking it seriously.

On my first visit, Danny had also invited Hélène Rochas, heiress of the perfume company, and she brought with her a Greek shipping oligarch, as you do. The oligarch, in turn, was joined by his solid gold worry beads. He spent the entire evening playing with that clattering chain of gleaming balls, noisily running his fingers along them. I mean, he played so much with those worry beads that it worried me.

Danny had three or four maids, and this is how the Kaye cooking routine worked. The maids would chop up the ingredients and do all the prep. Then Danny, the Sun King, would step forward in his apron and perform the grand art of cookery. His guests – us – were required to perch on stools and witness him as he made the meal and showed off his skills. Behold, the maestro! His stir-frying was impeccable; his food was delicious. Danny Kaye was one of those crazy people who when into something was really into it. He liked flying so had learnt to fly a jet liner, for instance. So when he cooked, he gave it his all. The result was impressive and, to the soundtrack of beating worry beads beneath the table, we ate magnificently.

It was said that Danny's wife, Sylvia, was domineering. I went for dinner once and he was eager for me to meet her. She came downstairs and we said hello, and then she went back upstairs and Danny took his place at the stove. She did not stay for Danny's exquisite food. That was the only time I met Sylvia. Perhaps she did not like to intrude on the Danny show. After one dinner, we finished the meal and he said, 'OK, follow me. Have I got an after-dinner treat for you guys!'

We stood up from the table and our host ushered us into his living room, telling us to take a seat on one of the luxurious sofas. He flicked on the TV, and then put on a videotape. It was one of his television shows. So we all sat there, with Danny, watching Danny on the box. That was strange. I'm not sure I would ever do such a thing. But Danny, who died in 1987, was fantastic company, very funny and curious about food. Have you eaten this, or have you eaten that? Ortolans, the tiny birds eaten whole in France, were one of his preferred delicacies.

He would ask me about food and I would ask him about Hong Kong. Danny, you see, had been there. Movies had paid for his trips to that faraway land. Whereas I only knew of Hong Kong through the movies.

Zheng Ji/Steamed Chicken

On my first visit to my ancestral home, as part of the ritual of paying homage to our ancestors, I had to prostrate myself before the household shrines. As I did so, my cousin was despatching a sacramental chicken in the yard. The bird was quickly plucked and cleaned, then rubbed with salt and steamed. We two then offered it up to our common ancestors, bowing three times before the shrines.

Then we quickly cut it up into small portions, and everyone in the family was served the chicken with a ginger and spring onion sauce that brought out the full flavour. The liquid from the steamed chicken was poured over the rice for an additional taste treat.

Let me assure you that even without ancestor reverence, this dish is delicious.

Serves 4 as part of a Chinese meal or 2 as a single dish
One chicken, about 3½ lb/1.5 kg
1 tablespoon Kosher salt (Maldon sea salt)

Dipping sauce:
Pinch of sugar
½ teaspoon salt
2 teaspoons light soy sauce
2 tablespoons finely chopped peeled fresh ginger
5 tablespoons finely chopped spring onion
2 tablespoons groundnut or vegetable oil
1 teaspoon sesame oil

I do like to rinse the chicken under cold running water – which is authentic – and then blot it completely dry with kitchen towels. However, we are told not to wash chicken, so, if you prefer, you can leave out this part of the method. Rub the salt inside the cavity and on the skin of the chicken. Place the chicken, breast-side down, on a heatproof platter, and set aside for 15 minutes.

Set up a steamer or put a rack into a wok or deep pan. Fill the steamer with about 2 inches (5 cm) of hot water. Bring the water to a simmer. Put the plate with the chicken into the steamer or onto the rack. Cover the steamer tightly and gently steam over medium heat for 1 hour. Replenish the water in the steamer from time to time.

Remove the platter with the cooked chicken and pour off all the liquid.

In a small bowl, combine the sugar, salt, soy sauce, ginger and spring onions, and mix well. In a small pan, heat the peanut and sesame oils until they are smoking. Pour the hot oils over the ginger mixture. Chop the chicken into serving portions and serve immediately with the sauce. 🍜

11

The Wild Child
of the Kitchen

OCTOBER 1961 IS a monumental point in gastronomy. It marks the publication of *Mastering the Art of French Cooking*. The book was written by Julia Child, Simone 'Simca' Beck and Louisette Bertholle, who had spent nine years researching, testing and crafting the recipes.

This seminal book, as I have mentioned, taught me how to create French cuisine when I was a student at Berkeley. It was my bible, and not just mine; millions of other cooks can nod in agreement. The authors followed up with a second volume in 1970.

These three women were also les trois gourmandes behind L'Ecole des Trois Gourmandes, a cookery school which gave French cookery lessons to American women living in Paris. Julia's husband, Paul, had received a posting to Paris by the American Embassy. After France, the

Childs returned to America, living in Massachusetts. However, they retained a foothold in France, building a house on land owned by Simca's husband, Jean. The building work took years and was finally completed in 1965. They had their own place in France, where they would spend part of the year.

Although Julia Child was my heroine, it seemed unlikely that our paths would ever cross. They would, I am delighted to say, but not in America.

In 1979, I cooked for a couple of fundraising events for a charity which had the support of a couple called Ivan and Dorothy Cousins. I had just been signed up by the publishers for my book, *Chinese Technique*. The Cousins lived in California, outside of San Francisco, and (pertinent to this story) Dorothy was Julia's sister. They were thrilled with my support and, when I said I was going to France, Dorothy said to me, 'Julia would really like to meet you.' She gave me her number.

A few weeks later, when I was in Provence, I phoned Julia Child. It was her voice that will live with me for ever. It was filled with confidence and a sort of happy-bossy tone, and it went up and down in pitch with almost every syllable. 'Come for lunch,' she told me. 'Take the train and we'll pick you up from the station.' I took the train from Marseille to Grasse, in the back country of the French Riviera, and waited as requested.

The day's heat was rising in temperature, and I looked at the little nearby shops and houses, which were colourfully festooned with cascading bougainvillea. A few minutes later, I saw a car heading towards me, the driver and passenger waving at me. Julia climbed out of the car, a great big smile, and while I had heard the woman's voice on the telephone, I had not envisaged her stature. Julia was huge. Like basketball player huge. (I later discovered that, as a schoolgirl, she had indeed played basketball.) I am reliably informed that she stood at six foot, two inches (1.88 metres). You can add another foot to that height, purely because of her formidable presence. If anyone was larger than life, it was Julia Child.

There were kisses and hugs – 'Darling, welcome to Grasse...' – and then, in the car, she said, 'I have to pick up some bread.' We went to the *boulangerie*, where there were more kisses and hugs and instructions to the baker from across the counter in high-pitched French. Julia's exuberance did not subside in the slightest at any point throughout the day. Back at the house, which was modest, homely and beautifully done, Julia turned to the subject of lunch. 'We are just having leftovers,' she said. 'Last night I had Michel Guérard.' I have talked of Michel, a founding chef of nouvelle cuisine. These leftovers would turn out to be an exceptional feast. I stood and watched Julia in the kitchen, and remember noticing that the work surfaces were so high. To me, that is, not her. Apart from food, we talked of politics. Julia was very left-wing; hated the Republicans.

There was a little twist to the meeting. Shortly before setting off for France, I had bumped into Professor Jean Bony, that famous medievalist who had taught me when I was at Berkeley. I mentioned that I was going to France, and added, 'When I am there I am going to meet a brilliant cook called Julia Child.'

'Ah,' he said in a casual way, 'I know Julia.'

'You *know* Julia?'

'Yes, I have known her for years. We were both living in Paris at the same time, and we used to attend the same study group. We would all get together to talk about medieval art.'

When I asked Julia if she remembered Jean Bony, she said, 'Of course.' We agreed that if she came to dinner at mine, I would also invite the professor. They had not seen each other for thirty-five years.

After lunch, Paul showed me his artwork and photographs. It was a lovely day, which ended with Julia telling me, 'When your book comes out, have your publishers get a hold of me.' Then she instructed: 'You have to promote your book. You have to push it.' She gave me a slap on the back: Julia was a tactile woman and did plenty of back-slapping. 'I will host an event at my house,' she added. Julia kept that promise. When my book came out in 1981, she held a reception at her home in Boston and invited along the press. From that evening, I still have a photo which shows me cooking with the wok, while Julia looks on, towering over me.

About a year after my book, Julia published another one of hers. I invited her for a celebratory dinner, and this would be the opportunity to reintroduce her to Jean Bony. It was a quite poor – some might say 'dodgy' – part of Berkeley in which I lived, but on that evening a sleek limo swept through the area, pulling up outside my door. Julia popped out. The whole atmosphere was wonderful, with the two of them reminiscing and recounting tales of Paris in the 1950s. I cooked Peking duck, my signature dish, and my heroine came in the kitchen to observe. I was thinking, *Oh my God, Julia Child is in my kitchen.*

She complimented my duck oven and wok burners and the design of the room, and as I cooked she talked about her days in China. During the Second World War she was stationed in Yunnan province, serving for the American intelligence services. Indeed, that is where she and Paul had met. She described it as 'a courtship over delicious food'.

'I do enjoy Chinese food,' she said to me. 'Beside French cuisine, it is one of my great loves. I could learn to cook French, but I could never learn to cook Chinese.' Silence. Then she said, 'But I do love to eat it.' And so we ate it…

I must confess that even at this stage in our friendship I still addressed her as Mrs Child. This was the Chinese within me: she was much older than me, and to call her Julia seemed disrespectful. Just before the meal was served, she enveloped me in her arms so that I felt my feet lifting off the ground, and said, 'Please, you can call me Julia.'

'I find it very difficult, Mrs Child.'

'Well,' she said, 'we made friends, nevertheless.'

12

~

Making Stir-Fry in the House of Chaos

T HOSE WHO LIVED in the Berkeley Hills, with its stunning views over San Francisco Bay, included Dr Yuen Ren Chao and his wife Buwei Yang, both elderly but with the energy of a young couple. She was a retired physician who had studied medicine in Tokyo. In fact, it was as a foreign student that she had discovered the enduring pleasures of cooking: she did not have a taste for Japanese food, and so had fun making her own.

He was a gifted linguist whose education had brought him to America, to study at Cornell and Harvard. He spoke many Chinese dialects. On returning to China, he had met Buwei and fallen madly in love with her and, I am sure, the gastronomic delights she cooked for him.

They were married in China in 1920, and subsequently became the parents of four daughters. A year before the outbreak of the Second

World War, and fleeing the Japanese invasion, the Chaos packed their cases, left Nanjing, the capital of the eastern Jiangsu province, and came to America, via Hawaii. They began a new life, first in Cambridge, Massachusetts, where the linguistics expert shared his wisdom with scholars at Harvard.

At this point their story takes an interesting turn. As the conflict raged abroad, they carried out jobs; roles that would assist the war effort. Dr Chao, who also spoke Japanese, taught languages to instructors in the US Army. Meanwhile, Mrs Chao – she was under five feet tall, but was never to be underrated – cooked frequently for her husband's 'pupils'. She shopped for ingredients in Boston's Chinatown, not far from their home, and the dishes she prepared were always Chinese.

Her creations were refreshingly impressive to an audience of Americans in the 1940s who had never seen, let alone eaten, Chinese food. The Chaos' house echoed with American voices saying 'Wow!' and 'Amazing!'

Indeed, when tiny Mrs Chao carried her dishes from kitchen to table, the reaction was so positive, the praise so recurrent, that she had an idea. 'I will write a book of recipes,' she decided and, forever a busy soul, she immediately set about the task of compiling a cookery book. The challenge, however, could not be completed by her alone. Although Mrs Chao was a talented cook, her English was not sufficient for her to write the recipes.

Step forward Dr Chao. He helped to translate the recipes into English. There was a third party involved in the production of the book, the couple's daughter Rulan (also known as Iris). Then in her twenties, she was another mighty intellectual, soon to have a formidable career as a professor at Harvard, and with remarkable talents for music and linguistics. She, too, would translate for the American audience.

And so it was that the three Chaos – mother, father, daughter – toiled away to produce a manuscript. Until then, there were few Chinese recipe books in America. (One book, *New Chinese Recipes: For the American Family*, was a slim volume, published in 1940 to raise funds to help the people of China.)

Now, being linguists, Dr Chao and Rulan reflected deeply on the descriptions of Mrs Chao's cooking.

First, there was this issue: in Chinese cooking, when you start to fry dumplings or wontons you will see that, instantly, they fasten themselves to the hot wok or pan. That's meant to happen. This process browns them and gives them an irresistible crispiness. Dr Chao had a eureka moment. 'We shall call them "pot-stickers".'

There was another issue, concerning rice. Many Chinese dishes require cold, steamed rice to be placed into a hot wok and then vigorously tossed around using chopsticks or a long spoon – the grains take on a nutty toasted flavour. Dr Chao had another flash of inspiration. 'This', he declared, 'we shall call "stir-frying".'

In 1945, Buwei Yang Chao celebrated the publication of her book, *How to Cook and Eat in Chinese*. The phrases *pot-sticker* and *stir-fry* began to work their way into the language and languages, not just in America but in kitchens, restaurants and cookery books all over the world.

The couple had another daughter, Lensey, who wrote her first book at the age of eight and, under her married name Lensey Namioka, she wrote prolifically about China and the Chinese-Americans, with an audience mostly of children and young people. Her works include *Ties That Bind, Ties That Break*, about a girl who refuses to have her feet bound. The name *Lensey* is unique. Her father established that there were two syllables that can be used in Chinese, but which appear in no Chinese words. They can be written in English as 'len' and 'sey': when joined together, they made a name.

—

IN 1947, the family moved to California, and to a large family house, high up at 1059 Cragmont Avenue, in the Cragmont area of Berkeley Hills. Dr Chao took up his post at the University of California, becoming Agassiz Professor of Oriental Languages.

He would describe their home as the House of Chaos, relishing the play on words. Maybe he did consider it a house of chaos, because he plotted an escape route. Or rather, he decided to build for himself a Chinese study in the grounds behind the property. When he sought planning permission, however, the building regulations prevented the development. Always one to accomplish his dream, Dr Chao got round the rejection by building a smaller dwelling – a cottage, with bedrooms, which could also be his study.

In time, this would become a property the Chaos could rent out. Mrs Chao particularly liked the idea of creating her own Chinese 'compound', where she could have people around her who would be supportive.

This takes us to the 1970s, and a young woman called Susie Maurer.

Susie worked in the travel industry and had gone through a messy divorce. Unlike one of those other divorces, which aren't messy. She had a daughter, Erika, and they lived in San Francisco. A girlfriend had said to her, 'Susie, you've got to get out of San Francisco. Come live in Berkeley.'

Somehow or other, she found herself viewing the Chaos' cottage, and Mrs Chao must have sensed Susie's supportive nature. Mrs Chao's instincts were flawless because, I would later discover, Susie is particularly supportive. Soon Susie and Erika had left San Francisco and were living in the cottage behind the Chaos. Cragmont Avenue would be

Susie's home for the next forty years, and she loved pretty much every moment of it, living in the shadow of that redwood grove and close to the big rock where people would come to practise mountain climbing.

There were many upsides. Susie had an uncle who said, 'China is the future,' and he paid for Erika to have Chinese lessons in high school. The world-famous professor Dr Chao, though, was her mentor.

They all got on well. Susie would describe Dr Chao as 'a sweet, unassuming intellectual, whose brain was so wonderful he could live with himself for ever'.

Later on, when China opened up, VIPs came to visit the renowned linguist and academic. One day, Erika phoned her mother to say excitedly, 'Mom, there's a big car just pulled up outside the Chaos'. It has flags on the front.' You never knew who you would meet there.

Mrs Chao, who was renowned to all the restaurateurs in the area, did not cook as much as she had done, but she enjoyed entertaining at home. Once, before a Chinese dinner, she took Susie to the dining table and said, 'Watch how I place the table. So and so thinks he is at the most important seat, but really he is not.' This amused the Chao matriarch. In the bathroom upstairs, she often kept a live fish in a bath of cold water to purge it – and maybe, just maybe, to shock visitors a little.

Squirrel Fish

Speaking of Mrs Chao's bath guest, perhaps this is an appropriate point for a recipe that involves a whole fish. Remember, serving a fish in its entirety will bring plenty of good fortune to those at the table.

Chinese chefs are masters at making foods appear not what they are supposed to be, and that playful attitude is apparent in this delightful dish. It is all in the technique of preparing the fish. Once fried, the fish curls up like a squirrel's tail, hence its name. This is the classic presentation of a banquet dish for a sweet and sour fish. It is worth doing and is impressive, to say the least.

Serves 4–6

1 whole sea bass, about 1 kg (2.2 lb), cleaned

salt and freshly ground black pepper to taste

cornflour or potato starch for dusting

900 ml (1½ pints) groundnut or vegetable oil

For the sauce:

300ml (10 fl oz) chicken stock

4 tablespoons Shaoxing rice wine or dry sherry

6 tablespoons light soy sauce

3 teaspoons dark soy sauce

3 tablespoon tomato purée

6 tablespoons Chinese white rice vinegar or cider vinegar

2 tablespoons sugar

2 tablespoons cornflour, blended with 4 tablespoons water

First, cut off the fish head behind the gills and set aside. With a sharp knife, fillet the fish on one side and cut until you reach the tail bone. Do the same with the other side.

Gently pull the two fillets intact and attached to the tail bone. Cut the bone that is attached to the tail bone. You should have two fillets held together by the tail bone. (Alternatively, you could ask your fishmonger to do this for you.)

Now score each fillet flesh side in a crisscross pattern. Season the fish with salt and pepper. Thoroughly dust the fish and the reserved fish head with cornflour or potato starch, shaking off any excess.

Make the sauce by combining all the ingredients, except the cornflour mixture, in a saucepan and bring it to a simmer. Slowly thicken the sauce with the cornflour mixture and set aside.

Heat a large wok until it is very hot. Add the oil and, when the oil is slightly smoking, quickly deep-fry the fish until it is crispy and cooked. Drain on kitchen paper. Now deep-fry the fish head and drain on kitchen paper.

Set the fish and head on a platter and pour over the sauce. Serve at once. ◗

13

The Cook on Crutches

MY COOKERY SCHOOL at home in Berkeley was popular with couples, as well as professional people who had their day jobs but were keen to improve their cooking skills. Along the way, I met people who became friends; I still know and am close to a few of them.

At one of my classes, I met the person who would become my lawyer. And I met the woman who became vet to my dogs, Zita and Molly. An insurance agent who came with his wife to my classes became my insurance agent. One day, a woman came in, and drew considerable attention because she was hobbling along on crutches. Actually, she had come not to my class, but to one that Jeremiah was teaching.

We got talking, and I asked about the crutches. Wouldn't you? It turned out that she had been in an automobile accident and had wanted to do 'something fun' while she recuperated, so she'd signed up for Jeremiah's class. And the conversation ended.

'Well, it's good to meet you. I'm Ken Hom.'

'And I'm Susie Maurer.' That lady, I would later learn, lived in the cottage behind the House of Chaos.

We met again, and then again, and our friendship developed on a mutual love of cooking. I would send her newspaper articles. She probably thought, *What's this all about?* And she would talk to me about her travels around the world. She also had a car, while my own travels were on my bicycle. One night I called her, and started with, 'What are you doing?'

She said, 'I'm not doing anything. Why?'

'Please can you come and pick me up because I need to get a pig from Chinatown? It won't fit on my bicycle.' An hour later we were in Chinatown, and Susie stayed at the wheel while a couple of butchers helped me load the hefty carcass into the trunk of her car.

—

COOKERY schools were still a rarity, even in the food revolution state of California, but people were becoming increasingly interested in good food. I was getting well-known and being asked to travel to other cities to teach and do demonstrations. There were others, however, who were travelling abroad – with their students – to teach about the food of foreign lands. For instance, Marcella Hazan, the woman credited with introducing Britain and America to Italian cookery techniques, was teaching cookery classes in Italy. Florence-born Giuliano Bugialli was also teaching Americans who fancied a cookery holiday in Italy. Susie had taken 'students' to cookery schools in France, so she knew the drill.

Nobody was doing cookery schools in Asia. What if I was to fill the void, with Susie helping me? We could get together, say, a dozen students who were curious about Hong Kong. Susie could arrange the travel and accommodation, and I could do the exciting cookery demos and masterclasses, and take the students on interesting tours of the markets and fun visits to restaurants. Erika would soon be starting college, and Susie was looking for a way to help pay for the schooling. This could be the way.

We talked about Hong Kong, and talked about it some more ... Nothing happened.

Meantime, Susie became sort of hooked up with Jeremiah Tower. He was trying to raise money to set up his own restaurant, Stars, and was on the look-out for financial backers. Susie had a rich client, to whom she had mentioned Jeremiah's hopes of becoming a chef-patron; and she was thinking she could leave her job in travel to manage the restaurant's front of house. Her rich client had said of Jeremiah, 'Bring him over one night. I'd like to meet him.'

Sure enough, one night it was time for Jeremiah to meet the rich client. He pulled up outside Susie's home, honking the horn, and out she came, beautifully dressed for the evening and carrying a jeroboam of champagne. That's the equivalent of four bottles of champagne in one bottle. When Susie wanted to bring a bottle, she really brought a bottle.

They set off for the rich client's home, and then they started to argue. Well, Jeremiah could be temperamental at times. Maybe he was feeling nervous about the meeting with the rich client, but the point is, he threw a tantrum.

Susie was saying, 'Grow up ... Get a grip.'

Suddenly, Jeremiah put his foot on the brake and said, 'Get outta the car ... Get outta my car.'

Susie: 'I'm not getting outta your car. Just calm down.'

Well, the drama developed. Jeremiah drove to the police station in Berkeley. And that's where *he* got outta the car. He went into the police station, while Susie stayed in her seat. A few minutes later, Jeremiah re-emerged with a police officer at his side. Susie wound down the window. The police officer blinked in disbelief. Was he seeing things or was that woman cradling the world's largest bottle of wine?

Police officer: 'Ma'am, Mr Tower would like you to get outta the car.'

Susie: 'That's fine, officer. Now?'

'No, ma'am. Mr Tower will drive you home.'

Susie, in unparalleled sarcasm: 'Oh! How kind!'

At that point, Jeremiah climbed back into the driver's seat, started up, and drove back to Susie's home, with his passenger almost invisible behind the jeroboam. A voice behind the bottle was saying to him, 'This is really baby-ish.' He turned up the radio to drown out the voice. At the destination, Susie hurriedly took herself and her champagne out of the car, and Jeremiah sped away. That was the last time ever that Jeremiah and Susie either saw or spoke to one another, which was a real shame.

The next morning I phoned Susie. She had a hangover. Jeremiah may have wanted to drown out her voice, but she was intent on drowning her sorrows. She had put a sizeable dent in the jeroboam's contents. She came over for strong coffee, and I said, 'Please don't worry, Susie. We'll get these tours going to Hong Kong.'

'Oh,' she sighed. 'After last night, I don't know if I can do anything with a chef.'

I told her, 'Susie, with me – what you see, is what you get.' She smiled sweetly, and I had the feeling we were in business. It would be Susie, the travel expert, and me, the cook and teacher. Oh, and I hired Erika, Susie's teenage daughter. She could teach us both how to use a computer.

14

The Boy Who Was Ip Man

THE MOVIE HOUSE was called Sing Sing and it was at the very end of Chinatown. It had concrete floors and cheap, wooden benches that were extremely uncomfortable.

At that time in the 1950s, most of the films were black-and-white and in Cantonese, as they had been shipped over from Hong Kong. Invariably they were tear-jerkers. Sad stories about people losing their loved ones. Death was a prominent theme. Some films told stories of people losing their children when they were young ... and then being reunited with them when they were older. Passionate reunions lit up the big screen, and lit up the faces within the audience.

Sure, the acting was hammed up. However, for those of us who were Chinese and living in Chicago – the entire audience – these productions were fantastic, and made the benches bearable.

On Sundays, and in return for $3, you would get to see four or five features, which would include Cantonese opera. Filmed operas are a strong part of Chinese entertainment and my mother was a devotee. Her favourite movie-opera star was Yam Kim-Fai, a woman who often played the role of a man. You've probably never heard of Yam but she made 307 movies and was worshipped throughout China.

I was less keen on the opera, which is an acquired taste. I preferred action films and, in particular, Wong Fei-hung. He was a renowned kung fu artist and played the character of Ip Man. He was also a mentor to Bruce Lee, the original kung fu movie star of the Western world. I would have loved to have learnt martial arts, but instead made do with the adventures on celluloid. People didn't have time to teach me the lightning moves of kung fu.

As a child I sat transfixed and on the edge of my uncomfortable seat as the lithe and nimble Ip Man leapt dangerously from roof to roof. The movie house was packed out, and there was food, though not the sweet ice creams, hot dogs or popcorn you might find on sale in your local cinema. There were Chinese sour-and-salty treats, such as dried sour plums, or little fish which had been fermented and dried. The cinema smelled old, musty and damp, and there was the whiff of the fermented snacks – the floor was littered with discarded food wrappers, which probably helped to keep the fermented smell in the room.

The large grocery store was the hub of Chinatown's community, but on Sundays the cinema became a secondary hub. People treated it as a place to meet and chat. At times it was difficult to maintain the crucial suspension of disbelief that is required when watching a movie. Just as Ip Man was launching himself onto another roof, the dramatic tension of the moment was destroyed by a couple of elderly women chitter-chattering about the price of water chestnuts.

There are always eating scenes in Chinese films, except for the operas. Whether it's a contemporary or ancient setting, the characters sit around a table, munching away. This reinforced what I was learning from my mother and uncles – that eating is fundamental to Chinese culture and social behaviour; that the Chinese are eating frequently and thinking of food non-stop.

After the cinema, I was in my own world of make-believe, pretending I was one of the kung fu guys. During winter, when the men came round to sweep up the snow, there were piles of the stuff on the pavements. These were my pretend mountains. I would leap from one mountain to another, kicking and chopping; deep in the fantasy that I was Ip Man.

The cinema was bad for me. It was bad because it prevented me from integrating. It stopped me feeling as if I was American. I never felt American and, today, I feel more British, which is ironic. When I go to Britain, I feel really at home, like it's the place where I belong. But the cinema was also good for me. It was a step back into a world no longer known to the audience. Like an island in the sea of America, Chinatown was disconnected from its origins. A visit to the cinema reconnected us instantly with our history. Others in the audience had known China. For me, it strangely formed a past that was intangible, even though my mother constantly told me that I was Chinese.

Going to the cinema made me … It made me feel real. And it made China feel real.

I would hear my relatives talk about parts of Hong Kong, such as Nathan Road – also known as the Golden Mile – or the district of Wan Chai. But what they said was meaningless as I had never set foot in Hong Kong. The meaning came once I saw these places on screen. From that hard bench in Sing Sing, my young mind was full of dreams, and my imagination was bursting with curiosity. I never imagined, however, that one day I would be there, in the places that I had first seen in that movie house. I never imagined such a thing but, still, I hoped for it.

15

Embraced by Hong Kong

I WAS AWOKEN BY warm light on my face. The light was comforting and, coming to my senses, I remembered the meal and a couple of glasses of champagne and a glass of claret. I must have nodded off. Darkness had given way to dawn, and the sunlight was powerful enough to bring me round. A stewardess offered me tea and as she poured she said, 'Stay awake for the landing. That's when it gets exciting.'

Kai Tak Airport was in Kowloon, and it served Hong Kong. In case you have never heard of it, let me explain. It was one of the most dangerous airports in the world. Pilots preparing to land first had to negotiate a particularly deep descent to reach the runway, taking the plane in between skyscrapers. They said you could look out of the window and see people brushing their teeth.

The overcrowded airport was located beside the sea – when coming in to land, a number of planes had over-run the runway and crashed into the water. The airport was opened in the 1920s but by 1998 the authorities conceded it was far too dangerous to keep open. They shut it down. The stewardess was right: it *was* exciting. *Harrowing* is probably a more appropriate description. I didn't see teeth brushers through windows, but the rooftops were scarily close and no sign of Ip Man. Word had it that, over the years, quite a few TV aerials were snipped away by the wings, wheels or fuselages of aircraft.

From that hard bench in the Sing Sing movie house in Chicago's Chinatown, I had hoped of visiting China, of being there; walking the bustling streets and eating the sort of food I had seen in the black-and-white movies. In 1980, I went. This was the trip, and I landed safely.

Usually, when you arrive for the first time in a foreign country, you feel like a foreigner. In France and Italy, I had spoken neither French nor Italian and had the sense of being a stranger. Hong Kong was entirely different, and quite magical. Everybody looked like me. I could understand what they were saying, of course, as most of them spoke Cantonese.

I'm home, I thought. I bought Cantonese pop music that I hadn't heard in the States, and Cantonese movies on video (still when I go to Hong Kong I buy DVDs so that I can catch up on the Cantonese cinema). It was peculiar to switch on the TV and hear people delivering the news in Cantonese. I remember flicking onto a variety show – again, people speaking in Chinese but, interestingly, I was struck by how confident they were. These were Chinese people, but they were poised and self-assured – attributes that were not always common in the Chinese-Americans. Hong Kong was a British colony, but the Chinese were running the show. I felt proud. I mean, there were times when I was literally moved to tears just to be there.

Everything I saw I liked. It was as if somebody had opened a door to a part of my life that had been hidden.

My first meal came after checking in to the Peninsula. I was hungry and ordered room service: a Chinese dish which shocked me because it was so bad; at that time, the Peninsula didn't have a Chinese restaurant and served Western food. Later, I went for a stroll and passed a funky little hole-in-the-wall restaurant. Steam was coming out of the door. People were gathering for whatever was being served. I double backed to take a look. Behind the counter, an elderly man was ladling up bowls of Wonton noodle soup. I joined the queue. It was simple, wonderful and delicious. So much so, it makes me want to cook Chinese food for lunch.

I am going to make Chinese sausage with stir-fried eggs, which takes about 5 minutes. A friend brought the sausages, all the way from Hong Kong to my flat in Paris.

If you were eating them for the first time, you might expect these sausages to be spicy. In that case you would be surprised, as they are quite sweet and richly aromatic. They are deep burgundy in colour, with white flecks of fat. They are made from pork meat, pork liver or duck liver, and are a little longer than your middle finger. Chinese sausages look a bit like thin, dry salami or British chipolatas. First, they are steamed before being used in other dishes.

Into a hot wok goes a splash of groundnut oil and I let it heat to smoking point. I toss in three sausages – they've been steamed and sliced into bite-sized pieces. I stir and fry for a couple of minutes. Next, I add six beaten eggs – stir-frying for 2 or 3 minutes, until the eggs begin to set. Six spring onions – sliced – join the party in the wok. Another minute of stir-frying. It's done! Ready to feed two people.

I cannot eat this dish without thinking of my mother, who often made it, adding seasonal greens, like chives or garlic shoots in the spring. 🥢

AS I wandered Hong Kong's streets, which were packed with stalls and markets, I was drawn in by the sights and sounds of people simply loving their food: the clatter of spoon against wok or the chop of cleaver on wood; the comforting waft of soups and stir-fries; the Cantonese shouts of stallholders pitching their wares. The climate was semi-tropical, so the streets were hot and humid, which added to the heady atmosphere.

The Cantonese like their food to be fresh, which means much of the produce is alive: water-filled tanks of fresh fish and shellfish, cages of clucking poultry, and even tanks of bouncing frogs. For the first time I saw fresh bamboo shoots. Until then, I had only known them in tins. There were spices and pastes which had not made – could not have made – their way past border control and into the Chinatowns of America.

This was street food that I had never come across. Early on Sunday mornings, my mother and my aunt used to go to the Jewish quarter, where they would buy a live chicken and bring it home to be despatched. The sound of the chicken clucking was my wake-up call. However, there were no market stalls in Chinatown Chicago, perhaps for two reasons: first, it would have been too unhygienic to be legal; second, it was too bloody cold.

The markets of Hong Kong did not offer cats and dogs. The sale of such meat was banned by the British authorities. I have never eaten these animals, which are taboo in the Western world, although my cousin in China has a restaurant that specialises in dishes of cat. The Chinese believe that we can obtain the qualities of an animal by eating it. For the Chinese, dragons and tigers are auspicious. They symbolise great strength and, by eating them, their strength is passed on to the consumer. Of course, dragons and tigers are hard to come by. Snakes and cats are the next best thing. Similarly, for those seeking virility, tiger penis is recommended as the solution. Most stallholders are all out of tiger penis, but deer penis is considered a good substitute.

I remember a subsequent visit to Hong Kong with Ron Batori. We went to a restaurant; the dining room was like a large, grand ballroom. We were waiting to be seated, and standing next to an American couple at their table. They were having trouble with the menu as there was no egg foo yung or chop suey, but plenty of alligator and other strange (to them) dishes. The man put his menu down on the table, looked up to his wife and said, 'Darling, I think I might have the double boiled deer penis. It looks like the safest bet.'

I had lamb in a Chinese restaurant, which was a new experience for me: lamb has a powerful, pungent smell which is not pleasant to many Chinese and is rarely on the menu. I found only one butcher's store which sold it. I also had real Sichuan food. At Uncle Paul's restaurant in Chicago we did one or two Sichuan dishes, but this was the real thing.

I discovered a lot of the regional cooking of China. This included Shanghai cuisine, and ingredients such as hairy crab, of which I had heard but never seen. It is a variety of the mitten crab – so called because of its furry legs. There were rice birds, which are tiny little birds that appear during the rice harvest. These days it is forbidden to eat them, but then they were captured and roasted. I ate roast goose – quite popular in Britain, but I'd never come across it in the Chinatowns of America.

It was like stepping into an Ali Baba cave of food treasures ('open sesame oil'), and I was fascinated by all the cookery shops, too. They sold utensils I had never seen before and I returned from that first trip with two suitcases that were filled only with cookware and ingredients that were unavailable in the States.

———

IT helped enormously that I spoke Cantonese, though I spoke it in an archaic way because I had been locked away in Chicago's Chinatown. In Hong Kong, people would ask me, 'How long have you been away? When did you emigrate?'

'I was born in America,' I'd respond, and they were astonished that someone who was born in America could speak Cantonese, and in a strange, old way.

The tours became a regular fixture, organised by Susie. We acquired connoisseurs along the way. Willie Mark, the esteemed restaurant critic in Hong Kong, came on board, introducing me to the finest chefs in the province and suggesting restaurants that had to be visited. I had expected to discover a Hong Kong that felt repressed because it was under British rule. Quite the contrary. The Chinese got on with their lives and went about their business as if the Brits weren't there. Hong Kong was a fantastic discovery for me, and our trips were an instant success.

Susie has a lot of class, and she sorted out a sponsorship deal with Singapore Airlines. Until then, the route was not direct but went from San Francisco to Hawaii and then on to Hong Kong. Susie also arranged rooms at the Peninsula, an iconic hotel.

Then there was the programme for my students. I went ahead of them, and they would arrive on a Saturday to be greeted by yours truly. On the first night there was a dinner, and the following morning I'd take them to the New Territories, for a taste of rural China at a time when most of the country was closed and therefore inaccessible to tourists. The rice fields and fishing villages of the New Territories were such a contrast to the urban sophistication of Hong Kong. It was time-less China.

We would visit a temple and then go to a fishing village near the border. Next, we would head to a market that sold live fish. This was in a street lined with inexpensive restaurants – the fish is bought live and taken to the restaurant, where it is then cooked. Such moments were extraordinary and special for my students, who had never seen anything like this. Lunch was followed by a trip to a farm which was experiment-ing with crops; what would grow best in the climate, and how best to improve the crops.

The day would end with dinner in the New Territories, and at a res-taurant that specialised in a dish of pigeon. The pigeon is partly braised in a sauce, then dried for five hours in front of a fan, and then it is fried to look like crispy Peking duck. The sauce in which the pigeon is braised is a 'master stock', which has been cooking for about eighty years and is regularly topped up. There were, say, fifteen of us, each receiving a pigeon. So fifteen pigeons were carried out on a tray and the custom is to eat the birds with your hands, a tradition that met with no resist-ance from my crowd. The dish is sensational and the students would return to the hotel shattered but with an understanding of my vision of Hong Kong.

I was finding my identity and Hong Kong was finding its identity. When I first went in 1980, Hong Kong was just taking off, not only financially. It was becoming more sophisticated and international. Chefs were arriving from all over the world to cook in Hong Kong, and foods that were un-Chinese, such as asparagus, were appearing in the markets. People in Hong Kong were educated in the ways of the world as well as in the ways of China. Until then, everyone had wanted to get out of China, but now people were coming to visit. For the first time, Chinese chefs were also returning to set up their own businesses in a land that was not foreign to them.

There was an air of sophistication about the place. In Chinatown in San Francisco, the Chinese knew, of course, that they were not in their country and kept their heads down. You could sense their anxieties of being the minority. The confident inhabitants of Hong Kong were stylish and worldly, and knew about everything. They knew of restaurants in Tokyo and New York.

I was surprised by the influence of Japan upon Hong Kong. It was here that I started to buy Japanese pop songs, which the Cantonese liked. I could buy clothes by Japanese designers. And these were clothes that fitted me – in America everything was jumbo-sized because I am too small. People were much more aware of Japanese food, plus there was Thai and Vietnamese food on a scale that we did not have in California.

I was forever fascinated in the markets, there was so much I had not seen or did not know. I am aware that we continue to learn until the day we die, but in the markets I realised how much I did not know. In America, these foodstuffs were often forbidden. Here, I tasted Chinese ham, which was not allowed to be imported into the States. Apart from eating proper Sichuan food, I had Shanghainese food, too. The Shanghainese boast that Hong Kong was a sleepy backwater until they arrived in 1949, after the People's Republic was established on the mainland. There is some truth to this claim, as the Shanghainese did indeed bring with them their great commercial and manufacturing skills. They also brought their style of restaurants: pass the windows and you will see the cooks preparing specialities such as dishes with broad beans, or steamed Shanghai dumplings.

These dumplings are made using dough of flour and water, which must be allowed to rest after mixing. This is laborious and time-consuming. Instead, I use wonton wrappers. The filling is finely minced pork, dried Chinese black mushrooms (first soaked), finely chopped spring onions and coriander, light soy sauce, rice wine, sugar, sesame oil, white pepper and potato starch mixed with water. The dumplings are steamed for fifteen minutes in a tightly covered wok.

Seafood was very popular and expensive, its supply never quite catching up with its demand. Many restaurants had tanks to keep the fish alive before they were ordered. Meanwhile, dried seafood such as shark fins, dried scallops, dried abalone and dried salted fish were prized for their intense taste and flavours and were among the most costly types of food in Hong Kong at that time (especially in restaurants because of the long preparation time).

There was a restaurant that had just opened and it was beautiful, but it specialised in shark fin. I found it bizarre to see bowls of shark-fin soup – not the most elegant of dishes – being consumed in this opulent setting. Shark fin, as I have previously mentioned, is an acquired taste (and I do not condone or approve of its consumption). The fin requires four days' preparation, from soaking it to cooking it in at least three batches of good stock, and, aside from its chewy, gelatinous texture, its taste depends on the quality of the stock.

One evening, I wandered into a restaurant, took a seat at a table and smiled as the waiter asked if I would like to try the house speciality. 'What is it?' I asked.

'Drunken shrimp,' he said.

As a child in Chicago's Chinatown, I had listened – I was mesmerised – as my mum and uncles sat around a table in the King Wah and spoke often and excitedly about drunken shrimp, a curiously named dish they had left behind in China. Now I was being offered it.

The moment has never left me. Live, medium-sized shrimps – what would be called prawns in Britain – were brought to the table in a crystal bowl, flipping and jumping around. Rice wine was poured onto them, just enough to cover. Then a transparent lid was placed over the bowl to prevent the shrimps from jumping out. Nothing happened for about ten minutes. Nothing except that the shrimps got 'drunk'.

Then the lid was lifted, and the shrimps were spooned out and poached briefly in a clear chicken stock. Finally, they were served, shells and all, with a sauce consisting of soy sauce to which hot, fresh red peppers and heated peanut oil had been added. Three decades is a long time to wait to try a dish, but it did not disappoint.

I was out all the time, exploring every part of the city. I had cousins there, so I saw them as well. Hong Kong would become my part-time life, and every year I would spend at least two months there.

 One of the most fascinating dishes I came across in Hong Kong was the so-called deep-fried milk. Milk custard is cut into diamond shaped pieces which are then lightly battered and deep-fried until crisp. They are dipped into sugar.

Milk dishes were interesting to me because the Chinese do not enjoy milk with the same gusto of Westerners. A glass of cold milk is enjoyed by a Westerner, but is not appealing to the Chinese.

So I was surprised to find many popular milk dishes in Hong Kong. The chefs ingeniously combined milk with evaporated milk, thereby reducing the milk smell and taste. How milk got into Chinese cuisine is an intriguing question. One theory, perhaps the most plausible, is that the dishes spread to Hong Kong from the Portuguese recipes of Macau, where milk-influenced fare started appearing in the sixteenth century.

There is also fried milk with pine nuts, made in the wok. The nuts are stir-fried for a matter of seconds, until golden brown. They are removed. Then the milk mixture – milk and evaporated milk – is poured into the hot wok. The milk curdles. Its chemistry changes to something which is digestible, and palatable to Chinese. It also takes on a new flavour and taste. The pine nuts are returned to the wok, stirred with the curds and served with bean thread noodles. There's a garnish of coriander and ham, both finely chopped.

Many shops specialised in bean-curd custard or steamed milk with ginger juice. The latter combines whole milk with sugar and ginger juice, which is steamed. The result is delicate custard with a refreshing ginger bite, which is sweet and spicy, and served warm with slices of mango or orange. 🥣

SUSIE and I rented a professional cookery school in Hong Kong, where I would cook and teach and the students would cook and learn. Our days were jam-packed – in the most enjoyable way – with cooking, eating and shopping for produce in the colourful, heaving markets. The dinners were carefully considered, as I wanted to show the students different techniques and styles of cuisine.

The only problem was the wine. It was the early '80s, before Hong Kong had discovered a fascination for the great wines of France, and there was little available. Susie and I decided to cut our costs by taking wine from California, which we could buy at bargain prices through our contacts (who thought it sounded like a great way of spreading the word in Hong Kong). Friends, including Ron Batori and Belle and Barney Rhodes, swung into action, donating cases of wine for our cause.

For that first trip, Susie managed to sweet-talk Singapore Airlines into letting us check in cases and cases of wine, and then we boarded the flight to Hong Kong. At Hong Kong, there was a chauffeur waiting, very kindly sent by the Peninsula to take us to the hotel. He saw that we were travelling with five cases of wine, which he duly loaded onto a trolley, and took us to our car. Our cases were loaded into the trunk of the limo and we thought we saw a dribble of wine at that stage, but said nothing and submerged ourselves in the air-con luxury of the back seats.

When we arrived at the Peninsula, a regiment of bellboys took our suitcases and boxes of wine, and Susie and I stepped from the car and started walking towards reception. We were behind the bellboys, and realised we were following a trail of Cabernet which had tarnished an otherwise glinting marble floor. It was acutely embarrassing. Susie took charge of the wine, putting the cases in her room. Then she contacted the Peninsula's food and beverage manager, and went to talk to him about Californian wine, of which she knew very little.

He agreed to store the wine, and Susie's job thereafter was to collect it and take it to restaurants, at which point there was another headache. The restaurants in Hong Kong were not used to serving good wine, and they did not have many wine glasses. So it was not merely a matter of bring your own wine, but bring your own wine glasses, too. We arrived at restaurants clinking.

Once we had the wine and the glasses, there was another difficulty. Waiters did not know how to serve the stuff. When you think about it, why would they? After all, they did not drink wine, did not sell wine, did not possess wine glasses and had no interest in wine. It would have been odd had they known how to use a corkscrew, how to pour and how to pour in small quantities. Sometimes they would pour red wine into glasses half-filled with white wine, and I'd leap up in horror: 'Please don't do that!'

The response? 'Oh, it makes a nice colour.'

So aside from me teaching the students, the waiters also learnt a thing or two about wine. And to think that Hong Kong is now one of the largest wine auction markets in the world. The finest Château Lafite Rothschild vintages grace the cellars of restaurants in China, should you happen to be there and have a barrow-load of cash when the sommelier comes your way.

There were a few sartorial issues. I wore a white suit, which, Susie said, made me look like John Travolta in *Saturday Night Fever*. On our first visit to a duck farm, I was with my students, and in my white bell-bottoms, traipsing through duck mess (no, not very John Travolta). Glancing down at my splattered trousers, Susie said, 'Ken, this day will be a highlight or a disaster. How are we gonna make it the former?'

Susie and I took a new group of students on a tour of one market which was on levels, with different produce on each one. On the first level there were stallholders selling live fish that were being pulled from water tanks and gutted on big boards. On the next level there were hundreds of tanks filled with thousands of bouncing frogs. As we passed, we could see them being taken from their tanks and despatched.

We walked up to the next level to find hundreds of stalls with live chickens, again being slaughtered as we strolled along. I thought this was thoroughly interesting for the new students, but then Susie turned to me and said, 'Ken! Enough! Your audience is not ready for this.'

'Susie,' I said, 'you need to get in touch with your food.'

'Yeah, right,' she said. We did not venture up to the next level.

At a restaurant in Stanley Market I went into the 'restroom' and, as I stood at a trench letting nature take its course, my brand new pair of extremely expensive sunglasses fell from my face and into the trench. I had a choice: leave them or fish them out. As I said, they were extremely expensive so you can guess which option I took.

—

THE cookery school tours in Hong Kong were so successful that they would continue, year after year, for a decade. They appealed not only to devoted cooks. Some of America's finest chefs became 'students', joining us on trips. After the first three years I had the hang of it; Susie was already an expert at top-line tours, so I was in good hands, and she advised me on what to do and what not to do. The knowledge would later come in useful when, for instance, I organised a truffle tour in France. Many chefs came on that, too.

Our American students were intrigued by the Chinese way of life and their aspirations. Importantly, the trips were about more than just food; they were about understanding food within the context. There was an immersion in Hong Kong's religion and history, how Hong Kong came to be, and its different ethnic groups, like the Hakka people. I always want things to be educational; it's a crucial aid to culinary awareness.

They were magical mystery tours, which ended up on a junk – we'd pile on board and have drinks and sushi as we sailed, before winding up at a pleasant restaurant. To help us out, we hired a few staff: a lady who worked for an American company and was the wife of a CEO; a businessman and his wife; oh, and the wife of the Chief of Justice. The final day ended with the Peninsula's Rolls-Royces whisking us off to a restaurant for a spectacular feast of Peking duck.

All of this was crammed into one week, and the students returned home having enjoyed a wonderful, memorable taste of Hong Kong. They had seen and experienced food as a mirror of society and history. I always felt that through food I could give people a glimpse into another society and how they could benefit from such insight. They were not the only ones to benefit. After the first trip, Susie and I sat in silence on the plane, preparing for take-off, and she said, 'Ken, a penny for those thoughts.'

'Susie, you know, for the first time in my life I don't feel like a minority.'

Crispy Shrimp Paste Chicken

I first enjoyed this chicken dish in the company of Willie Mark, Hong Kong's most knowledgeable food critic. We were at the Sun Tung Lok restaurant in Harbour City, and I was unprepared for the excellence of what I thought would be a simple fried chicken dish. I immediately set out to duplicate the dish in my own kitchen and have ever since incorporated it into the repertory of dishes I make frequently.

The distinctive flavour comes from the shrimp paste, which gives an aromatic and exotic taste: it must be used with care, as it is quite strong.

The secret to the extra crispness of the chicken is in the double frying. Marinated and then fried the first time, the chicken is fried again just before serving, making it ideal to serve at a dinner party. This use of a seafood paste to flavour chicken is a typically southern Chinese touch: a Chaozhou inspiration.

Serves 4

1.1 kg (2½ lb) chicken, or boneless thighs chopped into bite-sized pieces

For the shrimp paste marinade:

1 tablespoon shrimp paste

1 tablespoon ginger juice, squeezed from 2 ounces ginger

2 teaspoons sugar

2 teaspoons Chinese sesame oil

1 teaspoon light soy sauce

All-purpose flour or potato starch, for dusting

2 cups groundnut or vegetable oil, for deep-frying

3 tablespoons finely chopped spring onions

Chop the chicken into pieces with a heavy knife or Chinese cleaver. In a medium-sized bowl, mix the shrimp paste marinade ingredients, add the chicken and let it sit at room temperature for 30 minutes.

Heat a wok or large, deep frying pan until it is hot and add 2 cups of oil. Lightly dust the chicken pieces with flour, shaking off any excess. When the oil is hot, deep-fry half the chicken for 5 minutes or until golden brown. Drain it on kitchen paper. Then fry the rest of the chicken.

Just before serving, remove any debris from the oil with a fine mesh ladle. Reheat the oil until it is very hot and re-fry the chicken for 1 minute or until golden brown and heated through. Drain on paper towels, sprinkle with chopped spring onions and serve at once. 🥣

16

A Product
of Sunflower

START AT MEMPHIS and chug south along the Mississippi for a hundred miles or so, and you'll come to Sunflower County. Within it is the town of Sunflower. It's more like a village, with only a thousand residents. About 800 of them are African-Americans; their ancestors were slaves who toiled until death on the vast corn fields and cotton plantations of the South.

Strangers don't tend to come to Sunflower just to browse or take a look around. There are a few churches in the town, but no hotels. If you want to eat in a restaurant you'll have to go further south to Indianola (formerly Eureka), to the Blue Biscuit for rib-eye and Delta beignets – square, puffy, hole-less doughnuts – dusted with icing sugar, and then maybe mooch around the BB King Museum, which is just across the road.

Not much goes in to Sunflower, some might say, and not much comes out. But things took a distinct turn on 4 September 1920, with the birth of one more inhabitant. He was Craig Claiborne and he'd outgrow Sunflower on his journey to greatness in the world of gastronomy. Though the folks in Sunflower never quite forgot him. In fact, they are reminded of him most days – head down Craig Avenue and you'll come to Claiborne Street.

Craig Claiborne was, for many years, the most powerful figure in the world of American food. He had fought in the Second World War, and again in the Korean War, but was determined to make a career of his two great passions: writing and cooking. He paid to learn about cooking at Ecole Hôtelière de la Société Suisse des Hôteliers, the hoteliers' learning post near Lausanne, in Switzerland. He dabbled in PR before becoming editor of *Gourmet* magazine. Then he received the ultimate honour when, in the late 1950s, he was made food editor of the *New York Times*. Food, cooking, fancy restaurants; at that time these were not supposed to be a concern for men. Craig's appointment was a brave one, but it was the right one, as time would show.

Craig was masterful in several ways. He possessed an extensive, ever-growing knowledge of food and had a flair for teaching about foreign cuisines – at that time French and Italian – that might have seemed intimidating to the American audience. Craig was a restaurant critic and gifted food writer and also wrote (often with his dear friend Pierre Franey) a score of cookbooks, as well as an autobiography, *A Feast Made for Laughter*. He was a kind, gentle man who was determined to champion the young, up and coming chefs.

His culinary passion was ignited as a child when he would cook with his mother in the kitchen of her boarding house in Indianola, after the family moved from Sunflower. One of his books was an endearing nod to his roots: *Craig Claiborne's Southern Cooking*.

Craig was a famous socialite, and I had first met him in 1980, albeit briefly, through the New York-based cookery writer Paula Wolfert. We hit it off. Then an eight-page feature came out in *Bon Appétit* magazine and, at the risk of sounding ridiculously smug, it was all about me and what I was doing in California. *Bon Appétit* was the largest-circulation food magazine in the States, and I remember that my summer cookery classes were filled within hours of the magazine hitting the stands and informing readers of my existence.

'I want to come to California and write about you for the *New York Times*,' said Craig. His article, published on 6 February 1981, featured the headline: 'A Chinese Chef Rings in the New Year'. Running over two pages, it included an interview with me along with a few of my recipes, and was a remarkable raising of my profile. And then some! Not only an endorsement from the *New York Times*, but one from the deity that was Craig Claiborne.

Publishers in New York didn't and don't think much counts until it appears in the *New York Times*, and when mine saw Craig's piece they increased six-fold the print run of my new book. This was to be my first book, *Chinese Technique*. The publishers, Simon & Schuster, were delighted when I suggested a book tour of twenty-eight cities throughout the States.

You know me by now – I assessed the cities that had the largest book sales, plotted these cities on a map of America, worked out the time it would take to travel from one place to another, and then returned to my publishers to say, 'It'll take three weeks.' Now, see, you can't just sit on your ass and expect things to come. I don't care how talented you are, you've just got to go out there and you've got to work hard for it.

New York was the first stop of the book tour, and the *New York Times* held a sensational party for me, attended by the newspaper's editors, and I started to meet a new crowd of people. I was interviewed by a then-unknown Martha Stewart, who was writing for *House Beautiful*. A young woman in Baltimore named Oprah Winfrey invited me on to her early morning chat show. Julia Child, as she had promised, threw a party for me at her home in Boston, inviting influential members of the press. The attention was phenomenal and, when I reflect on it now, the privilege was substantial. Coming from an impoverished background, I was now the guest of honour – and it was an honour for which I always feel grateful.

I remember, for instance, that the book tour took me to Chicago, where I stayed in the luxury of the Ritz-Carlton. The publicist phoned to say she'd messed up on something or other, and then there was a knock on my door. A waiter was standing there, beside a trolley upon which there was a silver ice bucket in which there was a bottle of Louis Roederer Cristal. There was a note from my publicist: 'Sorry for messing up.'

The tour was an eye-opening, dream-like experience as I flitted in stretch limos from one signing to the next, and stayed in the finest hotel suites. *I can get used to this*, I thought. Instead, I returned to California and then went to Hong Kong for one of my tours, which were now overbooked due to the media attention from the book tour. In June of 1982, Craig Claiborne got in touch to talk to me about his party. He had his own book, an autobiography, to launch.

———

I must tell you a story about Craig, just so that you have the full measure of the man. In June 1975 there was a TV channel fundraising event, for which American Express kindly offered a spectacular prize: to fly the highest bidder and a companion anywhere in the world for a meal of their choice. No catches, no limits. That's not quite true. There was one condition: that the restaurant took American Express.

Craig put in a bid of $300 but thought, as I would have done, that he would be outbid. Surely someone would offer thousands for such a prize. But no, he won. It makes you wonder where you would go, doesn't it? Craig gave the most serious deliberation to the choice of restaurant.

He sought counsel from a friend in Paris, who suggested Chez Denis in Rue Gustave Flaubert, close to the Arc de Triomphe. Next, Craig took a flight to Paris to check out the restaurant, having ensured first that it would accept American Express. This trip was merely a recce, ahead of the real deal. He loved the food and told a little white lie to the owner, Denis Lahana. Craig did not mention Amex but said instead that a wealthy friend had offered to treat him to the most expensive meal in Europe. 'What would you charge?' he asked Denis. The response: $4,000. Once American Express had agreed to the restaurant, Craig returned to Paris with Pierre Franey. They embarked on the meal they would never forget for as long as they lived.

Beluga caviar and champagne began the feast as an *hors d'oeuvre*, and then came three soups, a parfait of sweetbreads, and tarts of quail and ham. There were oysters, followed by lobster with truffles, and then ortolan – the tiny birds which, when legal, were a great delicacy and eaten in one mouthful, usually with a napkin over the head, either to capture the scent or to prevent God seeing you eat a small bird.

There was duck and loin of veal, and so it went on and on, one dish after another being carried to the table. Over four and a half hours they worked their way through three courses composed of twenty-four dishes (not including the *hors d'oeuvre* and the first things they were served on being seated at the table – little Parmesan cheese toasts and a small dish of toasted almonds from Mallorca). Pheasant, foie gras, woodcock; the whole caboodle. Desserts included *îles flottantes* – that classic French dish of poached meringue 'islands' in a sea of vanilla-infused crème anglaise. With this dish they savoured a glass of Château d'Yquem, from the 1928 vintage. Try buying a single bottle of that honeyed wine today and it will cost you about the same as their entire lunch. So maybe don't try buying it.

Of the other wines, there was a Château Latour, produced in 1918, when the French were cheerfully celebrating the end of the First World War, and which Craig and Pierre deemed to be the finest Bordeaux they had ever tasted. There was also Château Pétrus from 1961. Their favourite wine of the feast was Romanée Conti from the 1929 vintage – if you can find a bottle today it will cost you about $25,000 or £18,000. There was Madeira from 1835 and cognac from 1865.

When Craig wrote about the feast, there was outrage from about a thousand readers of the *New York Times*, who sent letters of complaint: how could he indulge in such extravagance when people all over the world were starving? It was the middle of the '70s and the end of the war in Vietnam, and orphans were being brought over from Vietnam to find foster homes in the States.

Anyway, Craig argued that his meal had not deprived anyone of a single mouthful of food. Julia Child dropped him a line to give support, saying, 'Does anyone object when some rich bitch buys a $4,000 mink coat?'

———

SO it was '82, and Craig's party for the launch of his autobiography, *A Feast Made for Laughter*. He had invited what he regarded as the best chefs in America to come and cook for him at the party, and I was delighted to be one of those chefs. It was a sumptuous affair, and the guests included his literary friends Kurt Vonnegut and Betty Friedan, as well as Hollywood stars such as Lauren Bacall. But the place was particularly notable for the number of chefs who had come from far and wide to raise a glass or three to the esteemed Mr Claiborne.

One of them was Madhur Jaffrey and, thankfully, through the heaving crowd in which paths could not possibly cross, ours did: we managed to meet. It was entirely my pleasure, because I admired both Madhur and her books. She told me how she had recently made a series for British television – the BBC, no less – and that it had been a great success. 'Congratulations!' I said. 'I'm thrilled for you.' And I was.

I thought little more of it. Within a day or so I was on a flight to France, where I would spend a couple of months of the summer cooking, eating and trying out new restaurants. When I returned to California at the end of August, there was a small pile of telegrams.

You must remember, this is '82. There were no mobile phones, few people had faxes and I was considered ahead of the game simply because I owned an IBM computer, on which the cursor had a mind of its own and the characters appeared in green on the screen. Anyway, I started to go through the telegrams. One of them was from my new friend Madhur, and was to the point. It read: 'Please call me. English TV is desperate to talk to you.' Well, we all had landlines, so I called Madhur.

What came next was to be the beginning, as they say, of a new chapter.

17

The New Chapter

MY HOME WAS in sunny California (you may be tired of me reminding you). I did not live in Britain, did not watch British television and therefore did not know what was on offer in terms of food programmes. Pretty much zilch, it turned out.

When Madhur sent the telegram there were, at that time, three British television channels – BBC One, BBC Two and ITV. Channel 4 was a few months away, broadcasting for the first time on the afternoon of 2 November 1982. Eight years later – to the day, funnily enough – Sky would launch.

Just to set the scene, here is a brief overview of the year...

Margaret Thatcher was Prime Minister. Prince Charles and Princess Diana celebrated the birth of their first child, William. Terence Higgins died of Aids, spawning a charitable trust that would become one of the largest in Europe. And when the news did not centre on the war raging against Argentina, over ownership of the Falkland Islands, there was the grim reality of life for many in the UK: unemployment was at three million. Life, as we know – and the British certainly knew it back then – is not always a bowl of cherries.

On paper, this did not necessarily seem like a nation eager to find out more about food. They had other things on their mind, and round about this time looked to comedy from *The Young Ones*, *'Allo, 'Allo!* and the American import, set in a Boston bar, *Cheers*.

Today, you will see the primetime slots filled with cookery and food programmes. Every channel covers food in some way. In those days, things were very different. Cookery programmes were confined to BBC Two, and they were broadcast in the morning or, perhaps, during the afternoon although it had yet to dawn on the broadcasters that many people would ever want to switch on 'the box' during the day.

British television viewers had seen food cooked by Fanny Cradock, a stern lady who delivered instructions to her bumbling husband John-nie. 'Pass me a bowl, Johnnie,' and that sort of thing. He was, I suppose, a bit like her sous chef or even her kitchen apprentice, and he didn't pretend to have a clue about food. Next came *The Galloping Gourmet*, a good-looking cook called Graham Kerr, who'd been born in London but moved to New Zealand in his twenties. Kerr spent about thirty minutes (the duration of the show) cooking a meal. When it was done, he would dash into the studio audience, extend a hand and pull an admiring lady from her seat, whisking her onto the stage, where the table was laid and the meal awaited. They ate as the credits rolled. His programme was fast and fun, even if a studio stage is not the most romantic location, and it was strangely compelling and colourful in the otherwise grey and drab world of cookery on British television.

By the early '80s, the outlook of television cookery was changing, albeit slowly. Delia Smith was on the scene, though cookery was still hidden away in odd times of the schedules. So if you were interested in seeing the programmes you'd have to set your video recorder, if you could work out how to set your video recorder.

There was also Sarah Brown, who had been a dancer but now made vegetarian food in a BBC series. Madhur Jaffrey, the sender of the telegram, had added a dimension. As she had mentioned to me when I met her at Craig Claiborne's party, her BBC series was a huge success. Behind the scenes, producers and decision-makers at the BBC were trying to analyse its popularity.

Madhur was beautiful and charming and cooked delicious Indian food. Through the creation of dishes, the viewer was taken to a faraway country – indeed, another continent – with all its mystique and exotic allure. The British have long had affection for Indian food, and Madhur showed them, encouraged them, to cook it because it tasted sublime and was not difficult to cook. Often, Delia and Madhur inspired women (most men did not cook in those days) who were searching for inspiration: what can I make for my friends when they come for supper on Saturday?

—

WHEN I called Madhur, she said, 'Ken, you must talk to the BBC. They changed my life.'

'Madhur, what am I going to do in England? My career is finally getting started here and nobody knows me from Adam in Great Britain. I mean, I would be starting from scratch.'

She said, 'Will you just talk to them?'

I said, 'Yes, of course.' I was grateful to Madhur but to be frank – and you've probably gathered from the dialogue – I was not the voice of optimism.

Madhur explained that a TV crew would be coming to California to make a documentary and, while in the area, would like to take the opportunity to interview me. So a couple of weeks later a producer, Jenny Stevens, came to my home/cookery school. She was a New Zealander and had been the assistant producer on Madhur's series. Jenny and I talked for about an hour and a half, and she recorded me. She told me how the series would work – cooking in the studio, and being filmed out on location. As for the location? 'I'd like to come and film you in Hong Kong when you have finished one of your cooking tours,' said Jenny.

She asked if I could extend my time in Hong Kong, adding on a week, which would enable some filming. I said that would be fine, and her parting words were: 'We'll get back to you.'

Jenny Stevens did not get back to me. I assumed it was because: a) I lived in California; and b) she considered that my English was not *proper* English. Nothing ventured, nothing gained, I reckoned. But I did not think I had a chance, and when 1983 came around I resumed my cookery class, carrying on with life. Then one day, in the middle of January, I received a frantic call from England. It was Jenny Stevens, the producer from the BBC. 'We'd like you to come over and audition,' she said. 'We'll fly you over.'

I said, 'That's wonderful but I can't just drop what I'm doing. I have things already booked. I can come to you in early February.' We agreed that I would fly there for three days, do the audition and fly back. Economy flights, of course. This was the BBC.

18

The Test (and Testing Times)

BAYSWATER IS A part of west London which has enjoyed its fair share of romantic history. In the early 1900s, for instance, J. M. Barrie spent three years writing *Peter Pan* at his home at 100 Bayswater Road. However, it is absolutely packed with large, expensive houses that have been turned into cheap hotels.

The BBC had put me up in one. Yes, *moi* – the man who had, quite recently, indulged himself in the lavishness of the Ritz, Chicago, opening the door to waiters with bottles of expensive champagne on trolleys, courtesy of Simon & Schuster. Here in Bayswater, the room was so small that this is what had happened on the first morning...

There was a knock on the door. It was my breakfast tray arriving. I tried to open the door but it banged against the bed. So I had to manipulate the door in order for the tray to be passed to me. I saw only hands, one on each side of the tray. 'Just leave it outside the door when you've finished,' said a male voice on the other side of the door. *Just?* He made it sound easy.

Once the tray was inside, it reduced the room's volume by about a third. I crouched on my tiny bed in my tiny room, eating cold scrambled egg on cold toast, wondering how I would remove the tray, and saying to myself, 'What the hell have I got myself into?' And then I tried to get myself out of the tiny room, moving the bed so that I could open the door.

The producers had managed to find a free (as in available, not as in cheap) studio, and I was told it was where Winston Churchill had delivered his broadcasts during the Second World War. Apparently, this was where the great British Prime Minister had stood at a microphone, addressing the nation of wireless listeners: 'We shall fight on the beaches, we shall fight on the landing grounds, we shall fight in the fields and in the streets...'

Meanwhile, I was there to do an audition for a cookery series. I was struck by the shabbiness of the studio, and I was polite but still thinking, *What the hell am I getting into?* It was bordering on decrepit. However, I was an admirer of the BBC, knew of its reputation and had watched BBC productions that were broadcast on American television. I did the audition.

I stood behind a 'kitchen worktop', against a backdrop of sky blue, and looking quite snazzy in slacks, a striped shirt and a purple cashmere jumper. There was a cooker, which had two burners and was one step up from the sort of device you'd take on a camping trip. Nowadays camping is trendy and posh, so the cooker would be considered a few steps down. It looked like the kind of thing you'd have seen in a caravan. I had a wok on the heat, but the heat did not reach my version of high, which, as you know, is ferociously high. I had brought my own meat and vegetable cleavers, but not a chopping board.

Which leads me onto the BBC chopping board. It was not particularly heavy or sturdy, which was fine. However, there had been a price label stuck to the wood and this had been removed, but in a cack-handed manner, leaving the sticky underneath of the sticker on the board and clearly visible to me, at least. For this – my first experience behind the cameras – I pointed at the remnants of the sticker, looked at Jenny behind the camera, and said: 'Shall I remove that? It looks very tacky.'

She replied: 'Oh, don't worry about that. Nobody is going to see it.' I did. This dialogue was never cut from the audition tape, so anyone with the sense of sight could have seen it. Having lost that battle, I moved onto the struggle of being a presenter. 'Hello. Today I am going to show you how to cook…' My mind went blank. I knew I was going to show the 'viewer' how to cook but, momentarily, I could not for the life of me remember what I was going to show them how to cook. 'Can we start again?' I stammered. Then I remembered. I was going to show them how to cook dark chicken meat with shallots.

After that, it seemed to go quite well. I relaxed into my natural comfort zone of cooking, demonstrating how to bone the thigh and leg of a chicken, before turning to my slightly heated wok on the caravan cooker and stir-frying the thinly sliced meat with whole shallots and fresh, finely sliced ginger. I cooked with chopsticks, as I do, and this must have seemed new and different to my small audience behind the camera. I talked about the wok and how to cook with it, and demonstrated knife skills, showing how to slice the ginger in a neat, professional, cheffy way.

I sense that I am sliding – for only a few seconds – into ginger but cannot stop myself. In traditional Cantonese cooking, fresh ginger is as ancient and essential as the wok.

Ginger from Canton is said to be the most aromatic and, like garlic, it is an indispensable part of much Chinese cookery. As I had seen on my travels, this knobbly, golden-beige rhizome is used in many dishes in Hong Kong, even if in the early '80s it was unfamiliar in its fresh form to the British. As a powder, the Brits used it in ginger cakes and ginger biscuits.

In Hong Kong, the markets sold fresh ginger which had been peeled, as well as the older, shrivelled ginger which was intended for use in medicinal broths.

Young stem ginger – the newest spring growth – was also available in Hong Kong's markets, and stir-fried in dishes or pickled. As it is young and tender, peeling is unnecessary and it can be eaten as a vegetable. Pickled young ginger is served as an *hors d'oeuvre* in Hong Kong restaurants, or eaten as a snack with preserved Thousand-Year Duck Eggs.

Peeled ginger will keep for several months when it is stored in a glass jar and covered in rice wine or dry sherry. You will be left with a flavoured wine that can be used instead of rice wine in some recipes. This is different from English ginger wine, made from ground ginger root, raisins and brandy; mix ginger wine with Scotch whisky and you'll have a whisky mac. Cheers!

Dried ginger or dried galangal is a member of the ginger family, used by the Chinese for medicinal as well as culinary purposes, often to counteract the strong odour of meat. Keep it in a jar at room temperature and it will last indefinitely. 🥣

—

A decision was made quickly. Very quickly. That night, the executive producer invited me out to dinner, and over the meal he broke the news. 'We would like you to do the series,' he said, and we toasted the deal, clinking glasses of warm chardonnay (BBC expenses). Initially, I did not absorb what was happening. I did not have time to consider its potential effect upon my life. I said, 'OK.' And when he talked about publishing a book to go with the series, I said, 'OK.'

At this point, I did not know of the extent that the BBC had gone to in order to find a presenter for their series about Chinese cookery. Much later on I learnt that many others had been considered, and there had been auditions with potential hosts, ranging from British-based Chinese chefs to ones on the other side of the world, in places like Australia. All of them had been screen tested. They had failed. They had been given the thumbs-down because their cooking abilities were deemed to be insufficient or their accents were so strong as to be incomprehensible to viewers.

There was also the job itself. Often, it is thought that presenting a cookery programme is an absolute doddle if you can cook quite well. People think that all you need to do is stand at the stove and make some food. However, there are chefs who are good at cooking but, alas, cannot cook and speak at the same time. It is made to appear easy so as to encourage the aspiring cook at home, but it is not as easy as it is made to appear. The producers were not out to make a silent cookery show. They had been unable to find a British-based chef, and so looked to America, where the Chinese-American chefs tended to have an English mother tongue.

A contract was drawn up. I signed and checked out of my miniature hotel room. On the return flight to America it hit me. I thought, *Oh my gosh, my life is going to change.* But I didn't realise how much it could and would change. Yes, I felt it was another opening or an opportunity but I never dreamt how the series would turn out and how it would shape my life.

It is funny; I always feel my life has been a progression, that I have taken opportunities not knowing where they would lead. Others say, 'I want to do this, I want to do that.' They plot the coming steps. By contrast, I had no idea what I wanted to do. I was thirty-three years old and, in hindsight, I felt that my audition went well because I had behind me quite a few years as a teacher. I wasn't just a chef or a cook – I wanted to teach. Had I been younger and with less experience of teaching, I would (and could) never have survived the audition.

The discussions in London had been upbeat. The series would be called *Ken Hom's Chinese Cookery.* 'We want to make it terrifically exciting,' they had said, and they had adventurous plans in store. We would film for a week in Hong Kong. To take a cookery programme out of the studio and to another country – let alone another continent on the other side of the world – was a new and almost sensational proposition. It was beyond terrifically exciting. From the comfort of your armchair, you, the viewer, could almost taste the food and travel to explore China.

In October 1983, the film crew joined me in Hong Kong and we filmed for a week. It felt entirely natural. Paul Levy, the pioneering food writer, sensed a story and flew over from London to write a piece for *The Observer.* Then, in the summer of 1984, I went to London to shoot the studio work. It was quite a painful experience. I did not have a restaurant, had never done television, and was unknown in Britain.

Why then did the producers want me – or anyone, for that matter – to present a series about Chinese cuisine? The answer is that the department fell under the category of 'continuing education'. There was an agenda, hidden, to show viewers the multicultural aspects of Britain and how another nationality has lived within the nation. Madhur's series had done this with Indian food, showing indirectly how Indians had contributed to British culture. I was doing the same with the Chinese.

The British liked Chinese food, as they still do, but they knew little about Chinese culture. The notion of continuing education meant that viewers could be educated, but in a way that was not pedantic or preachy. This approach, you could say, was so successful that it remains to this day. The best and most successful cookery programmes are educational.

19

Dipping a Toe into Japan

A S WE WERE greeted at the door of the restaurant, I glanced into the dining room beyond and saw waiters wearing wellies. *A new one on me,* I thought. *Could be interesting.* We're in Japan, by the way, mid-'80s.

The room was filled with small pools of water and we were shown to a table beside one such pool. One of the waiters, squelching in his shiny green knee-high boots, came to our table to take our order. We asked for fish and then watched as the waiter turned, grabbed a net, climbed into the pool, splashed and waded for a few seconds and then climbed out of the pool. He had a big fish wriggling in his net. This would be our lunch or, at least, one course of it.

In Hong Kong I had seen a similar approach. There, waiters took the order before hauling the required fish or seafood from a large tank of water; this was then brought to the table in a bucket. Of course, the point is that you, the customer, know that what you are about to eat is as fresh as can be. Freshness is sacrosanct. And so fresh that the fish is actually alive when the order is placed.

Here in the restaurant in Fukuoka, the beautiful big fish was carried to the table, its eyes still crystal clear. All of the flesh had been removed and thinly sliced into sashimi. This had been put on a bed of finely sliced daikon, the crisp winter radish, which looked like waves on the side of the dish with the fish upon it. We all proceeded to eat. Ten minutes in, the fish's mouth started moving. It was still alive. What an extraordinary sight, though not to everyone's approval, admittedly.

A couple of years later, I was in Japan and at a restaurant, and the chef showed me how this was achieved. A thin, very sharp, metal chopstick is put through the spinal cord, which anaesthetises the fish and just before serving the chopstick is removed, keeping the fish alive, though not for too long. Since then, I have eaten squid or octopus in the restaurants of Japan, various parts of the body moving during the meal. Theirs, not mine.

—

THE great and the good came on the Hong Kong tours, and on one trip Darrell Corti joined the group. I mentioned Darrel a little earlier on in this story. He was a wine merchant and connoisseur, and he contributed (along with Ron Batori) the wine notes for my book *East Meets West Cuisine*.

Darrell said, 'After Hong Kong, I'll take you to Japan.' This is how I came to see waiters in green wellies. In fact, Darrell had put together a ten-day trip, including stop-offs in Tokyo, Kyoto and Nagasaki. We would eat, drink and see many aspects of Japanese food.

Some things were a bit edgy. For instance, up high on a farm in the mountains we had a dish of chicken sashimi. First, the breast meat was brought to our table. It was very thinly sliced and raw. The chicken had been despatched only shortly beforehand. The texture was unpleasant, or at the very least strange to my palate. Then, the chef took the legs and thighs of the bird and these were cooked in a broth. The broth was flavourful but, alas, the meat was tough and chewy: the flesh had not had time to 'relax' and soften.

Japanese food is fantastic, even if it does not have the breadth and variety of Chinese cuisine. This is because it is a small country, making the range of food specific rather than expansive. However, they are masterful when it comes to taking a something like tempura, which began life as the heavy, soggy Portuguese *tempera*, and then improving on it and making it deliciously light and superb. Deep-fried in hot oil, it is made by the chef right there, in front of the customer. Their cuisine is a refined art, with almost obsessive attention to detail. They have taken Chinese dumplings and turned them into superior dumplings: less stodgy and with garlic added.

The Japanese chefs are also brilliant at producing lots of different dishes with the same main ingredients. When we visited Tokyo, Darrell took us to a restaurant which specialised in gyoza, the pan-fried dumplings. It served nothing but these dumplings, though in different forms, be it boiled, pan-fried or steamed, and with a range of different fillings.

In Osaka, we visited Japan's largest cookery school, the Tsuji Institute, and were introduced to Shizuo Tsuji, the founder of this impressive school where Japanese chefs are trained. It was like having a meeting with the Pope. We did not eat with him, but just to have an audience with him was a great honour.

Tsuji was a remarkably cultured man who spoke French and English

– both fluently – and had a medal or two bestowed upon him by the French government for his exemplary services to the world of culinary arts. He was the extremely proud owner of the world's largest collection of Bach recordings on vinyl.

Among his massive library was one particularly fascinating tome: a seventeenth-century French cookery book which he had duplicated at a cost of $300, then a considerable sum. He was also, as you can imagine, an accomplished author who wrote in suitably magisterial terms about the philosophy of cuisine, as well as technique. His book *Japanese Cooking: A Simple Art* was published in the '80s and many consider it to be the bible of Japanese food.

Later, I worked in Japan with Cathay Pacific, creating dishes for the airline's passengers. This gave me the chance both to be with and to observe Japanese chefs. They would take my dishes and make them so that they were precisely as they appeared in photographs. But the food lacked taste. Meanwhile, the chefs of Hong Kong, Thailand and Singapore could copy the dish and make it tasty. I believe this difference arose because the Japanese palate does not require, or wish for, similar seasoning that you or I might want. And they do not like too much spiciness. (Even though I didn't grow up with spicy food, and my mother did not care for it, I love it.)

How did I deal with this palate issue? Well, when you are in Asia it is important to save face and to get people on your side. You never say, 'This is rubbish.' First, you must say, 'This is very, very good. You have done a super job.' Second, you say, 'However, what do you think to the idea of just adding a little more seasoning? Do you think it would be better?'

The response will be, 'Yes, chef.'

Asian chefs are used to Western chefs who taste and then get upset and become dramatic. No, no, no; that is not the way. Progress is obtained by showing a positive side so that we can all live in perfect harmony. To insult people is wrong. To me, this attitude is natural, thank goodness, because of my childhood.

Once the chef had added the correct amount of seasoning or spice, I'd say, 'I think *you* are right. It is definitely better.'

20

The Trials and Tribulations of Peking Duck

THE MAILMAN KNOCKED one morning. Note: mailman rather than postman. We are back in you-know-where, before heading to London to film *Chinese Cookery* for the BBC. The package was large and from London, and I opened it to reveal a videotape from my new friends at the Corporation. The accompanying note read something like: 'Here is a video of Delia Smith. Can you be more like her, please?'

I watched the video and despatched a letter of response, saying something like, 'No, I can't be like Delia. For starters, I'm sorry, but I don't talk like her.' Delia is clever and brilliant at teaching a recipe, focusing on the measurements and quantities. Madhur, meanwhile, was also an accomplished actress and learning lines came naturally to her. Sarah

Brown, presenter of the series about vegetarian food, had been a dancer so knew the principles of entertainment.

My style, however, was laid-back: add a bit of this and then a touch of that. Delia had a way of standing or turning her body, with the camera in mind. She did it so well. The producers also wondered if I could do the same thing. No, not really. It was so *non-me*.

When I returned to London to film the series in the summer of 1984, I stayed in the apartment near Sloane Square, which I mentioned way back at the beginning of this book. Although I had funny, fussy Mrs Kelly as the cleaner, I guess I had moved on and up from the hotel in Bayswater. Ron Batori – ever the fixer – knew the owners of the apartment and had secured a 'mates' rates' deal of £100 per week. We would film over eight weeks: one episode per week. This put the approximate £1,000 bill within the BBC budget for accommodation, so everyone was happy with the arrangement.

The basement flat had a sofa bed and a small kitchen, where I was testing the recipes. At my home in the States, I had already tested them. I wanted to repeat the testing process but with ingredients bought in Britain. So I would totter along the King's Road and see what was available in Waitrose. I had also bought about fifteen cookery books published in Britain, to see what authors were writing about and how they talked about food.

There was good news and bad news in terms of production.

The good news was that I had already completed the book, *Chinese Cookery*, which would tie in with broadcast of the series. This book was more or less the scripts of each episode, and I would have sessions with the producer and production team, discussing which dishes would go with each programme, thereby giving a theme to each episode.

The bad news? Although the book seemed to me like a script, there was, in fact, a real script for each episode. This included 'links' – the bits where the presenter introduces a segment – or delivering lines to camera. Most of the time I was ad-libbing because I was cooking. But the tortuous – and indeed torturous – part of this whole process was memorising the lines. Oh God, it sucks.

FOR me it sucks. Let's go back quite a bit. For three years during my childhood, from the age of six to nine, I was sent to a Chinese school. Along with the other kids of Chinatown, I attended for three hours, every evening after my usual day at the English-speaking school. The teachers thought I did not pay attention. If a pupil was naughty, the teacher would put a black ink dot on the child's face. The idea was, you would return home and your parents would see the dot and know that you had misbehaved during lessons.

Frequently, my teachers thought that I was not paying attention. Such was the frequency that it led to not one black dot but many on my face. I would emerge from the Chinese school and head home to my mother with a face covered in artificial freckles. At my English-speaking schools, things were no better. There, the teachers thought that I could not work well because I was Chinese and therefore did not comprehend as well as the other young students. They thought I couldn't speak much English.

Both schools were way off. I was paying attention and I did understand English just as well as my classmates. My problem was that I was dyslexic. This learning disability was rarely diagnosed and, throughout generations, dyslexic children were merely regarded as stupid. As with so many others of my age, I did not realise until later in life that my so-called inability to pay attention or understand – my trouble, as

I saw it, of absorbing words as I read them – is a common condition. Making the series, trying to learn lines or read from a script, made it even more obvious to me.

I was sent to the BBC's elocution sessions. At these classes I was taught to say marinade in the English way, so that it rhymes with lemonade, instead of marinade in the American way, which rhymes with lard. For tomatoes, I was not allowed say *toe-may-dohs* (American). Instead, I had to say *toe-mar-toes* (English).

The producers did not want people to misunderstand me. Or rather, they were keen to ensure that the viewers could understand me. They also wanted me to retain my accent, made not in China but in Chicago, or even Chicago's Chinatown. Funnily enough, when the series aired, many viewers thought I was from Hong Kong. Of course, people from Hong Kong don't have British accents unless, perhaps, they lived or went to school in Britain.

On the production team, Jenny Lo was well acquainted with Chinese food and cooking and, more importantly, knew what to say and what not to say, and she was a constant prompt should I happen to veer into Americanisms. 'Remember, Ken, the British say "spring onions", not "scallions" … Ken, over here we say "mangetout" – we don't call them "snow peas" … Aubergine, Ken. Not eggplant.'

Then there were my clothes. I felt that if I wore my chef's jacket it would discourage the viewers. They'd think, well, obviously he's a chef so he knows what he's doing. I wanted viewers to feel at ease and to see that the cooking was easy. There should be a sharing, casual tone; something to entice the viewers and illustrate that cooking is a relaxing pleasure rather than a chore.

My suitcases were packed with lots of different clothes. When I had money in those days, I loved shopping for clothes. Even though the

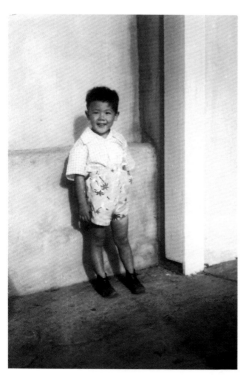

With my mother in Chicago in 1954, when I was six years old.

San Francisco's Chinatown, photographed in the late 1800s (courtesy of San Francisco Public Library).

One day the moustache, head hair and bandana will be gone, but for now… My days as a Maoist hippie (aka student in California) in 1971.

At my cookery school (in my home) in Berkeley, California, 1979.

Accompanied by my speciality, Peking duck, in my Berkeley kitchen, 1980. I never grow bored of cooking it.

In the bustling markets of Hong Kong in the '80s, shopping with my students.

At Craig Claiborne's party in 1982, where I met Madhur Jaffrey. Craig is in striped shirt at the table, Pierre Franey beside him. I'm standing, centre. Also pictured: Marcella Hazan, Roger Vergé, Florence Lin, Marion Cunningham, Diana Kennedy.

Where would I be without Jenny Stevens, the producer of *Chinese Cookery*? Here we are in a restaurant in Hong Kong. It was October 1983, and we were taking a break from filming segments for that first BBC series. Leaving the studio to film outdoors is commonplace these days, but back then was novel.

With my relatives in Hong Kong in 1983.

Chopsticks raised for the beginning of my TV career. It was 1984, and here I am with the crew, mostly male, on the set of *Chinese Cookery*, my first series for the BBC. The firemen stayed out of the shot!

'When your book comes out, I'll host a party at my house.' Julia Child kept her promise, and here's the evidence. She invited the press to come and meet me at her home in Boston in September 1984. Through her brilliant books, I learnt to master the art of French cookery. And, through immense respect, I addressed her as 'Mrs Child'.

October 1985, cooking for my Hong Kong classes. I'd say the wok was probably hot enough.

All I did was say I'd like to meet Eric Cantona. Next, I was cooking for the Manchester United football team in the '80s. That's Eric on the left, Ryan Giggs on the right and Alex Ferguson stretching over for a taste.

Filming an episode of *Hot Wok* in my Berkeley garden with producer Kate Kinninmont and my dog Titoune looking on.

John Cleese tucks into my crispy vegetarian parcels in 1995. We met when he was filming *Fierce Creatures* at Jersey Zoo and I was filming the *Hot Wok* series.

In Hong Kong in 1997, to film the BBC series *Travels with the Hot Wok*. It's a tough job but someone's gotta do it.

A mutual love of good food and wine united us. Alex Ferguson and me enjoying yet another glass together, this time at the launch of my Yellow River Café in London in 2000.

In 2001, I cooked for Tony Blair and Jacques Chirac at my restaurant Pacific Oriental. The French President sent this photo as a thank-you.

Celebrating my mother's 80th birthday in Chicago's Chinatown, June 2002.

Before lunch at Château Lagrézette, 2002. I'm with Tony and Cherie Blair, showing them the wines we'll be savouring with the meal. They certainly seem interested.

With Anton Mosimann outside
his restaurant in London's Belgravia.
Ever the kind and gallant knight,
he helped me get that confit of
duck to the world leaders.

I'd paid to see her sing at the Cheetah
in Chicago in the '60s. Four decades
later, Tina Turner and I were introduced
by Alain Dominique Perrin at his
seriously swell birthday party in
Paris in 2003.

Memories… The wine cellar at my watchtower home
in Catus, in south-west France. This photograph
was taken in 2006, just a few months before most
of the wine was sold at auction at Christie's.

The cherished kitchen at home in Catus, featuring
that enormous table that I acquired from the
shepherdess of the Scottish Borders.

In 2009, I was appointed an honorary OBE for services to culinary arts. To celebrate the award, I held a party for my friends in London. Here I am with lovely June Whitfield. We had met years earlier when I cooked for her in the *Hot Wok* series.

There's rarely a break from cooking at home in Catus. Here I am, in the summer of 2011, at my Maestro Bonnet hob. It took a dozen men to carry in the oven's mainframe.

It could have been a joke about how I don't like cold weather. The row of cooks, from left, Gennaro Contaldo, Antonio Carluccio, Giorgio Locatelli and me. We were enjoying Antonio's birthday party in London in April 2014.

phrase shopaholic was unknown, I had been one in the stores of Hong Kong and France. I felt that the atmosphere should be casual and relaxed – look how easy this food is to make – and my clothes should reflect the undisturbed comfort.

Madhur had told me that when she filmed her series she wore her hair in a bun. This, she was informed, made her look 'too Indian'. So she was told to wear a wig. This would make her look 'less Indian'. In astonishment, I said, 'Madhur, why did you agree to that?'

'I'm an actress, Ken,' she replied. 'I'm an actress.' Luckily, I still had my hair so I wouldn't need a wig to look less Chinese.

———

AS the viewer, you would see only me. My view was different. In front of me, and behind the cameras, there were thirty-six people. The costs were considerable, therefore, which meant there was no chance of running over by even a few minutes. We had to stick to the schedule.

These thirty-six people all had their eyes trained on my every movement. Three of them were large, burly men who were wearing blue uniforms, bordering on military, and on the floor at their side were a couple of fire extinguishers. I asked a producer, 'I was just wondering … Who are the men beside the fire extinguishers?'

'They're the fire officers.'

'The fire officers?' I asked, unsure I'd heard correctly.

'Yup. Just in case there's a fire.'

'Why? Are we expecting a fire?'

And the response was: 'Well, you know. What with the wok and stuff.'

When I made a mistake – and yes, I made a few – the team in front of me would roll their eyes and some of them would tut or sigh. The producer Jenny Stevens watched the different camera angles from television monitors in the gallery, a small room that was above the studio and accessible by a flight of iron stairs.

When there was a problem, when Jenny did not approve of what I had said or done, or if I had fluffed a line, the crew and I could hear her high heels clickety-clacking on the metal steps as she came down the stairs. She moved briskly, and that sound always meant trouble. Members of the crew, grown men, quaked in their Hush Puppies and cursed in whispers. They were not alone. I would tremble and then freeze at the clanking of high heel on iron, petrified by the prospect of the rollicking that was to come.

My timidity and fear were not justified. I was overreacting. Jenny may have had the demeanour of a headmistress but, boy, was she smart. Also, Jenny had a lot riding on this. She was working her way upwards, progressing through the ranks, having previously been Madhur's assistant producer. If this was a success, then Jenny was made.

When I presented her with a list of dishes to cook for the first episode, she said firmly, 'Scrap that. We'll do those later. For the first episode you're going to cook Peking duck. That will blow them away.' In retrospect, she was right – or 'spot on', as the British might say – and it did blow them away. In fact, we did not film in sequence as it was felt I would be more at ease as we progressed.

Also, Jenny instilled in me a sense of urgency and efficiency. I learnt to understand what makes interesting viewing. It was during this period of filming the first series that I learnt the skill of a cookery demonstration, which I have followed ever since: if you want to keep it interesting, then keep it fast and keep it moving.

—

THE duck for the Peking duck was due to come courtesy of Mary Cadogan, the home economist on the series.

I was very fond of Mary, though unaware of how she had landed the job under false pretences. When the producers were hunting around for a home economist, they asked the established food photographer Robert Golden if he could recommend someone for the job. Robert had worked frequently with Mary and, being a kind soul, he suggested Mary would be ideal. The producers had said, 'We need someone who's an expert in Chinese cooking.'

Without the slightest hesitation, Robert had replied, 'Oh, that's Mary. She's an expert.' Reassured, they signed her up.

Mary had experience of food styling for magazines and on advertising assignments, and a three-year tenure as deputy food editor of *Family Circle* magazine, but she did not know very much about Chinese cooking. In Britain, who did?

This meant that she would need to bluff her way through our time together. We would rehearse dishes in the kitchen of a college and one day I saw Mary making wontons, folding them in a way someone who had never made wontons might fold wontons. That is to say, incorrectly. 'Mary, they look good,' I said, though they didn't. 'But why not try them like this?' and then showed her how to fold them.

However, as we worked together she developed a love of Chinese food, and our bond was strengthened by a mutual acceptance that food is *the* central part of life. Mary came from a large family: eight brothers and sisters. Her father was one of ten; her mother, one of seven. Her parents were Irish and had left Co. Wexford to build a new life in the English county of Kent, where Mary was born. 'The heart of our home was a big kitchen table,' she told me as we cooked together. 'Mum was a good, plain cook, who made fantastic apple tarts and lovely puddings and roasts. She cooked everything from scratch.' Once she said, 'I was jealous of friends who had Kellogg's corn flakes for breakfast because we always had porridge.'

At college, where she did a three-year diploma in Home Economics, she was known for her sartorial style: female students were not allowed to wear trousers, but Mary would arrive for class in clothes bought from jumble sales, and skirts made out of old drapes. Her career began in the textile industry before she veered into food.

Before filming the Peking duck segment, she had visited her local butcher in Dorking, Surrey, and ordered eight ducks, the finest the butcher could lay his hands on. After collecting them the day before filming, she took them home, where she had a walk-in larder. She assembled a metal clothes rail, and hung from it the eight ducks on meat hooks. This would allow their skins to dry out. The following morning, she left early for the studio, accompanied by her eight well-hung (stop sniggering) ducks.

I would arrive routinely at the studio at 10 a.m., while others were in well ahead of me, preparing for the day. Once there, I would rehearse the dreaded links. Now, Peking duck must have a crispy skin. And by the time I arrived Mary had already put one of the ducks into the hot oven, but its skin had not turned crispy. She was one duck down and not quite sure what the problem was when I spotted her putting the second duck into the oven. This was, by the way, how Mary was spending her birthday, although she had not mentioned to any of us that it was a special day for her.

I said, 'Mary, is that a Cherry Valley duck?'

'No. It's from my butcher.'

'It's the wrong breed. It will never crisp.'

Poor Mary burst into tears when I pointed this out. I was horrified.

I loved Mary. I like to think I'm good in a crisis, I don't rant and rave – what good does it accomplish? 'Don't worry,' I said. 'We'll fix this.' We all hit the phones, ringing around to find the right duck. We sent a taxi to Safeway – or was it Chinatown? – to get the real thing. Peace and calm was restored. A kind member of the crew took Mary to the pub at lunchtime, but she continued to cry. It was a birthday she has never forgotten.

In China, the preparation and cooking of Peking duck is an art form. There, the ducklings are raised on a six-week diet of soya beans, barley, sorghum and maize. Then they are ready for the table. They are despatched, cleaned and air is pumped through the windpipe. This process slightly removes the skin from the flesh and means the skin will roast separately and the fat will melt and keep the meat moist. Pouring hot water over the skin will close the pores, and the bird is then hung up to dry. As it dries, a solution of malt sugar is brushed over the duck. Then it is time to cook it in a wood-burning oven.

Once cooked perfectly, the duck's skin is brown, shiny and crisp. The meat should be meltingly moist; no fat. Here is my recipe, which I have adapted over the years since cooking it on that first episode of *Ken Hom's Chinese Cookery*.

Peking Duck

Serves 4–6

1 x 1.6–1.8 kg (3½–4 lb) duck, fresh or frozen, preferably Cherry Valley

For the honey syrup:

1 lemon

1.2 litres (2 pints) water

3 tablespoons honey

3 tablespoons dark soy sauce

150 ml (5 fl oz) Shaoxing rice wine or dry sherry

◔

To serve:

Chinese pancakes

Spring onion brushes (see page 45)

6 tablespoons hoisin sauce or sweet bean sauce

If the duck is frozen, thaw it thoroughly. Rinse the duck well and blot it completely dry with kitchen paper. Insert a meat hook near the neck.

Using a sharp knife, cut the lemon into 5 mm (¼ inch) slices, leaving the rind on. Place the slices in a large pan with the rest of the honey syrup ingredients and bring the mixture to the boil. Turn the heat to low and simmer for about 20 minutes. Using a large ladle or spoon, pour this mixture over the duck several times, as if to bathe it, until the skin of the duck is completely coated.

Hang the duck over a tray or roasting pan and leave in a cool, well-ventilated place to dry for 4–5 hours, longer if possible. (If you wish to speed up the process, place it in front of a fan for several hours.) When the duck has dried, the skin should feel like parchment paper.

Preheat the oven to 240°C (475°F, gas mark 9).

Meanwhile, place the duck on a roasting rack in a roasting tin, breast side up. Pour 150 ml (5 fl oz) of water into the roasting tin. (This will prevent the fat from splattering.) Put the duck into the oven and roast it for 15 minutes. Turn down the heat to 180°C (350°F, gas mark 4) and continue to roast for 1 hour and 10 minutes.

Remove the duck from the oven and let it rest for at least 10 minutes before carving it. Using a cleaver or a sharp knife, cut the skin and meat into pieces and arrange them on a warm serving platter. Serve at once with Chinese pancakes, spring onion brushes and a bowl of hoisin sauce or sweet bean sauce. ◓

21

Cooking and the Books

THE SUCCESS OF my *Chinese Cookery* series was due, in part, to the speed of the cooking. Most dishes were cooked before the viewers' eyes, in real time. Indian food can be fast, but often it involves making elements of a dish in advance. Chinese food tends to be quick and simple, as well as healthy. Usually we did not have to depend on tricks such as 'Here's one I made earlier' or 'This is what it looks like half an hour later.'

The production team was overwhelmed by the simplicity of it all, thank God. 'Fantastic' and 'Wow' were the frequent verdicts as they stormed in to try the food once filming had finished and Jenny Lo said, 'OK' – the cue for the vultures to descend. One of the burly fire officers, who was there to ensure the studio did not burst into flames, went up to Mary Cadogan and asked her, 'Where can I buy a wok?' A sure sign that we were doing something right.

At rehearsals, the controller of BBC Two came to watch, and afterwards told Jenny that we would have a 7.30 p.m. timeslot. Peak-time viewing. We celebrated the wrap with a Chinese meal on a boat on the River Thames. There was a feeling of great excitement, that we had created something new.

My stint in London also gave me the chance to enjoy British food. I love fish and chips with tartare sauce, though am not a fan of malt vinegar. I have had fish and chips in other countries around the world, but it only ever succeeds when cooked and eaten in Britain. The owner of the flat in which I stayed during filming made the most delicious steak and kidney pie, the smell of which wafted through the building. He was German. I like British savoury puddings, but can only manage a mouthful of sticky toffee pudding.

Scotch eggs are a bit heavy for me, but Lancashire hotpot is a classic and bacon butties are moreish, preferably made with streaky bacon. When travelling, I always have a bacon butty in the British Airways lounge. Strange though you may find this, I think I would prefer pork pie hot rather than cold, but confess that I have never tested it. When I first visited London in the early 1970s, I believed that Indian food was part of British cooking as it was so popular.

A promotional tour was planned for the broadcast of *Chinese Cookery* and publication of the book. The PR people sent me here and there, to do interviews with the press and on television and radio. One day I went for a chat on a show on London radio station LBC.

I arrived early at the station's HQ and was told that I would be joined on air by a few other people. I didn't catch all the names, but one of them was the actor Michael York and another was Divine, the drag queen and actor. I had come across Michael at a charity event in San Francisco. I knew of Divine, but had not met or seen him.

Michael York was the next to arrive. He shook my hand and gave me a friendly greeting. 'Hi. We've met before.' I guess if you meet a Chinese guy you remember who he is. We were chatting away when the next person arrived. She had spiky, reddish-pink hair. I studied the face, the make-up and said to myself, 'That must be Divine. That's pretty damn good – looks like a real woman.'

At that instant, Michael left my side and dashed over to Divine and kissed him right on the lips. As I stood there, trying to unravel the scene before me, another guest arrived. He was wearing a robe and had a perfectly bald head. By now, I was totally confused. My view was of an English movie heart-throb kissing a drag queen, with a bald man in a dress standing next to them.

Only once we were in the studio, when the presenter introduced us on air, was I able to solve the mystery. Divine was the bald man in the robe. The intriguing woman with reddish-pink hair was, I discovered, the fashion designer Zandra Rhodes.

I tell this story because my mother used to say to me, 'If you keep your mouth shut, no one will think you are a mute.' The moral, therefore, is that it is better to be quiet and dumb, than to speak and say, 'Hello Divine, nice to meet you,' when you are meeting someone called Zandra.

———

THE book, *Chinese Cookery*, had been printed so that its publication tied in with the series. Unbeknown to me, the demand from the booksellers was so great that the publishers of BBC Books concluded they would break the £5 tag.

Until then the highest price for a cookery book was £4.95. I know; it's the price of a pint these days. Zilch. They put my book at a new record of £5.25. They were not acting on impulse, necessarily. Orders were so immense that the first print run was 350,000 copies. At that time, this was the largest initial print run of a non-fiction book in British publishing history.

I was in California, but from London Jenny Stevens had kindly kept me up to date with reports about the success of the series. My parting words to Jenny had been, 'I think some people will like the series, but I'm not sure it will be massively popular.' Now she was telling me about something called an AP index. This is the Appreciation Index, a research tool which enables broadcasters to assess the popularity of someone who has appeared on television. It is a range from 0 to 100. Jenny said, 'Anything above 60 is good and yours has been 78 and sometimes 80. That's unheard of. People just really love the series.' I'm sitting here smugly smiling as I tell you.

I was in an extremely odd situation. I was becoming famous in Britain, but did not live there and did not know the country very well, even though I had fallen in love with London. I guess I was watching from a distance, rather than being caught up in it. Soon afterwards I visited Britain and went with Jenny to the theatre in the West End. A stranger sidled up to me and said, 'I must say, I loved your series.'

I said, 'Really?' I was being recognised, and soon would find myself in a slightly confused state of wonderment.

Authors speak of a fear of book signings. A fear that no one will ask to have a book signed. The room will be virtually empty – just the author sitting at a table with three pens and a mountain of books waiting to be signed, but no one to say, 'Please will you sign it?'

The PR people at BBC Books asked if I would be happy to do book signings, and I told them, 'No, I don't think it would be good idea because nobody knows who I am.'

'Oh, don't worry about that,' they said. 'Even if it's ten people it will be well worth doing.' I agreed. The first signing, I seem to recall, took place at a bookshop in London. I went with Roger, the BBC Books marketing man. We took a taxi through the rain and pulled up at the shop where the signing would take place. Along the pavement there was a queue of at least 600 people, I am not kidding. Bewildered, I said to Roger, 'Look at all those people. What are they waiting for?'

Roger replied, 'They are waiting for you.'

'You're joking.' I could not believe it. They were waiting for me and I only had two hours to sign – luckily my name is short.

I was deeply touched when a Chinese-British postman, looking smart in his Royal Mail uniform, stepped from the queue to shake my hand. He had a proper cockney accent, and he said, 'Ken, it is so fantastic what you are doing for us, showing the British people our food. Thank you very much.' I was overwhelmed by this brief but meaningful acknowledgement. If nothing else, I had made this man happy. I was humbled by his words, and felt a tear run down my cheek. For the first time, I really felt that deep affection from people I did not know.

In a bookshop in Manchester, they took me into a large back room where they had hundreds of copies of *Chinese Cookery*. I thought, *They are never going to sell those.* I felt sorry for them. In the States I would be lucky if someone had a stack of twenty of my books.

They did, however, sell in that store in Manchester, and in many others throughout Britain. The recipes have endured the test of time. Three decades later, the book has sold one million-plus copies around the world. In 1985, the BBC would commission me to write another book, *Ken Hom's Vegetables and Pasta*, which was published in 1987 when *Chinese Cookery* was repeated on TV. Jenny was sending me the *Sunday Times* bestseller lists, which showed *Chinese Cookery* competing with *Vegetables and Pasta* for the number one spot. Each title alternated from number one to number two as the weeks went on. It was amazing but, again, I was watching from thousands of miles away.

Most people are detached from those who buy their books. We can't meet them all so they have questions and we don't know what those questions are. Nowadays we know those questions because they are easily asked on the internet, via Twitter or Facebook. But before the internet and social media you had to have people ask you the questions. In fact, nowadays I try to anticipate the questions.

Recently I was in Liverpool and met a woman who had a first edition of *Chinese Cookery*. The book was in tatters, covered in stains of tea, coffee, wine and maybe a little cornflour. How wonderful! It is a great accolade to see copies from the old days, with notes written on the pages. 'This one was sensational' next to one recipe. 'I'll do it again' written beside another, and then, 'A family favourite'. It makes me think, *Oh my God, this is something as ordinary as cooking that is connecting our lives.*

On those book tours in the '80s, it was helpful to visit supermarkets to see what was available so that I could suggest substitutes, and would know not to say 'use this' when 'this' was mostly unobtainable in Britain. I did not live in Britain, but was starting to see how the food scene was changing. Visiting the UK a few times a year had provided me with a clear perspective of the nation's progression, seeing how quickly things change and how the supermarkets met the challenge of supplying shoppers' needs and desires.

Then, of course, I always insisted on eating in the best restaurant in the area to see what the chefs were like. This was a way of meeting budding chefs, giving me a comparison with the chefs I knew in America. I wanted to see what they were doing in Great Britain, and how that was changing.

———

PICK up a cookery book and you tend to flick through the pages, stopping on the colourful photographs of dishes that catch your eye. Oh, that looks delicious, you think. I'll make that for supper on Saturday when Nick and Sally come round.

Such books, when done well, provide joyous escapism. For many of us, the cookbook moves from our bedside table to our kitchen counter, and back again.

The reader gets to cook new dishes and glean a few culinary tricks. For the author there are bonuses too: the simple pleasure of sharing with the reader; the feeling of bliss on receiving the finished product, hot off the press and sent by the publishers; and the contentment that comes from making new friends – friends with the other people who help to produce that single book.

I am still close to Ann Bramson, my first editor way back at Simon & Schuster in New York. Subsequently I have established equally happy friendships with wonderful photographers, food stylists, designers and other editors at publishing houses.

One of those editors was Heather Holden-Brown, who has since become a brilliant literary agent. She joined BBC Books in the late 1980s and, a few months into her job, she was 'put in charge' of me. It was Christmastime and, as I was visiting London, we agreed to hook up. Heather made her way past the throng of shoppers around Sloane Square and came to the flat in Chelsea where I was staying during the stop-off. This was our first encounter, and I only found out later that she was a little anxious about our meeting because she had not previously worked on food books. Maybe I sensed her slight apprehension, so I figured we should have a drink and she didn't object when I grabbed a couple of glasses and opened a bottle of Chablis, nicely chilled, and put on the coffee table between us a plate of golden-brown dim sum.

We chatted about books and food writing, of course, and then Heather told me a story which has stayed with me. It is a story, I suppose, which neatly illustrates how the immigrant remains faithful to the food of her or his homeland. Now, you and I can leave the country where we have been born and raised and lived for decades. We can move abroad to begin a new life. But can we leave behind the recipes? We cannot. After all, Britain is renowned for its food culture, which is founded on the recipes and food brought to the nation by immigrants.

Heather's story was about her mother, who was born and raised in Canada – Toronto, I think – and, in her late twenties, she came to London. I do not recall if she was specifically looking for a husband in England. Yet she found one.

Once married, they settled in Surrey and, in the early 1950s, my dear friend Heather was born. This is where we reach the interesting food angle of the story. You see, we all savour the new, exciting tastes of faraway lands, but we continue to crave the flavours and aromas that take us back to our kitchens at home.

So when Heather was packed off to school, she would have shepherd's pie or steak and kidney pie for lunch, but when she returned home, she ate like no other young lady in the county of Staffordshire, where her family were by then living. Heather's eyes lit up – mine, too – as she told me, 'My mother made chocolate brownies, big cherry pies, heaps of pecan pie and lots of chocolate chip cookies.'

They are all trendy now, but in the '50s they were unknown in Britain. A sip of Chablis and then Heather went on. 'She roasted ham and served it with raisin sauce … None of my friends had food like that.' Her mother even made an intriguing dish called spaghetti Bolognese, buying olive oil from Boots in the nearby high street.

I have no idea about the number of possessions Heather's mother brought to Great Britain from Canada, but I know that one of her suitcases contained her bible – it was *The Boston Cooking-School Cook Book* by Fannie Merritt Farmer. Ms Farmer was New England's answer to England's Mrs Beeton. First published in the 1890s, it is a classic, with hundreds of recipes for the aspiring home cook, ranging from oyster gumbo to a whole stack of muffin recipes, along with half a dozen chowders, Maryland chicken, Boston baked beans, and desserts of macaroon cream, peach custard, ice creams of banana, caramel and pineapple, as well as baked Alaska. Bedside-table stuff.

As we heard the high-pitched harmony of child carol singers making their way down the street towards the front door, my new friend added, 'One day I came home from school and my mother said, "Heather, we're going to make popcorn."'

'Popcorn?' said the daughter to her mother. 'What's that?'

I cherish Heather: she always makes me hungry.

———

TRUE, I had a career in Britain, but, as I had not planned to become a TV presenter in Britain, I returned to California after the promotional tour and resumed my life there. Like everything I do, I merely try to give it my very best. I had thought, *I'm not going to do something of which I will be ashamed.* As I was not from Britain, I did not think the British public would 'embrace' me. But I did not feel at home in the States, so I was used to being the outsider. I thought, *I'll give it all I've got, learn as much as I can, and take the experience.*

It was 1985, and I was thirty-five years old. Business for me was flourishing, and included a trip to Asia for the Potatoes Board as well as another for the Wheat Board. These corporations pay sensational money; I couldn't, and wouldn't, complain.

Meanwhile, I was receiving all kinds of proposals and propositions to endorse products. The most appealing and attractive offer was to endorse a wok. More than twenty companies tried to get me to sign up to it. Terence Conran, founder of Habitat, was one such person keen to sell a Ken Hom wok. The problem was that, while all of them wanted to sell a wok with my name on it, none of them wanted my involvement in its design. To me, this was ridiculous. For decades, I had been cooking with a wok. The companies, however, were usually run by people who had never cooked with such a utensil.

Also, I had form. In California I had already designed a wok for use in professional kitchens. Although offers were tantalisingly handsome, I was adamant, should there be a deal, that I would be intimately involved in the design and would sign off on everything. That was the clincher, the make or break. I figured that if nobody would agree to my terms, then why should I do it? Many meetings with companies concluded with me saying, 'I'm sorry, this isn't going to work out.' The thing is, a cook cannot cook Chinese food without a good wok.

———

THE wok is a versatile piece of equipment and may be used for stir-frying, blanching, deep-frying, steaming and smoking foods. The sides of the wok are deep. Its bottom is either tapered or slightly flattened, ensuring the wok is quickly heated and the food is cooked evenly. The deep sides prevent the food and oils from spilling over during cooking, although you don't need much oil in a wok. It's a healthy way of cooking.

Chinese cuisine has been described as 'a cookery of scarcity'. In a geographic situation of limited arable land and even more limited forests, providing food and firewood for a population of so many millions was an enormous challenge. Over the centuries, the Chinese learnt how to extract from nature the maximum of edible ingredients and to prepare them tastefully with a minimum of cooking oil and fuel. From these necessities, stir-fry cookery and the wok were conceived and fashioned.

The wok came into wide use about 2,000 years ago, and its appearance coincides with the progression of China's Iron Age, which came much later than Europe's. The word 'wok' is Cantonese. The word 'guo' is used in Mandarin or pinyin Chinese. As the Cantonese are the great travellers of China, it is their pronunciation of the term that has won worldwide acceptance.

Traditionally, Chinese kitchens are sparsely furnished, but the stove (usually rectangular) is substantial and has two circular openings above the fire chamber. Large, round-bottomed, cast-iron woks fit tightly on these openings so that all the heat is transferred to the wok and none is lost. So the proper cooking temperatures are quickly attained. Every tool in the kitchen is versatile, every technique extracts the full nutritional value and flavour from the ingredients, and the foods themselves are prepared so that they cook quickly in a little oil and don't waste heat. The wok evolved to its perfection in this environment, a warm stove and a wok becoming synonymous with heart and home at the centre of Chinese family life.

There are two types of wok: *pau* and Cantonese. The *pau* wok has one long handle which is 30 to 35 cm (12 to 14 inches) long, making it perfect for stir-frying. You hold it with one hand, while using the other hand to stir the ingredients – using a long spoon, spatula or chopsticks, that is, rather than your hand! The long handle saves the cooks from hot splashes of oil, should there be any. The traditional Cantonese wok has short, rounded handles on either side of the edge or lip of the wok. This type of wok is easy to move when full of liquid, so ideal when deep-frying or steaming.

———

Just the mention of steaming evokes memories of the kitchen at King Wah, Uncle Paul's restaurant in Chicago's Chinatown. Can we go back there, please? In the kitchen I would help to make steamed beef meatballs.

To make these meatballs, the beef is first minced by hand, using two cleavers, one in each hand. Egg white and cornflour are added during the chopping process, until they are fully incorporated into the meat. These two ingredients make the meatballs light and fluffy.

Next, the seasonings are added: light soy sauce, sesame oil, finely chopped coriander and spring onions, sugar and black pepper.

The chopping continues – Chop! Chop! Chop! – until the meat becomes a light paste. The meat is rolled into balls, and at King Wah we would sit around chatting while we rolled. A steamer or a rack goes into the wok, pour in water, turn on the gas, bring to a boil and lower the meatballs – on a heatproof plate – onto the rack or into the steamer. Reduce the heat to low, cover the wok and wait for 15 minutes.

Pour away the liquid from the plate, put the meatballs on a warm serving platter and serve immediately.

The washing of the wok is as easy as the cooking in the wok. Do not scour a seasoned wok. Instead, wash it in hot water without detergent. If you wish to store the wok for a long while, or if you live in a damp or humid climate, rub the inside of the wok with a dessertspoon of cooking oil. This will provide added protection against rust. 🥣

22

The Evolution
of the Wok
(Mine)

ONE DAY, I heard from a man named Michael Levene, who had a manufacturing business in Britain. As usual, I conveyed my wok terms – that I required the final say – and, as had become the way, expected that to be the end of the conversation.

To my astonishment, Michael said, 'OK, we'll do what you want.'

The company was set up by William Levene, Michael's father, who began as a street vendor in east London. The entrepreneurial spirit ran deep in the family veins. Michael had done well by selling cookware products on TV. One of these products was a can opener, MagiCan, which became a bestseller around the world (sales were boosted when Margaret Thatcher was photographed cheerfully testing it while touring the Ideal Home Exhibition in 1988). With that, he launched another product, and so on. MagiCan, by the way, is still a bestseller to this day.

Michael lived in a huge, gothic-looking house in the north London suburb of Hampstead with his wife Jean, herself an accomplished business-woman who had her own, eponymously named, PR agency. Michael was full of business ideas and liked to hear them from others, although he had a short attention span: if you couldn't spit out your idea in ten seconds, forget it, because he would be bored by then.

He was respectful of what I wanted, which was control and the authority to sign off on a product. There were moments when he would try to talk me into something and I'd say that I didn't think it would fly. He listened.

As he loved fine wine and good food, we spent many hours at the table together. There was an affinity, probably because he was Jewish and I was Chinese. My mother used to go to the Jewish quarter to shop and, when Chinese food was covered in the American press, it was always by journalists with Jewish bylines.

He was humorous, and our fun together was an essential bonus in our working relationship. He was never cheap and he put me up in good hotels. When I was staying in London, he would be sure to come and see me, even if it was over breakfast in my hotel, where he would always order kippers. I do not appreciate this smoked fish for breakfast, which is so popular in Britain. I can eat sushi in the morning, but not kippers. So I ordered eggs and bacon.

With Michael, I knew I had made the right decision. I have turned down many ventures that could have been incredibly lucrative, but I try to look at the long-term benefits of a project. I have a gut instinct which tells me when things do not seem right. Putting your name to everything that comes along can only devalue your brand. Integrity creates a strong brand. With the woks, as with everything in which I have been involved, I asked myself two questions. Would I buy it? And, if I bought it, would I feel ripped off? I was once asked to endorse a flavouring product which had no salt. 'I just wouldn't use it,' was my response. 'Why should I be involved?'

In August 1986, two years after I had filmed *Chinese Cookery*, I was back in Britain. Michael had flown me over to talk about the design and the weight of the wok, and we shot a video, a bit like a television commercial, which would be shown on TVs in shops and stores.

The wok was produced in time for Christmas and when I asked Michael to predict the sales, he responded, 'Probably about 12,000.' Come Christmas Day, more than 100,000 British people had each bought one of my woks. It just took off. The success was so overwhelming that I suggested returning to Britain in February 1987, to promote the wok around Chinese New Year.

This led to a two-week tour of cookery demonstrations, which I regard as the best thing I ever did. That is because it cemented my relationship with the British public. I got to travel around the nation, not just London, but north up the M1, visiting places such as Newcastle and Huddersfield and Derby, and, going west, to towns and cities that included Dorchester and Bristol.

People who had seen the series were able to come and watch the cooking, up close and personal. I learnt a lot about Britain and the British, whose sense of humour – packed with heaps of irony and an abundance of mischief – I find deliciously irresistible.

MICHAEL Levene provided me with an assistant, Sue Burke. She was also my driver and, as the road trip progressed, she became a funny, entertaining companion. As we drove, we sang – the oldies but goldies, mostly the Rolling Stones or the Beatles.

Sue is a northern girl, born in Southport, Lancashire, and grew up in the south, in Middlesex: 'Rayners Lane,' she told me. 'End of the Metropolitan line.'

She was, and remains, a lovable tough cookie, who said it like it was. She explained to me what I should and should not say: 'Ken, we don't do that here.' I learnt so much. It was through an education from Sue that I came to feel more British than American. Sue did not cook much and had little interest in food. It was merely fuel. She was not an adventurous gourmet. As we drove, I asked her what she would have for her final meal, and Sue said, 'For starters, shish kebabs. Then chicken madras with pilau rice and aloo gobi. For dessert, vanilla ice cream. And yours?'

I said, 'Caviar, steamed fish and Peking duck.' (And now, I think, I would eat it in Rio de Janeiro on the Copacabana beach at sunset, as the setting is perfect and extraordinarily beautiful.)

Although the wok sales were rapidly heading towards a million, Sue had not heard of woks until our meeting. She was blissfully unaware of my TV series and accompanying book. Quite simply, she was not the slightest bit interested in food. She considered me to be 'a nutcase' because all I talked about was the eating of the last meal and the planning of the next one.

In a fancy restaurant, as I studied the pages of magnificent Burgundian delights, Sue tapped the wine list in my hands and said, 'Don't know why you bother. Tesco's wine is as good as anything that costs a thousand pounds.'

During the tour she existed on a diet of steak; grilled or fried, she was not fussed, as long as there were chips with it. She did like fish, but only when it was battered and came with chips. At first I attempted to encourage Sue to explore a restaurant's menu, and to be enticed by the descriptions of each dish. Then the waiter would come to the table, to hear Sue's opening line, 'Do you have steak?' I tried, also, to lead her towards the love of a feast and, as the dishes arrived at the table, I said, 'It's all right, Sue. We can walk it off afterwards.'

Sue said, 'I don't think you're supposed to have a big walk after eating.'

When I treated her to lunch at Bibendum, that fine but pricey restaurant in Chelsea, I savoured the melting textures of calf's brain with sauce gribiche, while Sue got the kitchen to make her roast beef with Yorkshire pudding and gravy. Good for her. Sue's beef, by the way, could never be bloody. Her saving grace, in my opinion, is that she likes red wine.

Traditionally, the most celebrated roast beef comes from the rib cut. I also enjoy roast beef fillet, served with classic truffle sauce, which is simple to make. To feed four, I use a fillet that weighs 1.3–1.5 kg (2¾–3¼ lb), trimmed and tied (ask your butcher to do this, if necessary).

I preheat the oven to 220°C (425°F, gas mark 7), and while it heats up I season the fillet well with salt and freshly ground black pepper to my taste. I heat a roasting pan on top of the hob and add a couple of tablespoons of groundnut oil or vegetable oil. Once it is hot, I slowly brown the beef on all sides until is golden brown.

The beef goes into the oven for 10 minutes before the heat is reduced to 190°C (375°F, gas mark 5). It has 10 minutes more of roasting before it is removed from the oven, placed on a board and allowed to rest for about 20 minutes at room temperature before carving.

While it rests, the truffle sauce can be made. This is done by finely chopping 60g (2 oz) of fresh black winter truffles or high-quality tinned black winter truffles (cooked once). Pour off all the fat from the roasting pan, saving any bits and juices. The pan is returned to the hob and here comes the 'deglazing': add 3 tablespoons of Madeira, which will bubble, reduce in volume and collect the flavours from the pan. Add the reserved juices and bits, and finally the chopped truffles.

Serve the fillet with the sauce. Easy and elegant! 🥢

FOOD, like music, literature or the movies, is subjective. What you love may not appeal to me, and vice versa.

The pleasure of eating, however, is usually formed in childhood. Likewise, the displeasure of eating can be traced back to our early years. Sue and I both came from backgrounds where there was little money. In my case, eating well – experiencing flavours that would excite the taste buds – was of primary concern when I was growing up. In Sue's case, the process of sitting at a table and eating was nothing more than sitting at a table and eating, munching merely to fill an empty tummy.

As a child, she had eaten her mum's curries, chops and mashed potatoes, or roast chicken on a Sunday, followed by chicken soup (made with the bones) on a Monday. 'When we were very small we used to have bread and dripping, and Weetabix and sugar sandwiches,' she told me. 'I was a fussy eater. Sometimes my brother and I would have Weetabix for tea because Mum couldn't always afford to feed us.'

Sue grew curious about my food. She was at my cookery demonstrations, helping to set up, watching the preparation and then watching as I cooked. After each demo, she would pick at the leftovers, and acquired a taste for my food until, one day, she said she loved it. She had become a close friend, so I considered her compliment to be a great accolade. She still had to be careful, though. 'Ken, I am allergic to garlic,' she had warned me, early on. 'It gives me the runs.'

I enjoy doing cookery demonstrations and, in the early days, I was startled by the powerful impact of television. The demo audience included many people who had watched me on TV, and they chatted to me with such friendliness and familiarity, always calling me Ken, which I welcome. They had watched me, of course, in their own homes, on the television. This is different from how we regard those who appear on the big screen in a cinema.

Someone from the BBC explained it to me. He said, 'Up there on the cinema screen, they're only acting, and it's simply a story. When you are on telly, especially doing what you do, people either really like you or dislike you intensely. There are some people who appear on TV and just fall off the chart – viewers can't stand them, we won't mention names. Then there are others who are accepted by viewers as a member of the family.'

The demonstrations have helped me write books because people have so many questions, ones that I can address in a cookbook.

Rice is frequently the subject of questions from the lovely people I meet when travelling or strolling along the streets.

Long-grain rice is the most popular rice for cooking in China and as a child I recall the ritual washing of the rice under cold water as my mother started to prepare our meal. The required rice was put into a bowl that was then filled with cold water. Carefully, the cloudy water was poured away, keeping the rice in the bowl. This process was repeated several times until the water was clear. These days, it does not require washing, but if you want to be authentic, then that is the form.

Short rice is most often found in northern China and is used for making rice porridge, a popular morning meal. I find short rice to be coarse and rough.

Glutinous rice is also known as sweet rice or sticky rice, and is short, round and pearl-like, with a high gluten content. It is used for stuffings, for rice pudding and in pastries, and sometimes wrapped in lotus leaves and served at Chinese banquets. It should be soaked in cold water for at least two hours before cooking, and can be cooked in the same way as long-grain rice.

In southern areas of China, the New Year is celebrated by washing rice clean for several days before the feasts begin. This is known as 'the grain for ten thousand years' (wan nian liang) and eating it during the New Year festivities is hoped to bring prosperity.

WITH Sue at my side, I went on the talk shows, such as BBC's *Pebble Mill at One* and ITV's *This Morning*, which then was presented by the popular married couple Richard Madeley and Judy Finnigan. At *This Morning* they had asked me to cook a dish, but I was horrified when I saw their nasty wok and Sue kindly nipped to the shops to buy one of mine.

When Chinese New Year came around, Sue received a request for me to appear on Terry Wogan's popular chat show on BBC One. All I had to do was get from California to London. The saga began when the British Airways flight from San Francisco to London was cancelled due to mechanical problems with the plane. I told British Airways staff that I needed to be in London because of the show, so they re-routed me: first, I would take the red-eye to New York; second, I would take Concorde to London.

The show's producers worked out the timings and wondered if I'd be able to make it from Heathrow Airport to the studios in Shepherd's Bush, which can take anything up to an hour, depending on traffic. They contemplated putting me on the back of a motorbike to beat the rush-hour tailbacks. Thankfully, they went off that idea.

I took the red-eye to New York and was feeling quite knackered when I boarded Concorde. At Heathrow, I felt even worse. A driver collected me and we started on our way to the studios, around about the time the show was starting. All the while, Terry was telling viewers, 'Ken Hom should be with us very soon.' I arrived, all over the place, and they pushed me on stage. As I stood there in front of the cameras, in a dazed and exhausted state, Terry opened with the line, 'Well, Ken, great to have you. Now, tell us – how was the food on Concorde?'

I said, 'I was disappointed.'

No, not the best opener. The minute I said it, I thought, *Oh, now you've gone and done it.* The *you* being *me.* There had been talk, you see, that I would work with British Airways on a range of meals. I think British Airways might have hated me after that.

When the show finished I went with Michael Levene and his wife to their countryside home in Buckinghamshire. I slept for twenty-four hours. Now that I am not jet-lagged, let me explain: Concorde was small and short, and not like being in the first-class cabin of today's aircraft. That is why I was disappointed. I had expected something akin to first class.

Whenever possible, I travel only by BA and that is because I feel very British. Last time I flew to Brazil, the pilot said he grew up with my *Chinese Cookery* book, which is really touching. And I must admit I like it when they say, 'Will you have something to eat? It's not as good as yours.' I need that fix of the British sense of humour. It is as if I am as familiar to them as they are to me.

Sue and I travelled abroad, too. One of our trips was to Slovenia, and its capital Ljubljana. There was a company there that was selling the wok, and the bosses kindly invited us to dinner. Wherever I go, I try to respect the food and, for instance, in Finland I tried reindeer because that is what the Finnish eat.

As an aside, I must say that I try not to eat strange foods for the sake of strangeness. In 1988, when I was researching *The Taste of China*, I travelled to China with my friend Jenny Lo. As she is Chinese, Jenny could help me with the research. I could bounce things off her, especially how she grew up eating Chinese food. We worked our way through 800 dishes. Jenny beat me, by just a few, because one day I was ill and could not eat another thing.

At one of the restaurants we asked the waiters to make their speciality and were shocked by what they brought to the table. It looked like tripe but when we were halfway through the dish, I asked, 'What is this?' They said it was, in fact, elephant's trunk. The trunk was served in a sauce, and was gelatinous and lacked flavour. At another restaurant Jenny and I were shown the ingredient before it was cooked. It was dried up and extremely pongy. Bear paw. That, again, was gelatinous without much flavour. I have been told that it is best to eat the left paw since that is the one that the bear licks and therefore the more tender of the two.

Here, in Slovenia, a menu was passed to me. I waved it away, saying, 'I'd like to eat your country's most famous dish. Please give me what Slovenians would eat.'

They said, 'Well, that's fowl.'

I thought, *Interesting; could be chicken.* They looked at Sue, and I said, 'Oh, she'll have steak and chips, please. Not bloody.'

As I was eating the food, I thought, *I know chicken but the texture of this meat is strange.* It was delicious and sweet, but looked more like veal than chicken. I finished the dish and said to our host, 'What does this animal look like?' He used his hands as if they were hoofs in a gallop and started making neighing sounds. I had not eaten fowl. Instead, I had just consumed *foal*, a young horse.

Sue looked at me and said in her dry way, 'See. You should have ordered the steak when you had the chance.'

A postscript regarding *The Taste of China* (although knowing me it will end up longer than the average PS). I spent almost two years on that book, on and off. Apart from the adventure with Jenny in '88 – when I went to places in China that I had not previously visited – there was also a trip in '89 with the photographer.

The publishers wanted to use a famous Italian for the job of photographer, but I was adamant. 'No, I want someone Chinese.' In hindsight, that was one of the smartest demands of my life. Without it, we would not have had the book. The photographer was Leong Ka Tai, who had been recommended by my friend Lynn Pan, and he accompanied me, with his assistant, on part of this fascinating experience.

I wanted the book to be both thematic and personal; a departure from my other cookery books; not only about food but also about people and culture. It also turned out to be a remarkable insight into China before the sensational rise of the economy.

My extensive travels for the book included a journey with my mother from Hong Kong to visit my relatives in Guangdong, my family's home province. Laden with gifts for my cousin's family, we went first by high-speed hydrofoil to Macau. There we crossed the border and rented a car and driver to take us to Kaiping, and then through lush, deep country-side, to the village where the family lived, a warm, misty rain falling on the day that we arrived. It was dreamlike.

Firecrackers were set off and it was a happy, teary reunion, though I remember thinking how natural it all seemed. I speak our Cantonese village dialect, so I felt quite at home and as if I had been there before. A banquet was prepared and I saw first-hand what my mother's behaviour had always shown: the enjoyment of a meal comes not only from the food, but from the love and friendship at that table.

The meal began with the ritual washing of the rice, and this was rice grown in family fields and set aside for this occasion. My cousin went off to a small pond near the house, and returned with a net of grass carp for the meal. Twenty members of the family had helped in the preparation of this eleven-course feast. Food was set aside as an offering to the spirits of the departed members of the family. Whatever food the spirits do not eat is then consumed by the guests.

We consumed quite a lot. We ate bitter melon stir-fried with lean pork (a great favourite of mine). Chinese water spinach, plucked from the garden, was cooked with fermented bean curd. There was a stew of dried oysters and bean curd sticks, and the best long beans I have ever had, served with silk squash and crispy cloud ear fungus. With the special rice, we had braised goose, roast pig and roast duck. Reflecting on the banquet in *The Taste of China*, I wrote, 'The presence of so much meat and poultry demonstrated that this was indeed a special occasion … It certainly impressed me and if anything I overindulged during that long, delightful afternoon.'

That delight was later to change to despair when Leong Ka Tai, his assistant and I were caught up in the pandemonium of the Tiananmen Square protests and the after-effects of the massacre of hundreds, or maybe thousands, of students. We were moving from Sichuan and flying to Beijing on 5 June. We had been working for a month, and Leong had photographs which formed the illustrative crux of the book. Earlier, on 4 June, we were in our hotel in Chengdu, and there was a curfew. We heard gunfire; the first time I had ever heard gunshots, even though I had lived in America.

We knew something ominous was happening but there was a news black-out and the television was broadcasting only propaganda films of farming in rice fields. Leong Ka Tai said, 'This is not good.' He was right. We were totally unaware that the killings were being carried out by the army as they cleared the square of protestors. The following day, we flew to Beijing, where, unbeknown to us, the June Fourth Incident had taken place. When we landed, the place was chaos, with Hong Kong Chinese running around, yelling, 'Get out of here – they are killing everybody!'

Unable to find a flight (they were all full or grounded), we headed for the Great Wall Sheraton Hotel, where the foreign press were also holed up. As we drove to the hotel, we passed soldiers and tanks. 'What have we got ourselves into?' I asked Leong Ka Tai. Finally, we found seats on the last Cathay flight to Hong Kong.

We arrived at the airport, where there were more soldiers. 'What do you have in the bag?'

Leong Ka Tai showed them rolls of film – digital cameras were not then on the scene. If you lost the film, you were stuffed. 'What is on the film?' asked the soldier.

'It's about food,' said Leong.

The soldier stared at him and looked again at the film, grunting. For a moment it seemed like the film – the result of weeks of work – would be taken and tossed into a bin. But then Leong Ka Tai reached into his pocket and produced a little notepad. On the pages, he had made notes of everything that he had photographed. A true pro. We were waved through and I thought, *Somewhere, Buddha must be smiling.*

From Hong Kong, we sneaked back into China. Later on, I flew to England, where I was greeted by hurricanes, and finished writing the book in San Francisco, just when there was a big earthquake. *The Taste of China* did not win an award for the most dangerous cookbook ever written, but it was published in nine countries and shortlisted for a prestigious Andre Simon award. I was the lucky one: just thinking of the book instantly reminds me of those poor young victims who were murdered on 4 June.

Savoury Beef with Asparagus

This is a delicious, quick, wholesome dish that is very 'wok friendly'.

Asparagus is the favourite vegetable of many lovers of good food. It is easy to see why. The properly cooked stalks combine an earthy with an ethereal quality, a crunchy and a soft texture, subtle and distinct flavours. And in the spring, when it is in season and readily available, it is inexpensive.

Asparagus is congenial with almost any type of food but it goes uncommonly well with beef. The robust beef flavour does not intimidate either the taste or the texture of the self-assured asparagus. Both of these main ingredients stand up well against the hearty black beans and garlic seasonings.

Serves 4

450g (1 lb) lean beef steak

2 teaspoons light soy sauce

2 teaspoons Shaoxing rice wine or dry sherry

2 teaspoons sesame oil ·

½ teaspoon salt

¼ teaspoon freshly ground black pepper

2 teaspoons cornflour

450g (1 lb) fresh asparagus

3 tablespoons groundnut (peanut) oil

100g (4 oz) onion, finely sliced

2 tablespoons black beans, coarsely chopped

1½ tablespoons garlic, finely chopped

2 teaspoons ginger, finely chopped

3 tablespoons chicken stock, fresh or store bought

1 tablespoon Shaoxing rice wine or dry sherry

1½ teaspoons salt

½ teaspoon freshly ground black pepper

1 teaspoon sugar

2 tablespoons oyster sauce

Put the beef in the freezer for 20 minutes. This will allow the meat to harden slightly for easier cutting. Then cut it into thin slices 4 cm (1½ in.) long.

Put the beef slices into a bowl and add the salt, soy sauce, rice wine (or dry sherry), sesame oil and cornflour. Mix well and let the slices steep in the marinade for about 15 minutes. Meanwhile, slice the asparagus at a diagonal into 7.5 cm (3 in.) pieces and set it aside.

Heat a wok or large frying pan over a high heat until it is very hot. Add the oil and when it is very hot and slightly smoking, add the beef from the marinade and stir-fry for about 2 minutes. Remove the meat and drain it in a colander. Pour off all but 1½ tablespoons of the oil and reheat it over a high heat.

When the oil is very hot, add the onion, black beans, garlic and ginger and stir-fry for 1 minute. Add the asparagus and stir-fry for 1 minute. Now add the stock or water, rice wine, salt, pepper and sugar. Continue to stir-fry for 3 minutes or until the asparagus is slightly tender. Add more water as necessary. Quickly return the meat to the wok, add the oyster sauce and stir well. Turn the mixture onto a platter and serve at once. 🥄

23

A Moment
in a Château

THERE ARE TIMES when a chef appears on a radio show, to cook a dish. Being frank, I consider this a bit peculiar. To the listener, there are the sounds of chopping or bashing or sizzling. However, the result is odd. The listener, of course, cannot see what the hell is happening. There is usually only one person who benefits, and that is the radio presenter, salivating and fork at the ready. He or she ends up with a free meal.

So if I am asked to cook on a radio programme, I decline, politely. This was not always the case. My travels with Sue Burke, personal assistant extraordinaire, took us to Nottingham, where I had agreed to cook on a radio show. I would not be cooking in the studio but in the kitchen of a Chinese restaurant. There would also be a presenter and a technician, and the segment was due to be broadcast live after the 11 a.m. news bulletin.

At 10ish, Sue and I arrived at the restaurant to be greeted by the producer and soundman. They were standing on the pavement, and the producer said, 'We can't get in.'

We shook hands and I said, 'Good morning. What do you mean: you can't get in?'

She explained that the restaurant was locked, and when they had knocked there was no reply. We knew that the chef was in a flat above the restaurant and assumed that he was still asleep after a hard night's work. So we set about trying to wake him up, in order to let us in and do the live broadcast from his kitchen. In British parlance, this constituted *a matter of some urgency*. We rang the doorbell. We knocked. We rang lots of times. We knocked loudly. We shouted up at the window above the restaurant. Still, there was no response and we were getting close to 11.

The presenter was desperately anxious. Sue and I picked up gravel from the ground and started to throw it at the window. I said, 'Sue, look at us. This is crazy. We are throwing stones at a window.'

I turned to the presenter and said, 'Look, I've got an idea. This is radio. No one can see us. Why don't we just make some noises – bang a spoon against a drainpipe or something – and pretend I'm cooking?' She was having none of it.

Finally, the gravel on the glass was successful. There was a face at the window: the face of a bleary-eyed chef, whose long jet-black hair was sticking up messily like rigid tarantula legs. I shouted up to him in Cantonese, 'This lady beside me is having kittens,' I said, pointing at the presenter. 'Come down and let us in, please.' In a scruffy T-shirt and shorts, he was at the door. We managed to do the live broadcast, but that episode is another reason I don't like cooking on radio.

WHILE I was having fun in Britain, my connoisseur friend Ron Batori was building his wine business in California and, in 1987, he was out to make a big splash during Vinexpo, the annual wine expo in Bordeaux.

Ron's company had already established a good trade in the States. Now they were trying to build up the exports. So he got in touch and told me the plan. Ron has big ideas. He had rented an entire château, Château des Fougères, in la Brède, fifteen miles south of Bordeaux. Ron and his colleagues from the company would live there during Vinexpo. He would take me along as their cook. From the château they would be available to host dinners, lunches and parties, entertaining contacts from Bordeaux in an impressive style. You might think 'book a room in a comfortable hotel in Bordeaux'; Ron thinks 'book a château with a dozen acres of land'.

Yves Vidonne, whose father carried that pill box of laxatives (as mentioned in Chapter 1) was also drafted in. Yves ran a restaurant, so would be able to help with catering equipment, as well as supplying a head waiter and sous chef.

Ron rented a van and we packed up pots and pans and everything else, and threw them in the back of the van. There were a few minor issues on the way to Bordeaux. We put diesel in the rental car that was supposed to run on petrol. Then a bottle of wine broke in one of Ron's suitcases. Red, since you ask. Pelting rain followed us on the journey, which might mean nothing to you, but rain is calamitous and unusual to those who live mostly in California.

In Bordeaux, Ron and his colleagues went to a supermarket and did a massive shop that took ages. They reached the till, unloaded their trolleys, loaded up their bags, and then it was time to pay. None of them had any French money or acceptable credit cards. The store would not take traveller's cheques. One of Ron's colleagues produced US dollars, but there was a tut-tut and 'Non, non'. This caused a stink: 'Why don't you accept US dollars? If it wasn't for the US there wouldn't be any France.' That got them nowhere. So it looked like we would have no food. Eventually, somehow someone acquired some money.

On arrival at the château, Ron realised that he had overlooked two things that were very important. He had overlooked the hot water supply. Although there were eight bedrooms, there was only one water heater, indistinguishable in size from a kettle. Americans like to get up in the morning and take a hot shower. That was problem number one.

Ron had also overlooked the kitchen. That is to say, there was no kitchen to speak of. That was problem number two. There was a cooker which had two burners. We stood and gazed at it. Ron said, 'Ken, we're gonna have sixty people to lunch and dinner every day and night. How you gonna do it?'

I said, 'Ron, we're gonna do a lot of barbecuing.'

That is what we did. The barbecue came into its own, and meals were served in the dining room. Guests ate in the fading grandeur, alongside propped-up suits of armour. The château's owner, Madame de Montesquieu, didn't want to rent the place but she needed the money. So she planted some servants among us to make sure that we didn't do anything wrong. Well, I befriended them all and made them part of my team against Madame de Montesquieu. So when we wanted napkins they would say, 'Oh, the napkins are over there in that drawer – the ones with the big M on them.' The next day Madame de Montesquieu would find out and go ballistic about the fact that we were using her napkins and then she'd have them counted.

I would spend mornings shopping and on the last night we treated ourselves to a big dinner outdoors. Moral: you can always find a way.

24

The Table of the Shepherdess

I N THE EARLY 1990s I bought a house in the village of Catus, in the south-west of France. That is where I am today, and, to be more precise, I am sitting at a table, which easily seats fourteen. Many stories have been shared over lengthy feasts at this table. Those who have sat here include Tony and Cherie Blair, as well as Tina Turner and Fabien Galthié, the French rugby captain. There is an unusual story of the table itself, and how it came to be here.

In 1996, I was filming *Hot Wok*, and the brilliant Kate Kinninmont, who was the series producer, was looking for interesting people and settings which could feature in the series. Viewers saw me travelling with my wok and burner, making dishes for people in Britain and California, while showing the viewers how easy and versatile it is to cook in a wok; everything from curries to soups and even puddings.

Anyhow, Kate had read a newspaper article about a shepherdess who lived in the Scottish Borders. We thought she would make an interesting subject for one of the episodes in the six-part series. 'There really aren't many shepherdesses,' Kate pointed out, quite rightly. So off we trundled, equipped with a film crew, and I fell in love with this stunning, dramatically imposing part of Britain.

Viv was a glamorous shepherdess, chatty, warm and friendly. When she was four, her parents had taken her to sheep dog trials and, as she watched the shepherds at work, she decided there and then on her career. What a woman! She enjoyed good food but rarely found the time to make a decent meal. 'My diet is the odd bowl of muesli,' she told me as we wandered the rolling fields surrounding her home.

Within her beautiful cottage, there was a large, long table, which looked pretty ancient, too, and Viv explained that it had been in her family for generations. The table was carried out to the garden in front of her cottage, as our plan was to film outside. We set up my travelling gas burner and, from the boot of the car, out came the wok and ingredients. Then I went to a fishery nearby to catch a rainbow trout for our lunch.

Viv, who had invited a few friends over to watch the fun, was overwhelmed. 'I can't believe Ken Hom is cooking for me,' she said, and I was ridiculously flattered and delighted. Then I started to check the ingredients, while the cameras and lights were set up. These things take a little time, and while we were busy I could hear corks popping. 'Have a glass to relax yourself,' said her thoughtful friends. Dear reader, you are not stupid – you can probably see where this was heading, and it wasn't in the direction of sobriety.

The shepherdess became so relaxed that, as we neared the point of filming, I heard uncontrollable giggling and then glanced up to see Viv weaving in my direction. Had she tried to round up her woolly flock of sheep at that point, she might have had problems. Once at my side, she started to lean against me.

Kate, the perfectionist producer, was anxious, understandably. 'We're going to have to *deal* with this,' I could hear her saying to the crew. Now, we were working to a busy schedule so it wasn't as if we could postpone the shoot, to cook for a hung-over shepherdess the following day. The quick-thinking home economist, Anne Stirk, disappeared into the kitchen to make vats of coffee for the hostess. Viv, by this stage, was unable to stand without looking as if her body was wrapped around mine.

We decided to go ahead with the shoot. I was cooking an aromatic dish of five-spice trout with broccoli, and Viv found a corner of her magnificent table to prop herself against. 'Have you ever cooked in a wok?' I asked her.

'I've never *seen* a wok before,' she replied.

At one stage, the dish called for rice wine, and Viv was beside the bottle. 'Please can you hand me the rice wine?' I asked, and added, 'You can drink rice wine but you'd end up on the floor.'

To which she giggled, 'Can I be the one to add it, then?' She did, and was in the mood to be generous with it, too.

We managed to get through the cooking, although Kate had her work cut out when it came to editing. Many of Viv's giggles were discarded. I adored that shepherdess but – truth time – it was her table that won my heart. 'This is such a beautiful table,' I said to her.

'It is,' she agreed, 'but it's really awkward in my cottage. It's too big for my home. I can't get rid of it. Who would want to buy a table like this?'

I knew the answer. 'Well, I've got this medieval townhouse in a little village in France,' I said, 'and I would love to have this table.'

I bought the table, though you may well question my own sobriety of mind: the table could not be separated into smaller pieces and the gargantuan challenge lay in manoeuvring the massive piece of furniture up the steep steps and stairs, and through the tiny doorway into my home.

When Kate came to the house to film *Ken Hom's Foolproof Chinese Cooking*, she saw the table and was instantly reminded of the shepherdess. And then it was Kate who had uncontrollable giggles.

———

TRUFFLES, I suppose, led me to this house in the Lot.

When I came to France in the 1970s, I had tasted and feasted my way through the colourful markets and restaurants of the towns and cities, unable to resist one ingredient when it was on offer: the truffle. Studiously, I read about the mythology of black truffle of Périgord, which no one can quite decide is either a plant or a fungus, but all agree that it has a magical aroma and is one of the finest delicacies Mother Nature has given to us.

The Périgord truffle has a patron saint, St Antoine, and if you go to Richerenches in the Drôme you can attend truffle masses. Admittedly, they are not an ancient tradition: they were started a few decades ago, though the travelling scent of the truffles in the church draws in a crowd and fills the pews, and the local parishioners have trouble finding a seat. The truffle came to be a star of French food in the sixteenth century, when cooking with Oriental spices gave way to Renaissance gastronomy.

As I tasted and read up on truffles, I frequently came across the name Pébeyre. In the late nineteenth century, Pierre Pébeyre had been a school teacher, but his fixation with truffles took him out of the classroom and into a career in the truffle orchards. He set up business in the village of

La Chapelle Mareuil, in the north of the Lot, selling not only truffles, but foie gras, ceps and walnuts. His wife contributed to the business, looking after the bottling of conserves made from local fruit. After being brushed by hand, the truffles were sterilised in thick-glassed conical flasks and sealed with corks and metal wire.

Pierre sent his son Alain to study business in Switzerland and, indeed, the business moved to Cahors and prospered under Alain's reign. When Americans crossed the Atlantic on their way to Europe, they were treated to dishes that included truffles: the taste for this fungus spread to the States. Truffles became scarce in the First World War, when people left the countryside to find work in the towns and, with no one to maintain the undergrowth, the truffles could no longer form. Truffle oaks were not replaced. The soil suffered from degradation. Truffles became rare and extremely expensive.

Truffle markets, which were once a common occurrence in the south-west of France, have declined in number. Alain's son, Jacques, built commercial relations with Spain. He helped establish production, from upper Aragon to Guadalajara, which meant the Pébeyre business had an ample supply of quality truffles, to compensate for the drop in French production.

The family business took another step – and a particularly interesting one – in the early 1980s, when Jacques's son, Pierre-Jean, came on board. He revived his great-grandfather's trade, rediscovering the tradition of foie gras with truffles. He introduced new products, such as truffle butter, truffle sauce and oil infused with truffles. They supply truffles to the world's greatest restaurants. Now you can appreciate why I was so determined to meet the fabled Pébeyre family.

IN 1988, the year of the dragon, I was asked to do a pop-up restaurant in the Verandah restaurant at the Peninsula. Margaret Thatcher was running the UK, Ronnie Reagan was President of the US, the world danced to Kylie Minogue's 'I Should Be So Lucky', and the phrase pop-up restaurant had yet to be coined. Instead, I was the 'guest chef'. Plenty of guest chefs had cooked at the Peninsula, but they were the reigning, most sought-after French chefs. I was to be the first one who was Chinese, and was honoured to be asked.

Elegant and lavish, the Peninsula really is the grand lady of Hong Kong and, speaking of grand ladies, a particularly strange moment comes to mind: the moment I arrived with my mother. A mini regiment of bellboys gathered up our luggage. A doorman, pristinely attired in a uniform as bright as his smile, opened the door for us. Cooled by the much-appreciated blast of air conditioning, we stepped onto the gleaming expanse of marble that led to the front desk, and breathed in the welcome scents of the lobby; scores of pretty orchids and lilies rising from huge vases, the allure of Cuban cigar smoke wafting from the bar, the underlying hints of Chanel and new leather handbags. The smell of extravagance can really make a hotel lobby. We were thirty feet from check-in when my mother stopped suddenly and grabbed the cuff of my sleeve. She gazed around and then looked at me. 'I'm not staying here,' she said. 'It's too posh.'

'Mum, you don't have to pay. We are here as guests of the hotel.' We hovered in the lobby. She was shaking her head. There I was, using my most persuasive powers to convince her to spend a few nights in one of the world's finest hotels. For free. Boy, I would love to tell you I won. But she did – my mother never stayed at the Peninsula.

Meanwhile, cooking at the Verandah presented challenges, but of a different nature (and my mother was not there). I had settled on a theme to the menu: East meets West, featuring dishes from my then best-selling book. One of the evenings was to be a special meal for the Mayor of Shenzhen, which was then a fishing village but was about to be designated as a special economic zone. Today, it is a thriving metropolis with a population of seven million.

There were to be seventy guests – dignitaries with their wives and other well-to-dos – and I felt that the menu was suitably celebratory and opulent, but also affordable, even though the event was being hosted by a super-rich businessman. Eric Brand, the food and beverage manager, took me to one side.

'The menu is perfect, it's great. But please can you increase the cost per head?'

'I'm sorry?'

'Please can you increase the cost per head? Please can you make it more expensive?'

'Oh,' I said. 'Increase? Traditionally, people ask for the cost to be decreased. You know, save money rather than spend more of it.'

Eric explained. 'This is an extremely special dinner and the host wants that to be reflected in the price. He wants to show face rather than lose face.'

'Ah, OK. I get it,' I said. 'In which case, let's use truffles. Truffles aren't cheap.' Eric agreed.

Catering is a funny old business, which works best when everyone is happy. Eric was happy because I had found a way to make the meal cost a fortune. And the host would be happy because he was paying a fortune, which was precisely what he wanted to do. His guests would be happy because they were not paying. And I was happy because Eric was happy that the host and his guests would be happy.

That was all before the evening itself. We had lined up a real feast, and the dishes included chicken spring rolls with rice paper and sun-dried tomatoes, my East–West oxtail stew, and steamed fish … with black truffles from the south-west of France. The head chef (another Eric), Eric Shali, and his brigade did a fantastic job.

Now, the black truffles from France left that kitchen on seventy plates, adorning the steamed fish. Half an hour later, the waiters brought the same seventy plates back into the kitchen. They had all enjoyed the fish; there was nothing left of it. However, many of the guests had not eaten the expensive French delicacy. Instead, they had pushed the truffle to the side of their plates. The two Erics and I stared in arrant astonishment at a few dozen expensive and ornate plates, the rims neatly dotted with rejected slices of the black treat that had been touched only by fork prongs. What a strange sight. And what of the cost! Hundreds of pounds of waste right there in front of us.

Why on earth had this happened? 'It's the Chinese,' said Eric the chef. 'They don't know what it is. So they won't eat it. But the plates without truffles on the sides – those are the plates that went out to the Hong Kong Chinese. They know it's truffle.'

'There's no way we're binning it,' I said. 'Put it in a big bowl and we'll feed it to people who'll eat it. And that includes me!'

After service and over a glass of Chablis, I sat with the two Erics, giving a post-mortem (maybe the wrong phrase) on the meal. 'I've always been intrigued by truffles,' I said to them. 'I love them. When I had my cookery school in California, I used to go to a place called Pig-by-the-Tail. It was run by a woman called Victoria Wise, who was the first chef at Chez Panisse. Well, Victoria decided that she didn't just want to be a chef. So she opened a charcuterie right across the street from the restaurant. I'd happily browse and shop. And I'd also buy truffles from her. I'd use them in my dishes for the cookery school.

'And in that same cookery school,' I continued, 'I had a photo of a man who is holding a massive black truffle. It's a great shot and I pulled it out of *Gourmet* magazine and had it framed. Still got the framed photo in my kitchen at home. That man was called Alain Pébeyre, the son of the founder of the Pébeyre family. Truffle farmers. Now, what a family they are…'

Eric Shali interrupted. 'Yes, a fantastic family. I know Jacques Pébeyre…'

Eric Brand interrupted Eric Shali, 'I know Jacques, too.'

I recoiled in surprise, and then said, 'What? You both know Jacques? I would really like to meet him, if only to say hello and shake his hand.'

Eric B smiled. 'Leave it with me.'

In late December of the same year, I was in England, celebrating Christmas with the food writer Paul Levy. We stuffed ourselves full of fine food and wines, although at times the mood was morose because of a recent terrorist atrocity; earlier that month, Pan Am flight 103 had exploded in the skies over Lockerbie in Scotland. I returned to France and took a train south. True to his word, Eric Brand had spoken to Jacques, and I was the cheerful recipient of an invitation to visit the Pébeyre family. Jacques was there to meet me at the train station and I noticed how he smelled of truffle. We got into his car and there, again, was the truffle perfume. At home, the Pébeyres received me as if I were family.

A day or two later, I was joined by friends from Hong Kong, Grace Fung and Kendall Oei, and they too were taken into the fold. I was the honoured guest but truffle was the star of the show – we ate tons of it – and one lunchtime Jacques's beautiful wife Monique cooked up a truffle omelette to feed twenty-two guests, enjoyed with excellent wines, before we all hugged and kissed farewell on the doorstep.

—

I am a believer in the doors theory of life: in this corridor of existence, one door might close but another will open. Sometimes both doors stay open, which is even better.

My two-week stint at the Peninsula's Verandah restaurant caused a stir. Apart from being well received, I was the toast of Hong Kong's gourmets and food critics. I did not know it at the time, but the event was to lead to a succession of doors being opened.

The dishes were hailed as a resounding success and, shortly after the pop-up, or guest chef appearance, I was approached by Cathay Pacific. 'Would you like to help us with the meals we serve to our passengers? Would you like to meet to discuss it?'

Ever since taking my first flight – in 1968, when I was nineteen years old and travelling from Chicago to Florida on my own for my first ever holiday – I have noticed one constant: flying makes me hungry. However, there was also a constant in the quality of the food served on airplanes: it was dreadful. So I was looking forward to the meeting with the Cathay Pacific hierarchy. It began with them praising my tenure at the Peninsula and, in particular, the theme of East meets West. 'This is a brilliant concept … This is something that our passengers would really appreciate … More and more of our clientele are Chinese. They are travelling not only in economy but in business and first class. We want a concept that's innovative. East meets West is a concept that fits. What do you think?'

I took the opportunity to let off steam. 'The mistake airlines make is to pretend they are restaurants in the sky. They try to be fancy and ambitious – this can never work. Restaurants are restaurants with proper kitchens and a brigade of chefs who are just behind the swing doors, a few feet from the table. Planes are not restaurants. Of course, people want to eat on planes – I know that, I'm the hungriest person who ever flew. But do passengers really want a tough piece of meat with nasty sauce on it? That concept is all wrong.' My audience were shaking their heads in agreement. Of course they were. This was why they had called the meeting.

I continued. 'But passengers need comforting food, especially on a long-haul flight. Can you imagine how wonderful it would be to have a nice bowl of noodles, with maybe prawns and lots of vegetables? And in a broth that gives you that sense of well-being that you get from a homemade soup, full of flavour and steaming hot.'

In 1990, my happy partnership began with Cathay Pacific and would continue for three years. That was more than enough time for me to revolutionise menus, creating meals for passengers that met my comfort food criteria. Also, I learnt a lot about food, what can and cannot be served on a flight.

Many of the dishes that were served on flights were inspired by my book, *East Meets West*. They included fresh crab and lemongrass quiche, Asian-flavoured duck salad, Asian pear watercress soup, spicy ragout of ginger prawns, crystal prawns with fresh basil, peppers and garlic, steamed salmon in Chinese cabbage, and shellfish in black bean and butter sauce. Chicken dishes included ginger-orange roast chicken and chicken in rice wine with Sichuan peppercorn butter sauce. There was grilled steak with oyster sauce and bok choy and roast rack of lamb with Asian-style marinade. And for the vegetarians: Chinese ratatouille, rice noodles primavera, and pasta in black bean sauce with triple tomatoes. We served desserts of lychee sorbet with raspberry sauce, orange-ginger custard, and ginger crème brûlée.

I got hungry often because over that period I spent so much time in the skies, flying to airports on board Cathay Pacific in order to visit the chefs and the catering teams that worked for the airline. Over two years I went to thirty-five airports and one time I took a fifteen-hour flight from Hong Kong to Los Angeles, met the team and then, a few hours after landing, was back in the sky, returning to LA. An all-round trip of 15,000 miles.

The job took me all over the world: to Japan, the Philippines, Australia, New Zealand, Indonesia, Thailand and Canada. And more doors were opening. Hotels, such as the Oriental in Bangkok, and the Regent in Sydney and the Regent in Auckland, invited me to host pop-up restaurants. This meant that I was able to meet and work with interesting chefs, explore new places and taste dishes and ingredients that were new to me.

One of these trips was to the small island of Taiwan, where I cooked in the lively capital, Taipei, for the country's President. During the trip, I had time to eat in the local restaurants. One night I was taken to one by the legendary Chinese cookery writer and teacher Fu Pei Mei. The tiny restaurant was along Xinyi Road and she introduced me to Mr Yang, the owner of this very special restaurant, which I concluded was Taiwan's best-kept secret. Its speciality was xiao long bao, delicate soup dumplings. They were being made in the ground-floor kitchen, which had a window so you could watch the chefs folding the dumplings. They were the most magical dumplings I had ever put into my mouth. I ate twenty-five of them, at least.

Afterwards, I could not stop thinking about them, but by then I had left Taiwan so there was no way of curing the dumpling cravings.

In late 1992, I received a phone call from Nancy Newhouse, one of my editors at the *New York Times*, to which I contributed fairly regularly. 'I want you to write about the best restaurant you've eaten in,' said Nancy. 'One condition – you can't have a connection to the restaurant. Three hundred words, please, for three hundred dollars.'

Immediately, I thought of the dumpling restaurant in Xinyi Road. Sure, the readers of the *New York Times* would never have heard of it, and would never eat its extraordinarily good dumplings. But I was within Nancy's brief and I raved about the eatery, praising 'the world's tastiest dumplings ever'.

The short article appeared in January 1993, alongside the favourite restaurants of nine other chefs and cooks. The piece was headlined: 'The World's Top Ten Gourmet Restaurants'.

Among the readers was the executive of a Japanese business. He was curious about the little dumpling restaurant I considered to be the best in the world. And doors were about to open for the owners of that restaurant, which was called Din Tai Fung. Lots of doors. Today, Din Tai Fung is not a single entity but a chain, with about 120 restaurants in all corners of the globe. You may well have eaten their dumplings.

They never forgot me and my 300-word review which kick-started their phenomenal worldwide success. At some of their restaurants, my review is etched in large letters on bronze plaques. Beside the front doors, appropriately. I don't get royalties in return for their use of my critique, but they say I can eat free for life.

———

ON those flights from here to there and back again, my mind often took me to the medieval streets of Cahors beside the Lot river. Ever since Eric Brand had introduced me to the Pébeyre family, I visited them whenever possible. I adored Jacques, Monique and their family, and I was falling in love with this part of France, utterly entranced by its rusticity and the way that people lived by the seasons.

Until now, I had been used to an urban lifestyle, where all types of food were available throughout the year. The rural rules of gastronomy were entirely different, and I liked them. When white asparagus, for instance, came into season in this part of France, we had three weeks to eat it, and we ate a lot of it. Then we wouldn't see it again until the spring of the next year. For me, the south-west is the true heart of France. Another door was soon to open. An extremely old door, but one that was new to me.

One day, Jacques and I went for dinner at Restaurant Le Gindreau, St Medard, Catus. We had a magnificent meal in this one-star restaurant and, around about coffee time, Jacques introduced me to the chef, Alexis Pelissou and his lovely wife, Martine. I threw into conversation that I felt an affinity to the village of Catus and said that I was looking for a new home. 'I don't drive,' I said, 'so would love a place that's in a village and walking distance from the shops and bars, rather than an isolated house in the hills.' Pause. 'A large garden is essential,' I added.

'I know exactly the place for you,' said chef-patron Alexis. He took me to a beautiful, ancient watchtower. The foundations were laid in 1185, when the English King Henry II ruled over half of France, all down the west of the country. The chef told me how the building had been empty for five years, and that the owners, who had moved elsewhere in France, were eager to sell. One of the attractions was the grand cellar. I was – and am – passionate about wine but had never had a cellar. There was a beautiful courtyard in the middle of the tower, with a well in the courtyard's centre, and the property had a very big back garden.

The owners had a buyer. The English watchtower, which had also been a French watchtower, was now in the hands of a Chinese-American.

I never dreamt how much work it would entail. I bought it in 1991, and it took eleven years to get it to the right standard. I never want to do that again.

As you come through the front door, you find yourself in a massive hallway, with a large window looking out to the courtyard. The most impressive room is the kitchen, home to my fourteen-seater table. There's a massive hob, Maestro Bonnet, which makes ovens for many of the top chefs in France. To bring it into the house, it had to be dismantled, and it took a dozen grown men to haul in the mainframe.

The kitchen leads to the garden and a swimming pool. You would think you are on a Greek island, rather than in the middle of France. The chirps of birds compete with the ringing of the church bells. The house has three bedrooms, as well as a library on one floor, and the top floor looks out over the valley.

There is the most wonderful sense of community in the village, where everyone knows each other, and you cannot pass someone in the street without being kissed on both cheeks, French-style. The mayor brings me ceps and kisses both cheeks. There is the baker's wife who comes round to your side of the counter, to kiss your cheeks. Tuesday is market day, and Catus is flooded with people. The markets provide inspiration for cooking – see what takes my fancy, and plan the dish around it. It's also the only time when fresh fish is available. I have to stop myself diving into the sky-high pyramids of heirloom tomatoes.

At the market I always see my friend Ghislaine, who keeps ducks, and don't you know it – she sells superb foie gras and pâté. Usually she'd discard the duck wings and feet, but she keeps them for me, so that I can make confit to have with aperitifs. I always end up buying too much at the market, but that's all right, and it's a form of relaxation.

THEN there are *les fêtes*, the feast days when villagers gather in the square to eat roasted meats with couscous and drink the wines of local vineyards. Bastille Day is a national holiday on 14 July, and celebrates the anniversary of the storming of the Parisian prison, a historic moment of the French Revolution. The local farmers have a fête in the square, and villagers go from stall to stall, buying cheese and meats which you can grill yourself on a barbecue (be sure to take your own plates and cutlery).

The baker has his own fête, at which children bake and we all sit around eating the warm, crusty baguettes and large loaves with plenty of cheese, and washed down with carafes of *vin de pays du lot*. It's about sharing. People cook for you and you cook for them and, at times, Catus is one big fête. One year, I cooked a five-course Chinese banquet for about 150 people.

There was a four-year period when I lived here constantly. These days, however, I tend to spend a couple of months in Catus, during the hot summer, when the three-foot-thick walls keep my home cool inside. The village is in a valley and in the winter months the house can be cold and damp.

This is a house where I can truly entertain and cook a lot, and people have visited from all walks of life and all corners of the globe. Sometimes I think I could almost run the kitchen as a restaurant, serving forty covers a night. I have my woks, and thirty knives, made in Japan and Germany, but – probably like you – I wind up using the same ones: in my case, Chinese cleavers.

In the time it takes you to read this page, I could stand up, leave the table, walk out of the front door, along the street and find myself in the wine shop. Once upon a time I had a large cellar of expensive wines, but Jancis Robinson helped to change that. 'Drink local wines,' she told me.

So I sold most of my wine – more of which later – and I am extremely happy working my way through the vinous produce of the Lot. In the afternoons, I like to visit my friend at the wine shop and he is never short of suggestions. 'Try this' or 'Try that'. He's starting to get in saké for me. No, not very Lot, admittedly. Then I come home and start on my *mise en place*, as it is likely that friends will be coming for dinner. Friends are always coming for dinner.

Pierre-Jean Pébeyre became the brother I never had. I was amazed by his passion for the subject of truffles. In time, Pierre-Jean and I would come to produce a book together, which is entitled, appropriately enough, *Truffles*. He wrote of the fascinating history of truffles and the family business. I contributed the recipes, every one of them enriched by that special ingredient: truffle.

I can still taste, as I write, the truffle that was on the wedding breakfast menu yesterday; a glorious Friday in August 2016, when Jacques Pébeyre's granddaughter Caroline – whom I have known for twenty-two years – married her sweetheart Thomas.

The ceremony took place in the Lot, at l'Abbaye Sainte-Marie de Souillac, a magnificent twelfth-century abbey laid out on the plan of a Latin cross. I have known the building for more years than I have known Caroline. I photographed it in 1973 for the History of Art department during my days at the University of California, Berkeley. I photographed the abbey for a second time yesterday, although rather than being the main image, it was the background to the joyful newlyweds.

After the ceremony, we proceeded to Château de Pechrigal; the family had rented the entire place for a grand dinner and party. One hundred and twenty guests toasted the very happy couple, and we ate a feast which began with gazpacho and was followed by veal with a sauce Périgueux, a classic, extravagant sauce of reduced Madeira.

The pièce de resistance was what accompanied the dish: instead of small, thick slices of truffle in the sauce, we were each given one whole truffle, served on the plate alongside the veal. What an amazing sight. Panache, Pébeyre style! We all ate the whole truffle. And boy, was it good. Better than sex (at my age).

There was cheese, of course, and then pièce montée, that impressive tower of profiteroles so traditional at French weddings.

My head hit the pillow at three-thirty in the morning, a wide smile on my face.

And what of my cherished framed photograph of Alain Pébeyre, sniffing truffles through his white beard? It had been with me for ever, it seemed. Shortly after moving to Catus, I was unpacking boxes and came across the picture that had hung in the kitchen of my house in Berkeley. It needed a new home. And I knew just the right place for that old photo on a page torn from *Gourmet* magazine. It is not I, but Pierre-Jean and Babé – uncle and aunt to Caroline – who now see it every day, as it adorns the wall in their kitchen.

 We have come this far without a single mention of cucumbers. Now is the time to introduce them.

This is a luxurious purée, should you happen to have 1.5 kg (3¼ lb) of cucumbers, 900g (2 lb) of potatoes, 250g (9 fl oz) of double cream and 125g (4½ oz) of unsalted butter. I nearly forgot – you will also need 80g (2¾ oz) of fresh black winter truffles or high-quality tinned black winter truffles (cooked once). These ingredients, along with a little salt and pepper, will make the most wonderful companion to a perfectly fried veal chop.

Begin by peeling the cucumbers, and then slice them in half lengthways and use a teaspoon to remove the seeds. Next, cut the cucumber halves into slices. Sprinkle these with a couple of tablespoons of salt, and mix well.

Put the salted slices into a colander and let them drain for 45 minutes. This process rids the cucumber of excess liquid. When the slices have drained, rinse them in water to wash away the salt, and turn them into purée with a hand blender or in a food processor. In a tea towel or kitchen paper, squeeze any excess moisture from the puréed cucumbers. Set aside.

Now peel, slice and cook the potatoes in salted water for about 20 minutes, or until tender. Drain the potatoes and allow them to cool, before passing them through a ricer or food mill. Reheat them in a large, heavy pan.

In a separate saucepan, bring the cream to a simmer before whisking it into the potatoes. Incorporate the butter, mixing well. Add salt and pepper to your taste, and set aside.

All that remains is to chop the truffles, and chop them finely.

Just before serving, reheat the potato purée, fold in the cucumbers and truffles and serve at once. Your guests will be astonished by the transformation of the humble potato. 🥣

I have said that the house in Catus has a swimming pool. When I swim, I work out menus and recipes. What will go with this? Or, if I add this, how will it taste?

Swimming has not always been a part of my life. When I was child, aged about twelve or thirteen, we had swimming lessons: one class for girls, another for boys; we all swam naked, though not together. I was standing on the diving board when I felt a hand pushing on my back. The force sent me from the board into the deep water. I was petrified and flailing around, one second above the surface, the next beneath the surface. Then another hand, this time that of a Good Samaritan, grabbed me and helped me to the side of the pool. The trauma – the fear of drowning – had a lasting effect. For decades, I did not want to learn how to swim.

One day, I went on a boating trip with the Pébeyre family. It was in the middle of the summer, a glorious day, and we were canoeing along the Dordogne River. We were all wearing life vests, but I had not tied mine tight enough. This was to prove a problem when we came across some very rough rapids. The canoe capsized and my vest went up over my head. I could hear a voice – someone was shouting, 'Ken is drowning.' They were not wrong. I was not under the water for too long, thank God. Pierre-Jean's sister, Catou, got to me, reached out and pulled me up. She dragged me through the water, out of danger, to a small island.

Now it was time to learn how to swim. Today, I will not stay in a hotel that does not have a pool.

I stayed in a hotel with a pool in March 2011. It was in the city of Tokyo and, on a Friday afternoon, I fancied a swim in the twenty-metre pool on the sixth floor. A couple of days earlier there had been a small earthquake and now, as I front-crawled my way through the water, a major quake struck. The entire pool began to sway and then the water splashed left and right in huge waves. There were two of us in the massive pool and we gripped the pool's floating plastic separation cord. The shocked pool attendants scurried about. The earthquake lasted several minutes and was terrifying. We had to wait two hours until we got the all-clear to use the lifts to our rooms. Later that evening, there were a few after-shocks and the hotel room would shake occasionally but less violently.

———

FROM time to time, I am asked to go and cook a dish for passengers on a ship. One such request came through in 1996: would I do a seven-day trip from Japan to Hawaii? I said yes. I was packing for Japan when I got a call from Pauline, a dear friend in the States. I was best man at her wedding to Jim, who is half Native American. We had lost touch, you know how it is. She said, 'I know we've not spoken for years, but I was ironing and heard a voice on the TV, and I thought, it's Kenny.'

I was rushed and said, 'I'd love to talk more but am on my way to Japan. I'll call you the minute I'm back.' So I set off on the voyage, which includes entertainment acts such as jugglers and a clairvoyant. The clairvoyant said, 'Come to my cabin and I'll give you a free reading.' Well, there's an offer I could not refuse. In the cabin, the clairvoyant took my watch, touched it, and said, 'I see you alone on a boat … a canoe … in the Midwest.' I thought, interesting. I'd never been on a canoe in America's Midwest.

Back in California, I called Pauline and apologised for the abrupt end to our last conversation. 'How's Jim?' I asked.

'I have some bad news,' she said. 'Jim died a couple of years ago. A canoeing trip in the Midwest.'

25

Have Wok, Will Travel

THE *HOT WOK* series included segments in which I cooked for well-known people, as well as unusual and interesting characters such as the shepherdess of the Scottish Borders.

At first, the BBC had said the series would be a fixture in the daytime TV schedule. Then Kate Kinninmont had a meeting at the BBC and was told, 'Well, you could always throw in some celebrities if you want to make it primetime.' So that's what we did. I might add that I was so badly scarred by the process of memorising lines for my first series that this time round I insisted: no script!

For one episode, I went to Trinity Hall, Cambridge, where, in the beautiful grounds and on a sunny day, I cooked for Terry Waite. He was a hero of mine. He had spent five years as a hostage in Lebanon, much of it blindfolded. He told me that during the ordeal he was mostly chained to a wall and he was fed badly by his captors. 'The food, you had to see it to believe it,' said Terry. 'One day I said to my guard, "Can't you vary this diet? What have you got in the kitchen?"'

When the guard said there were potatoes, Terry pleaded, 'Get one. Bake it. Cut it in half, and put some cheese on top of it.' Terry recalled excitedly, 'He did it. He did what I said. And it tasted *really* good.' A heart-wrenching tale of taste.

He also recalled, with good humour, a story told to him by Terry Anderson, the journalist who spent seven years as a hostage of Shiite Hezbollah militants in Beirut. One day the cell door opened and a guard carried in a big pot. Anderson and his starving cellmates dashed to the pot, lifted the lid, and there inside the pot was a sheep's head. It had been boiled and the eyes in their sockets seemed to be staring back at the hostages. 'Well, if it's got the eyes in, at least it will see us through the week,' joked the American to his captives.

Terry Waite stood at my side, towering over me, as I made him a wokful of Burmese-style chicken, a dry-braised dish slowly cooked in spices and its own juices. Although I had never been to Burma, I had visited a number of Burmese restaurants which had opened in California. The food seems to be a cross between the cuisines of China, Vietnam and Thailand, and is an aromatic and fragrant style of cooking that uses spices to charm the flavours from the other ingredients in the dish.

———

 For Terry's dish, which would serve four, I used a couple of pounds (900g) of chicken thighs, blotted dry with kitchen paper and seasoned with salt and pepper. I peeled a couple of stalks of lemongrass, crushed them and cut them into 3-inch (7.5-cm) pieces. I heated the wok, added a few tablespoons of groundnut oil and, when it was smoking hot – you know the drill by now – turned down the heat and added the chicken, skin-side down.

Gently, I browned the chicken on both sides and, once that was achieved, I removed the chicken from the wok, drained it on kitchen paper and put it to one side. I drained off all but a tablespoon of the oil and chicken fat.

Then into the hot wok, I added 6 oz (175g) of thinly sliced onions, 6 crushed garlic cloves, 1 tablespoon of finely chopped ginger root, and the lemongrass. I stir-fried for 3 minutes, give or take. Next, I added a teaspoon each of turmeric and chilli powder, a tablespoon of light soy sauce and 3 tablespoons of water.

The chicken thighs were returned to the wok and stir-fried to ensure they were coated in the spicy mixture. I turned the heat right down – as low as it would go – and put a lid on the wok. Terry and I chatted for 20 minutes, by which time the chicken was cooked; the dish was done and ready to be eaten in the grounds of Cambridge on that warm summer's day.

A brief PS regarding lemongrass. It looks like a dried, oversized spring onion, and imparts a lemony fragrance to dishes. It is widely used in south-east Asian cookery (south-east Asian immigrants took it with them to Hong Kong in the 1970s and early '80s). When shopping for lemongrass, look for pale-green tops and avoid the dried-out lemongrass. Cut off the fibrous base and peel off the outside layers, and trim off the tops – save them to flavour oils or soups. It can be sliced and frozen for future use. 🥣

I went into the garden at the home of the actress Prunella Scales and her actor husband Timothy West. There, I cooked a vegetarian stir-fry dish of bean curd with shredded Chinese mushrooms, shredded ginger and spring onions.

I added dark soy sauce, a touch of sugar, black pepper and salt. Then I added the water from the dried Chinese mushrooms and covered the wok with a lid to let it simmer away. The bean curd was first fried to brown it, and it acts like a sponge so absorbs all the other flavours. Chinese emperors ate bean curd as a way of cleansing their bodies.

I cooked for the guards of Edinburgh Castle, and for firemen and nurses. And in Whitby, on the Yorkshire coast, I cooked for a fisherman called Joe and his wife Sue, who would sell her husband's catch from a stall at the harbour. Sue showed me how to tell the male crab from the female: turn them upside down, and the cock crab has a small apron, while the hen has a large apron.

When I told Sue that I would be cooking crab with garlic, she slightly surprised me by saying, 'I've never tried garlic.' Later she said that she should try it, 'bearing in mind we're in Dracula country ... This is where Bram Stoker came, and he was inspired to write *Dracula*.' Fisherman Joe pointed out that the best crabs are the heaviest ones; a tip worth sharing.

I made them a Singapore-style crab curry – using lots of garlic, which first I browned with finely sliced onion and spring onions and then added the crab, which I had chopped in its shell. I added coconut milk, a medium curry paste, a little sugar to balance the heat – whenever you are cooking something spicy hot, use sugar, just a touch, as a balancer. Twenty minutes later, it was done. Now, Joe had originally told me that he didn't like spice, but, as he tasted, he said, 'It might have been better if it had been spicier.' Sue tasted, and loved it.

Although I say that it was cooked within twenty minutes, there were a couple of hiccups along the way. First, I insisted on using a live crab, and one that was not despatched before it went into the pot. That is the way I was taught, and I appreciate it is not to everyone's approval. Second, there can be trouble with filming outdoors in public. In this case, a few teenage boys in swimming trunks thought it would be fun to disrupt the flow of filming on the quayside. As I was cooking and talking to camera, the teenagers leapt into the water behind me, screaming mid-jump, 'Ken Hom's wok is not hot!' I can assure you, it was.

Kate asked Annie Stirk, our home economist, to deal with the situation. As the boys climbed out of the water, Annie was waiting for them. 'We're trying to film. Can you keep the noise down, please?' Of course, a few minutes later, they were at it again – leaping from the quay into the chilly waters, while shouting with the projected volume of a Welsh choir, 'Ken Hom's wok is not hot!' At this point, the crab that I was cooking decided that the wok was too hot, and it shifted the lid with a claw and started to make a run for it. The noisy boys and the crawling crab were cut from the final edit.

———

I cooked a spicy curry of halibut for the wonderful actress June Whit-field, and we ate in her garden, over a nice bottle of chilled wine. And the actress Jean Boht and her husband, the conductor Carl Davis, also featured in the series.

I visited Jersey Zoo, which was also the temporary set of *Fierce Creatures*, to cook crispy vegetarian parcels for John Cleese, who had written and was starring in the movie. In a large bowl, carrots, mangetout, celery, chillies, ginger, garlic, dried Chinese mushrooms, bean noodles, a touch of rice wine and sesame oil are mixed well, wrapped up and slowly cooked in hot oil in the wok. I christened the parcels Fierce Creatures, as the chilli was a bit fierce.

Kate Kinninmont came up with the idea of filming part of the series in California, and she managed to stretch the budget to make it possible (though, to save a bit of money, Kate and her assistant stayed at my place, sleeping in the spare room and on the sofa). So, for the series, I also rustled up dishes at my home in Berkeley and ventured out to cook for others.

Against the backdrop of the Golden Gate Bridge, I made stir-fried fish with black bean sauce – with garlic and spring onions (scallions, as they say in the States) – for a couple of Hawaiian-shirted yellow-cab drivers in San Francisco. One of them told me that he had three woks and said, 'My pride is I can cook dinner for six in thirty-five minutes.'

They were really chilled out and when we wrapped up, one of them said, 'Gee, is that the time? I've really got to get back because my nephew and his son are coming to my apartment and I don't want them touching my gun collection.' Come again? Gun collection? 'Yeah, well, man, it's kind of my hobby. My apartment is full of guns.' Kate was pleased we hadn't asked to film in his home.

Kate found two great San Francisco-based writers who said they would be delighted for me to cook for them. One was Amy Tan; the other, Armistead Maupin, whose series of novels *Tales of the City* had recently been dramatised for television.

Armistead was an absolute gentleman, though when we arrived at his house and started to talk, it made me wonder about his peculiar relationship with food. When I asked what he liked to eat, he said, 'I have been on a low-fat diet. Well, it's really a no-fat diet, and most of my food comes in horrid little frozen packets. It keeps me fairly happy, but it keeps my appetite under control. In the Bay Area, there are a lot of cottage industries run by hippies who will make a lot of this food...' He took me to his freezer and, sure enough, it was crammed with scores of small boxes, which seemed identical and were filled with fat-free breakfast, lunch and dinner. He did not seem to own any real food.

Armistead invited friends over and, with bowls of salad and saffron rice, I served steamed chicken, which had been marinated in soy sauce and rice wine. I used a non-stick wok to make a French-inspired dessert of pears gently poached until tender in vanilla syrup (it takes about twenty minutes). 'Armistead, have you seen a vanilla bean before?' I asked (they are vanilla pods in Britain).

'No,' he replied. 'I don't know what a vanilla bean is.'

Pears, in Chinese culture, are a traditional symbol of longevity and fidelity. Indeed, the appeal of the pear extends beyond the grave, to the dead who cannot forget the pleasure they brought.

When I was a child, I was told never to bring home pears on the fifteenth day of the seventh month. That is the time when ghosts would be roaming the earth, seeking pears, among other goodies. So, on that day the pears might contain ghosts who would bring bad luck into the house. I did not doubt it at all.

Traditionally, pears also bring happiness. This means they should be eaten whole, never divided. Chinese pears are quite different from Western ones. They are round and crisp, like apples, rather than the soft and pear-shaped fruit with which we are most familiar.

———

THE day with Amy, author of *The Joy Luck Club*, was unforgettable. She came to my home, and was delightful. When I asked her if she liked to cook, she was honest. 'I don't,' she replied. 'I am a miserable cook but an extremely talented eater. I grew up in a home in which I enjoyed wonderful Chinese food, three times a day. My mother was a marvellous cook and because of that I developed low *cooking esteem*. Even when I was rinsing rice I somehow managed to burn it. In the end, I became the family's dish washer.'

This was intriguing, as she writes so frequently about food. She explained, 'I find myself growing hungry as I'm writing and that's why there are so many references to food in my books. People think there's some hidden symbolic meaning, but really my stomach was rumbling as I was writing and I imagined the meal I would be eating ... If I could cook, that is.'

Amy arrived on my doorstep carrying a designer bag. In the bag there was a small Yorkie, the name of which escapes me. It could have been Bombo. The bag was specifically designed with the dog in mind – there was a little comfy bit, where the animal could sit and peer through a grille, which also allowed ventilation and prevented the mini beast from suffocating. Amy and that dog were inseparable. She insisted that the dog would sit on her knee as we ate a meal of steamed scallops. Now, if we had been there without a film crew, it would have been fine. But when you are filming, you are acutely aware of all the sounds around you. And that dog yapped incessantly. I have since read an interview with Amy (in *The Bark* magazine) in which she said Yorkies are ranked as the noisiest dogs in the world. We had the footage to prove it.

When Kate tried to remove the dog, it yapped even more. Kate thought,

It's fine, we'll do a huge sound edit job. However, what no one noticed at the time was the dog's misbehaviour at the table. Amy would eat and then place her chopsticks on the table, at which point her pet would extend a lengthy tongue to lick the chopsticks, before Amy then picked up the chopsticks again, collected a scallop and placed it in her mouth. This meant that it was licks as well as yaps that had to be edited out.

When Amy left, one member of the crew said to me, 'Were you tempted to put that little thing in the wok?' No, not at all. I adore dogs and have had several as pets over the years. The following day, the San Francisco papers covered a glitzy dinner event. There, in the photos, was Amy walking along the red carpet. She was holding a designer bag, and clearly visible was the head of that chopstick-licking, yapping Yorkie.

—

BEFORE *Hot Wok* was broadcast, Kate was eager to drum up some press coverage for the series. She figured, *It's great that I've managed to make it an evening show, but how many members of the press can actually be bothered to come to the launch of a cooking series?*

She came up with the idea of launching it at the Chinese Embassy. The previous year had seen the broadcast of *The Dying Rooms*, a terribly sad and highly controversial documentary which unearthed China's attitude to orphans. China was on people's minds, and Kate reckoned that people would love to see inside the Chinese Embassy. So, with Tom, her husband and producer partner, and a girl from the BBC's publicity department, she went to the Chinese Embassy in Portland Place. Kate found it a bizarre experience, and afterwards she said, 'It's terribly grand on the outside. On the inside it is full of people with ill-fitting suits, and a couple of chairs in a huge room.'

The staff asked her to explain the political aspect of the show. 'There is no political aspect,' she said. 'Ken Hom is a Chinese person and he wants to bring Chinese food to the ordinary man and woman, the working people and the mothers and children.'

She presented a list of the guests who were due to attend the launch. They included June Whitfield, star of *Absolutely Fabulous*, but the official was more interested in another name. 'Ah,' said the man, 'you have Terry Waite and you tell me there is no political aspect.'

Kate said, 'He is somebody who has suffered and he thought about food all the time he was away. He loves Ken's food, and he's now got a wok.' The man then asked Kate, Tom and the girl from publicity if they would like some tea. 'Oh, that would be lovely,' said Kate.

At that, he reached under his chair and brought out a flask and a few mugs. He poured out the black tea and handed it around. There was no milk or sugar or even a table. At that time, China's poverty was tangible.

Kate said, 'It would be wonderful if your staff could cook for the press. And while we have the press in we would like to show some clips from the series. Do you have TVs here?'

'No,' said the man.

The publicity girl chipped in, 'We could bring a couple of sets. We could put one there and another one over there…'

The man said, 'Yes, we will agree to this. The press will come, but it's not political, it's positive.' There was a pause, followed by, 'We will require the money now.'

Kate said, 'Normally, you would do it and itemise everything – all the costs – and then you would send us an invoice and then we would pay.'

He came back with, 'No. We have to buy ingredients, we need the money beforehand.' Kate agreed.

They were about to leave, when a member of the staff asked if they would like to see the building, adding, 'We have a cinema downstairs.' It was like, *We're having all this discussion about how we're going to show the programme, and you've got a cinema downstairs.*

Sure enough, there was a cinema downstairs, large enough to seat about 100 people, and that is where we showed the clips. The press came in their droves, along with some of those who had featured in the series. Terry Waite – by now a wok enthusiast – was there, doubtless with official Chinese eyes upon him. The Chinese Embassy had created a banquet, but there were none of my dishes. Kate saw this as a snub, as she had explained in advance to the embassy officials that the food should be from my *Hot Wok* cookbook, which accompanied the series. 'It's OK,' I reassured her. 'It's a pride thing. They have only made what they know how to make.' At the Chinese Embassy, they were delighted with the positive outcome in the media.

IN those days I was often mistaken for Ken Lo. He had a well-known restaurant, Memories of China, in Knightsbridge and another in Chelsea Harbour. He was called Ken and I was called Ken, and we were both Chinese men involved in the business of food. However, we were certainly not the same man, and Ken, by the way, arrived in Britain in 1938, some eleven years before my birth.

It was not unusual for people to tell me they had eaten in one of my restaurants when, in fact, they had eaten in the other Ken's restaurants. Most of the time I'd correct them, pointing out they meant Ken Lo. Other times, someone would say, 'I had a fantastic meal at your place in Chelsea Harbour.'

And I'd say, 'Oh, thank you. I'm so pleased. It's always good to get feedback.'

Kate was in her office one day when she received a call from a journalist who said, 'I am so sorry to hear about your presenter.'

Kate said, 'Ken?'

Journalist: 'Yes, Ken.'

Kate: 'What about him? What have you heard?'

Journalist: 'Oh, I'm sorry. Didn't you know? He's died.'

This might have alarmed Kate had I not been sitting opposite her at the time. She said, 'I am right across the table from him, and he's very much alive.' When she put down the phone, I asked what it was all about and she explained that once again I had been confused for the great Mr Lo, may he rest in peace.

I had first met Kate when I was looking for a TV production company with which to work. She took the Eurostar to Paris, and came to my flat for lunch. When I raised the subject of dietary requirements (if such a phrase was in use then), she said she could not eat chillies, 'perhaps because I'm Scottish'. The slightest hint of chilli makes her throat close up and her eyes water, and later I would always make her a separate version of any dish, minus the chillies.

One year she came for Christmas in Paris, with her husband Tom, and their daughter Jane, who is vegetarian. I made vegetarian dishes for young Jane, though constantly reminding everyone that 'we Chinese eat everything with two legs or no legs'. The flat was full of tins of caviar, and she decided, 'I don't eat anything with a face – so caviar is OK.' On Christmas Day, when the city was cold but brightly lit by the sun and enchantingly romantic, we went to mass at Notre Dame, and then back to mine for the big Christmas lunch.

We could sit and talk about food for hours and hours. Kate had grown up in Glasgow, raised on a diet of working-class Scottish comfort food. This diet included huge slabs of roasted meat, but the vegetables – potatoes, turnips, cabbage or carrots – were usually overcooked. There were big, hearty puddings too, warding off the icy blast of the winds. Her childhood meals at home finished with a steaming cup of tea and a biscuit, or two. She did not know of ginger, though that was not unusual at that time in Britain. 'Where I come from,' she said, 'ginger is pop – as in ginger beer.' (By the way, if you don't know what *pop* is: it's a general, ancient term for a sweet, fizzy drink.)

Glasgow is the home of the deep-fried Mars bar, though Kate had never seen nor tasted one. 'My mother was at home and she always cooked good food, but it wasn't spiced and full of flavour, so we didn't have anything fancy. It was all quite bland.' She went to a convent school where the nuns had decreed, 'The girls shouldn't have very much to eat because it will make them sleep in the afternoon.' Yet she loved to eat, and during the religion class just before lunch, she would sit at her desk, daydreaming of food. 'I might have looked like I was thinking intently about Jesus,' she told me, 'but really I was thinking, *I wonder what the pudding will be?*'

Unlike Kate, I am not sweet-toothed, but whenever we came to plan the recipes, I'd say to her, 'We better have a couple of puddings – just for the British people.'

Kate did not enjoy cooking: 'The cooking that I knew was the way my mother cooked – and that's basically quite a tedious process of peeling things and then boiling them to their death.' However, her husband, Tom, was cooking with a wok long before I met him. Men like to cook Chinese food. It is speedy, and satisfies man's primeval instincts: the bashing of a sharp object against an ingredient, followed by fire, and lots of it.

Years ago, Kate bought a Ken Hom cleaver for Tom (if only she'd asked, I'd have happily given him one as a gift). Her friends said to her, 'That's ridiculous. Can't believe you're buying your husband a cleaver.' She explained to them that he did not want to 'ponce about with knives' and that the cleaver had therapeutic qualities: slicing vegetables with a cleaver is a form of relaxation for Tom. Then there is the finished product. A bowl of finely sliced, stir-fried vegetables – all shades of red, green, yellow and orange – is more appealing on the eye than a plate of mashed tatties, overdone cabbage and gravy. One is *technicolor*, the other is monochrome (with shades of brown). Then again, you may well disagree.

When we were close to finishing *Hot Wok* in California, I thought about how we could celebrate once we had wrapped up. Kate had invested so much of her time in the project, and was fantastic in every respect. We were both born in 1949, and I had an idea. I said, 'Kate, this has been such a wonderful experience. I've got a bottle of Château Lafite Rothschild 1949. And when we finish this series I'm going to open that and we're going to drink it at Chez Panisse.' The vintage is one of the finest for Bordeaux wines, and the producer is one of the best in the world.

She phoned Tom back in the UK and told him. He said, 'Oh my God, that's a chance in a lifetime. I'm flying out for the weekend.'

Kate said, 'You weren't even born in 1949. You weren't born until 1950, stay home.' The line may have gone dead by then; Tom caught the next flight over. We all had a taste of the great wine, and the chef emerged from the kitchen to enjoy a glass, too. After a spectacular meal, we breakfasted in style the following morning before Tom departed, catching his return flight to London.

Chicken Sun-Dried Tomato Spring Rolls

My first culinary experience with Vietnamese rice paper wrappers convinced me that they were more interesting in taste and texture than even the Chinese flour versions I knew. They are lighter, crisper and have a more delicate, parchment-like quality, which I love.

I find Vietnamese wrappers most suitable for this dish, in which I combine Western herbs, sun-dried tomatoes, chicken and distinctively Asian bean thread noodles. The noodles, which are made from mung beans, absorb any excess moisture and add substance without heaviness.

You will find this makes a wonderful appetiser, and much of the work can be done ahead of time.

Makes 35 to 40 spring rolls

55g (2 oz) bean thread noodles

225g (8 oz) boneless chicken breasts, cut into thin strips about 3 inches long

Salt and freshly ground pepper to taste

2 teaspoons olive oil

1 tablespoon finely chopped spring onions

2 tablespoons finely chopped fresh chives

2 teaspoons finely chopped fresh coriander

2 tablespoons finely chopped sun-dried tomatoes

One package Banh Trang dried rice paper 22 cm (8½ in.) cut into rounds

Sealing mixture:

3 tablespoons plain flour

3 tablespoons water

300 ml (10 fl oz) groundnut or vegetable oil

Soak the bean thread noodles in warm water for about 15 minutes, or until they are soft. Drain them well in a colander and cut them into thirds. Squeeze out any excess moisture in a tea towel.

Meanwhile, in a medium-sized bowl, combine the chicken strips with the salt, pepper, olive oil, spring onions, chives, coriander and sun-dried tomatoes. Add the soft noodles and mix well. This can be made ahead of time.

Make the flour paste by mixing the flour and water together.

When you are ready to make the rolls, fill a large bowl with warm water. Dip a rice paper round in the water and let it soften for one minute. Remove and drain on a tea towel or kitchen paper.

Place a large spoonful of the filling on top and roll the edge over the filling at once, fold up both ends of the rice paper, and continue to roll to the end. Seal the end with a little of the flour paste mixture. The roll should be compact and tight, rather like a short, thick finger cigar about 7.5 cm (3 in.) long. Set it on a clean plate and continue the process until you have used up all the filling.

(The rolls can be made ahead to this point; cover loosely with a tea towel and refrigerate for up to 4 hours.)

Heat a wok or large frying pan over a high heat until it is hot. Add the oil and, when it is hot and smoking, turn the heat down to medium and deep-fry the rolls, a few at a time, until they are golden brown.

They have a tendency to stick to each other at the beginning of the frying, so only fry a few at a time. Do not attempt to break them apart should they stick together. You can do this after they have been removed from the oil. Continue frying them until you have cooked them all. Drain them on kitchen paper and serve at once. 🥢

26

Men United

WAY BACK IN the '90s, I was being interviewed over afternoon tea, and the journalist asked me whom I would most like to meet. 'For instance,' said my interviewer, 'would you, perhaps, really like to meet the Queen?'

I said, 'I would love to meet the Queen, but to answer your question truthfully – I'd most like to meet Eric Cantona.' Yes, Eric Cantona, then a footballer. I enjoy watching football and had seen Cantona playing well in a few matches for Manchester United. He was an excellent player and I was interested by his story: the French connection, what with my own French connection. I admired the man, as did the fans. During games, the stadium was filled with the chant, 'Ooh aah, Cantona.'

Shortly after the interview was published, Sue Burke received a call. On the other end of the line was the personal assistant of Alex Ferguson, the football legend and then manager of Manchester United.

The assistant said, 'Alex saw that Ken was saying he would like to meet Eric. We can make that happen.' Then there was a PS from the PA. 'It would be great if Ken could come up and cook for the team.'

When Sue relayed the phone conversation to me, she threw in her own advice: 'You better do it.' Well, when I was next in the UK, I travelled from London to Old Trafford, the club's football ground. It was a bit of a photo opportunity. They had invited the press and there were about a dozen photographers, ensuring that I appeared in the following day's sports pages: a first for me.

I met a young footballer called David Beckham, aged fourteen or fifteen – and he was very polite, I recall. 'Extremely nice to meet you, Mr Hom.' I met Ryan Giggs, and we got along very well. And I met, of course, Eric Cantona, who had inspired this unusual event. Eric was slightly surprised when he said, 'Hello,' and I took the conversation politely from English into his native language. I could see him thinking, *Hey, a Chinese guy who speaks fluent French. I love it.* A week or so before our meeting, Eric had been in trouble for slugging a fan who had insulted him. I said, 'I figure you did the right thing.' And he laughed. I was being serious.

I unpacked my wok, cooked for the whole team, and then the Man United chef, Jasper, joined me and we cooked a carb-rich dish. It was huge fun. The following day's newspapers ran photos of the get-together. Headlines included 'Ooh aah, Cantonese'.

There is one bond of friendship that was sealed on that day and has remained ever since. It is with Alex Ferguson, the club's figure-head. Sir Alex Ferguson OBE is a true gourmet: a man who loves and lives for excellent food and exceptional wine. Alex and I got talking about food, and we have never stopped. On that day, it quickly became clear that when Alex was not delivering the team talk or barking orders from the side of the pitch, he was rustling up a dish in his kitchen at home in Cheshire, or pleasing his taste buds at the tables of fine restaurants.

Aside from being a great foodie, it emerged during our chat that he is also a wine connoisseur of some note and keeps an impressive cellar. 'Do you know, Ken,' he later told me, 'I always drink one bottle of good wine before a match.' As I was considering the effects of a bottle of wine, Alex added, 'For luck.'

Wine drinkers are divided: there are those who prefer wines from Bordeaux to wines from Burgundy, and those who prefer Burgundy wines to the ones from Bordeaux. I am a Bordeaux man; Alex is a Burgundy man, a fan of the pinot noir grape, which makes the finest red Burgundy. Our friendship was founded, I suppose, on a mutual passion for eating good food and drinking interesting wines, and we help each other with charity events.

Since that day at Old Trafford we have shared many meals, and I gave him one of my woks so that he could work on his stir-fries. He eats often at the Yang Sing, that legend of a five-storey restaurant, set in Manchester and serving Cantonese dishes.

On occasions, Alex's lovely wife Cathy has joined us, and, in contrast, she likes her food plain, with neither salt nor pepper to season it. Unlike her husband, she does not drink alcohol. This has worked out perfectly as I have sometimes invited Sue Burke, whose well-done-steak-and-chips approach to food means that she and Cathy can opt for the unfussy dishes while Alex and I enjoy the chef's specialities and Burgundian beauties from the wine list.

When I sent him a copy of my latest book, he wrote back to say thank you and added, 'I can't say that the book has helped my cooking skills, but I certainly know what to order when I visit Yang Sing!'

—

AT one point in the early '90s, I was asked to appear on a show called *Hot Chefs*. The series was presented by Antony Worrall Thompson, and is where Gary Rhodes was 'discovered'. I would have to cook a dish in front of the cameras and a studio audience, and the producers said I should have a 'sous chef'. Well, I did not have a sous chef, and did not really need one, but the producers were adamant that there should be two people working on the dish. So I asked Sue to help out. 'You won't be my sous chef,' I said, 'but my Sue chef. This is your chance to become a star!'

There we were, I was cooking noodles in the wok and Sue was slicing this or that. She had not realised that she had left a tea towel next to the gas. Suddenly, the tea towel went up in flames and there was a fire to put out. When they called that show *Hot Chefs*, they could not have realised the appropriateness of the title. At that moment, when I felt the burning tea towel scorching my skin, I was indeed a very hot chef. I put a wok lid on top of it, extinguishing the flames. It did make me realise why the BBC had sent three fire officers to stand guard during *Chinese Cookery*.

The fire incident was cut out of the final broadcast but passed on to a show that featured TV bloopers. My agent phoned me and said, 'They need your permission to run the clip. They'll pay you £400.'

I said, 'Sign for me and take the money – it's more than I got from *Hot Chefs*.'

—

Braised Pork Belly, Shanghai-Style

Pork belly is an inexpensive cut of pork which is very popular in Chinese cuisine, and it has always been a favourite of mine. At first glance, it might look rather fatty and unappetising, but its gelatinous texture is highly prized by the Chinese and, when it is properly cooked, the taste is fantastic. In this recipe, the long simmering process renders down most of the fat, leaving a juicy, delicious dish which goes very well with plain steamed rice.

Serves 6

1.5 kg (3 lbs) belly pork, including the bones

1 tablespoon salt

3 tablespoons groundnut or peanut oil

For the braising liquid:

6 slices fresh ginger

1.2 litres (2 pints) chicken stock

600 ml (1 pint) Shaoxing rice wine or dry sherry

150 ml (5 fl oz) light soy sauce

150 ml (5 fl oz) dark soy sauce

150g (6 oz) Chinese rock sugar or plain sugar

2 teaspoons five spice powder

2 teaspoons freshly ground white pepper

3 tablespoons whole yellow bean sauce

3 tablespoons hoisin sauce

6 spring onions, whole

This joint can be cooked with its bones left in. If you get your butcher to remove them from the joint, be sure to add them to the pot with the braising liquid for greater flavour. Rub the fresh pork belly with the salt and let it stand for 1 hour.

Then carefully rinse off the salt. This helps to clean the pork and to firm it up by drawing out some of the meat's moisture. Dry the meat with kitchen paper.

Heat a wok or large frying pan over a high heat until it is hot. Add the oil and, when it is very hot and slightly smoking, brown the pork belly, rind side only, until it is crisp and brown (cover the wok to prevent splattering). Add more oil if necessary.

Cut the fresh ginger into slices 7.5 cm x 0.5 cm (3 inch x ¼ inch). Put the ginger together with the rest of the braising liquid ingredients into a large pot or casserole. Bring the liquid to a simmer and then add the browned pork belly.

Cover the pot and simmer it slowly for 2–2½ hours or until the pork is very tender.

When the pork is cooked, remove it from the pot and let it cool slightly. (The braising sauce liquid can now be cooled and frozen for re-use. Remove any surface fat before transferring it to the freezer.) Then slice the meat thinly. The Chinese would serve the pork rind and fat as well as the meat, but do remove it if you prefer. If you like, some of the braising liquid may be thickened with a little cornflour and served as a sauce over the sliced pork. If so, be sure to remove all traces of fat from the sauce before thickening it. 🥄

27

At Home with Hom

THERE MUST HAVE been a point when Alex Ferguson was chatting to Alastair Campbell and the topic veered from politics or football to food. The Prime Minister's director of communications may have mentioned that he was looking for a chef. Or perhaps the manager of Manchester United was talking about a Chinese meal that he had enjoyed. Either way, the two men found themselves discussing food and me.

It was early 1998, and Tony Blair had been in power for less than a year. He was due to host his first Asia–Europe Meeting, which would take place in London and bring together twenty-two heads of state: twelve from Europe, ten from Asia. They would all need feeding, of course, and Britain's leader felt they would need feeding well. He wanted the meal to be a special part of the day, rather than merely a fuel stop punctuating the talks.

The leaders would be seated at one long table in a room at the Lord Chancellor's residence in the House of Lords. It is substantially grand and splendid, and then even more so: Derry Irvine, the Lord Chancellor, had just caused national outrage when it emerged that he had spent £650,000 of taxpayers' money extravagantly redecorating the place, including hand-printed wallpaper at £300 a roll. Anyhow, Alastair was in the middle of scouting around for the right chef to feed the leaders. And Alex said, 'Ken's your man.'

No. 10 phoned Sue Burke, my personal assistant in Britain. 'We'd like Ken to do this meal. Can he come up with something that's interesting? A meal that everybody can eat.' They had a point, as I realised when I studied the list of dignitaries. Pork was probably out of the question, as the Sultan of Brunei is Muslim. Then there was the President of Indonesia. He, too, was Muslim, so I definitely couldn't do pork. There was a lengthy catalogue of dietary no-no's; people didn't like this and they didn't like that.

For the starter, I decided to serve fish, which was wrapped in rice paper and then pan-fried. A quick double-check that everybody could eat fish, which they could, and so that was fine. As a main course, I would serve Asian duck confit, a nod to the French classic. For dessert, I settled on warm mango compote, served with vanilla ice cream and basil. It is an unusual dish, but one that I have served to guests all over the world, Asians and non-Asians, and it always pleases everybody.

I liked Tony Blair even before meeting him. He seemed to be on a mission to rectify some of the excess of the Thatcher years, and ready to invest in the NHS, schools and education. He was dynamic and very smart, and a refreshing change to his predecessors. Along with everyone else around the globe, I had watched when Tony Blair stood outside church in the late summer of 1997, hours after the horrific death of

Princess Diana. In a heartfelt tribute, he called her 'the people's prin-cess' and said all the appropriate things to a nation – indeed, a world – in shock. He was not a distanced politician, but in sync with the public.

As a child, I had seen another young, sharp, dynamic man become President. Tony Blair reminded me of John F. Kennedy. Many of our leaders are old farts, aren't they? Blair was passionate and enthusias-tic, and with a young family. He was inspiring. This was like the new Camelot, if you will, of Britain, with a premier who would change the way things are done. He was hugely popular.

With that in mind, you will not be surprised when I say that I was thrilled by the invitation to cook for Tony Blair and the summit leaders. Regarding his plan for a special and interesting menu, I figured, *I like it. That's innovative. He's thinking outside the box.*

Derry Irvine may have spent extravagantly on the rest of his resi-dence, but the kitchen did not seem to have benefited from his splurge. Ahead of the function on 3 April, I had made enquiries about the kitchen space and equipment, and concluded that it was small. Therefore, it would be best – and would save time – if I prepared the confit of duck at my home in Catus, before leaving for the event in London. I strive to be organised, as you know.

I asked my friend Alexis Pelissou – chef-patron of Le Gindreau near Catus – to help me prepare this dish. We used thirty pieces of duck in the confit.

 Asian duck confit is not only fit for a world leaders' banquet but is also an excellent dish to serve at home for your guests at a lunch or supper party. Imagine you are cooking for six; in which case you will need to begin with six pieces of duck thigh and leg.

Lay the pieces of duck on a tray and evenly sprinkle both sides with a generous amount – 50g (2 oz) – of coarse sea salt. Cover the duck with a tea towel and store it overnight in a cool place, or in the fridge.

The next day, the fun begins. Wipe off the salt and use kitchen paper to pat dry the duck pieces. You will need 4 x 350g (12 oz) tins of duck or goose fat – heat this fat in a large pot. When it is hot, add 8 whole, unpeeled garlic cloves, which you have crushed slightly. At the same time, add – here comes the Asian twist – 8 slices of fresh ginger root, 6 whole star anise, 3 cinnamon sticks or bark and 2 tablespoons of whole roasted Sichuan peppercorns.

Now add the duck thighs and cook slowly for an hour over a low heat. The duck should be cooked and tender. Let the duck cool in the fat. Refrigerate, with the fat covering the duck, until you are ready to use it. The confit will keep for months in the fat in the fridge.

When you are ready to cook the duck confit, preheat the oven to 180°C (350°F, gas mark 4). Scoop the duck from the fat and cook on a roasting tray for 40 minutes, or until the duck is crispy. Remove the duck pieces from the hot fat and drain them on kitchen paper. Strain the hot fat and keep for future use. Serve at once. The fat can be used to sauté potatoes. 🥣

ALEXIS and I vacuum-packed the confit, 'sous-vide' style, so that it was ready to be roasted in London. The following morning I began my journey. I checked in for my flight with unusual hand luggage: a large bag that contained confit of duck for twenty-two world leaders, as well as my cherished Chinese cleaver. This was, remember, before 9/11.

The great chef Anton Mosimann assisted me when I arrived in London. Everyone who came close accepted that baggage had never smelled as appetisingly fragrant as mine on that day.

The lunch was a resounding success, and I was not disappointed by the Prime Minister. After the meal, he was kind about the dishes and he went out of his way to introduce me to each one of his important guests. 'This is Ken Hom,' he said. 'He's one of our most famous chefs.' He insisted that I have a photo op with the world leaders. I gave him my most recent book as a gift, obviously not knowing if he would find time to flick through the pages, although I would later discover that he was a fan of mine and had watched my first series. Later that day Ron Batori called me to say, 'Jeez, I saw you on CNN!' I headed back to France, via a couple of interviews with reporters who interrogated me about Derry's wallpaper.

A few days later I was delighted to receive a note of thanks from the Prime Minister. 'Ken, your meal was a big hit, everybody loved it … The flavours were wonderful … Thank you for the book…' It went on and on, heaps of praise.

I wrote back, along the lines, 'Thank you very much, Prime Minister. I'm glad everything worked out.' I added, 'I know you come to France on holiday, and if you happen to be there during the summer I would be delighted to have you and your wife Cherie, and your family, come and eat.' Sure, so I said it, but I did not think it would happen.

FOR the next part of the story let's go to a beach on the Canary Isles. That's where wonderful Sue Burke was on holiday. (She was born in Southport, as I have mentioned, which means she is grateful for any sun she can get. For many years Sue lived in the warmth of Spain.) As she was tanning herself, as the Mediterranean waves lapped at her ankles, her mobile phone rang. 'Hello, this is No. 10 calling … The Prime Minister would like to come to Ken's home in France.' He'd received my letter, then.

Should you ever invite a British Prime Minister to lunch at your home, and should he accept the invitation, then prepare yourself for the kerfuffle that ensues; not that I would wish it any differently.

As I was trying to absorb the notion of cooking for the Blairs at my home – will it be Peking duck and what about Chinese wonton soup with truffles? – there were agents of the British secret service who were busy scrutinising the security of chez Hom. They were gathering 'intel' about my medieval watchtower: doors, locks, windows, walls. Heaven forbid there was an assassination attempt while the salad was served. The French police were also despatched, garnering glances from villagers and curtain-twitchers when they arrived on my doorstep to ensure the house was 'clean'.

When word reached the Mayor of Catus, he, too, was keen to receive an invitation. World leaders don't drop into the village often. The butcher, the baker, the candlestick maker; they were all ready and well preened, awaiting Tony Blair's visit. And then … a catastrophe happened in Britain. Tony Blair had to stay on that side of the Channel. He could not come.

Although Tony couldn't come – and he was 'Tony' to me by then – his family came en masse for a fabulous lunch. There was Cherie and the children, as well as Cherie's lovely mother, Gale, and Cherie's sister Lyndsey and her husband. We had a fine time without Tony.

WE thought we would try again. In the following year, 1999, I invited them to Catus, hoping Tony would be free. Once more, they accepted. I suppose I kind of treated the first year like a dummy run. This time around, I knew the drill. Things were slightly altered, however, as Tony's presence meant the level of security was increased. The town was practically sealed off by police officers and men in dark, mirrored sunglasses.

There were also stricter regulations about the meal. For instance, nobody could set foot in my watchtower unless they were on the list of invited guests. A few weeks before the event, the mayor (who was on that list) had button-holed me to ask, 'Can we have a reception in the town hall for the Prime Minister? Do you mind?' I said that I would have to ask No. 10. I phoned my contact at Downing Street.

'Oh, hello. The Mayor of Catus would like to have a reception for the Prime Minister.'

Pause.

I continued. 'I'm so sorry to have to ask this.'

My contact: 'No, it'll be fine. It's OK. As long as it's not...'

I could see where this was heading and jumped in, 'Oh, it won't be a long thing. Don't worry.'

The day began with the mayor's reception in the town hall, with scores of dignitaries eager to shake the Prime Minister's hand and pose with him for a shot (if it happened now, the shots would be selfies). This event in the town hall was filled with VIPs from the land of Lot, not confined merely to the pillars of Catus society.

The Blairs had flown in to Toulouse, where they were greeted by a few dozen photographers. In Catus there were more. When we emerged from the town hall, to walk a few hundred metres to my house, we were surrounded by about sixty photographers, clicking away. From the air, we must have looked odd. *What am I talking about?* From the ground, we looked odd.

For lunch, I made crispy spring rolls, with duck confit and truffles. It's really good, though the kids did not like the addition of truffle. Of course, I also served a platter of aromatic, crispy Peking duck, which is Tony's favourite Chinese dish. He is a good eater, and he and Cherie both enjoy Chinese food. Over lunch, I dipped into my clarets, and opened a bottle of Château Latour 1953, a premier grand cru Pauillac from the year that Tony was born. It was the only one I had, and I recall that it was rich and velvety, and its sweetness coated the tongue. It was entirely appropriate for the British Prime Minister and a pleasure to share it with the Blairs. That was the day Latour met Labour, though only one bottle meant only a small taste for each of us, alas.

———

I really warmed to Cherie. She is a remarkable woman. Since that first meeting in Catus, we have sat often, talking of life, its triumphs and its struggles. I say *struggles*, though we both see them as episodes that make us the people we are today. Nevertheless, Cherie endured a difficult childhood and, like my own upbringing, much of hers was without a father.

In fact, Cherie's father was the actor Tony Booth. He walked out of the family home when Cherie was aged eight, leaving her mother to pick up the pieces. Mr Booth went to London to make a name for himself, notably playing the young radical son-in-law in the BBC sitcom *Till Death Us Do Part*. Mrs Booth, meanwhile, and her family were engulfed in the acrid stench of scandal. They lived in a Catholic community in a suburb north of Liverpool; marriage vows were to be obeyed, and separation and divorce were unusual at that time.

Cherie and her younger sister, Lyndsey, were raised by their mother and grandmother. From their story there is much to be learnt about the strength of women (and perhaps the weakness of men).

Often Cherie and I would talk about food, of course, and she told me about the role it played in those early years of her life. 'My grandmother was always the cook in our house,' she said, 'as Mum went to work. You see, my grandmother's father was a barber. But he was the renegade in his family because he came from a family of cooks – they had eating houses in Harrogate. So Grandma obviously had some kind of innate ability, and was a great pastry cook. She had a repertoire and she stuck to it. She didn't like going out to restaurants because she felt that was just a waste of money. "You can buy things and cook it just as well at home," she'd say.'

Cherie's grandmother kept to a weekly routine of meals. 'On the Sunday, we would have shoulder of lamb roasted. On Monday, we'd have leftovers. Tuesday meant stew and dumplings, or Scouse. That's Liverpool stew with potatoes in, as opposed to stew and dumplings, which would have potatoes separately. On Wednesdays, Grandma always baked. So we would have steak and kidney pie followed by apple pie. She often made scones or rock cakes, and I'd help with the baking.

'Thursday, we would have lamb chops. Come Friday, it was fish and chips because we were a Catholic family. Saturday was a slightly more moveable feast, possibly shepherd's pie. And then we would start again.' Oh, it made me hungry just listening to her, though she said, 'The portions were quite small. A little would have to go a long way.'

As little girls at primary school, she and Lyndsey walked home during the dinner hour and their grandmother cooked them lunch. 'We might have fried eggs and chips, cold tripe and chips, pig's trotters, spare ribs. It was very working class.

'When I went to grammar school,' said Cherie, 'I didn't like to eat anyone else's cooking, so I didn't actually eat my lunches. By January I had fallen ill and they decided I was malnourished. So at that point they arranged for me to go be with my aunt, who lived nearer the school. And all because I just couldn't stand the school food. Eventually, by the time I was in the sixth form, I'd eat the school food … but didn't particularly like it.'

At the London School of Economics she stayed in halls of residence for the first year, and was therefore committed to the halls' food. Finally, at the age of nineteen or twenty, she moved into a flat and that's when she could start cooking for herself. Cherie and Tony were married in 1980, and used to watch my TV series when it was broadcast four years later.

'I had your early books,' she said, 'I loved cooking and did a lot in the '80s. In fact, right up until Downing Street. I loved to experiment. God knows what I cooked. In those days just the idea of stir-frying vegetables was quite a big thing.' She had also eaten food cooked by her Chinese sister-in-law. In the constituency home in Sedgefield, Cherie inherited an Aga 'and that opened up a whole range of dishes'.

I was curious: had there been times when Tony donned the apron? 'Tony once tried to cook something, I can't remember what it was,' Cherie told me. 'But he was following the recipe, and ended up putting in sugar instead of salt. That wasn't a great success.' She said, 'He can cook breakfast and carve chicken, but that's about it. Actually, he's always said he would like to learn to cook but hasn't got around to it.'

Cherie and I became very good friends (after that first visit I gave her a wok, which she still has to this day), and I am so fond of her. Sometimes

I feel that people don't realise how actively involved she is with charities, and she has made an immense contribution to women's issues on
an international scale. She cares deeply about others and, apart from
being a highly successful QC with her own law firm, she also works hard
to promote and fundraise for the Cherie Blair Foundation for Women,
which supports entrepreneurial women around the world.

Subsequently, I have always been delighted to help her with charity events, be it breast cancer awareness or Save the Children or her
Foundation for Women. When I was a consultant chef for a group of
restaurants in the City of London, we would host lots of events there.
She supports many of my charities and she came to Oxford Brookes
University to deliver the Ken Hom lecture. Cherie and I have what I
would describe as a nice, equal relationship.

———

THE Blairs came to Catus two or three more times. One year they were
due to visit on their way to a holiday in Tuscany. We would be joined
for lunch by an eclectic group of friends. There was Pierre-Jean Pébeyre,
the truffle farmer, Jancis Robinson, the wine writer, and Angus Deayton,
then host of *Have I Got News for You*, as well as friends who lived locally.

I had recently filmed my *Foolproof* series, which was produced by Kate
Kinninmont, and I invited Kate along. 'I've had such a great experience
working with you,' I said to her, 'so I'm going to sit you beside Tony.'

Kate was nervy. 'Oh gosh, I feel I don't know enough about politics,'
she said. 'Put me anywhere else at the table.'

They arrived, Tony walking into the kitchen, past the shepherdess's
table, holding their baby, Leo, in one arm. Someone attempted to give
Tony a glass of champagne as the Prime Minister tried simultaneously

to shake everybody's hands. He put my other guests at ease by saying, 'Hello, I'm Tony.' First-name terms.

Kate said, 'Should I take Leo?' As she put the baby over her shoulder he started to cry. Tony said, 'Thanks very much, but can you turn him to face out? He likes to see everybody.'

I disregarded Kate's nerves and put her right beside the Prime Minister at the table. They could discuss Scotland, Kate's homeland. Tony was a student at Fettes College in Edinburgh, and he was chatting away, 'Oh, I still miss Edinburgh.' They talked about student jobs he'd had in the East End of London. Once he worked for somebody who did not pay him and, as a young man, he did not know what to do, but had never quite forgotten the uncomfortable experience. The table came alive with hard-luck tales and funny stories.

Meanwhile, I set about decanting the final bottle of Château Lafite Rothschild. There was, as you can imagine, a sort of religious rite associated with the opening of the wine. That is because it is rare. You can't just open such a magnificent bottle and pour without an introduction. There must be an acknowledgement of what is about to be drunk. I talked about the wine to anyone who would listen, and then turned to my right at the table. 'Jancis, would you mind pouring, please?'

Jancis started to pour, working her way around the glasses on the table, beginning with Kate. As she poured, she talked about the wine. My guests started to taste, while she continued to pour, and there were cheerful slurps and sounds of approval as the wine went down. Having poured this glass after that glass, Jancis then reached Tony. There was not a drop left in the decanter.

For a moment – it was just a split second or two – there was tension at the table. Something was not quite right. The British Prime Minister was missing out on a gastronomic experience. Then we all burst into laughter and settled on communion: each of us poured a splash of our wine into Tony's glass. Equality was restored.

—

Warm Mango Compote with Basil and Vanilla Ice Cream

This is the simple dessert that I served to the world leaders at the Asia–Europe Meeting in London, back in 1998. Often I made it for promotions at The Oriental in Bangkok. Mangoes are popular and abundant in Thailand, and their rich, fleshly and satin-like texture transforms this recipe into an exquisite finale. Shop-bought vanilla ice cream is of a high quality these days, and so convenient. The combination of the cold ice cream and warm fruit is unbeatable.

Serves 4

1 vanilla bean, split in half

110g (4 oz) sugar

150 ml (5 fl oz) water

☙

750g (1½ lb) (2 medium) mangoes

tiny pinch of salt

2 tablespoons unsalted butter

6 basil leaves, coarsely chopped

a tub of your favourite vanilla ice cream, to serve 4

Scrape the inside seeds of the vanilla bean into the sugar and mix well. Using a non-stick wok or pan, bring the sugar and water to a boil, add the vanilla bean halves and simmer for 10 minutes.

Remove the vanilla bean, dry it thoroughly and save for future use by storing it in sugar. Peel the mangoes and cut the fruit into ¼-inch-thick slices.

Add the mangoes and salt and simmer for 2 minutes, just enough to warm and not to cook through. Remove from the heat, stir in the butter and the basil, stir gently and serve at once with scoops of vanilla ice cream. ●

28

Meals, Ready or Not

ASK LEE WILLIAMS about his childhood and he will tell you that he was useless at school, but he will steer the subject towards his grandmother, on his father's side. She was Burmese. 'When I was a kid she used to cook traditional Burmese food,' says Lee. 'So, some people go round to their gran's and eat cake and scones. I used to go in there and was met by the smell of freshly steamed basmati rice, ginger, garlic. I remember walking to her house and getting really excited about that Sunday lunch experience.

'For me it was phenomenal, all the little snacks she used to do, traditional Burmese food – curries, stir-fries, fantastic fish. That was the sensory experience of food – the smell, the taste, the excitement around meal times.' There began his affection for Asian and Indian food.

So he went through school, and 'I'm not gonna lie,' he says, 'I was a numpty. I just had no interest in anything. It wasn't until I dabbled with cooking that I found a place in life.'

His parents had separated when he was young, and Lee's father had a pub in Oxfordshire. 'I used to go and see him at the weekends. When he was working I sort of dipped into the kitchen to help out and earn a bit of pocket money, you know, doing kitchen portering. Then I got into cooking a little bit. I started off as a commis.'

The pub food was popular, and soon Lee realised his vocation. He knew he could never be 'one of those guys who's in a shirt and tie and an office every day'. He was absorbed into the environment and energy of the kitchen. 'I flunked out of school, went into catering college and that's where I really thrived.'

His career began at a restaurant in Wimbledon, followed by gastro pubs in the Channel Islands, and helping to open a restaurant called Broomes ('We got a Michelin star within the first nine months, which was fantastic'). Stars come and go. It has since changed hands and is now the Salty Dog. He travelled around on a chef's tour and found himself in Asia. Inspired by Chinese and Asian food, he went to Australia for a year and a half and then came back to Britain, but not before stopping in South Africa.

By the year 2000, he was at Monkey Island Hotel, a romantic spot on the Thames in Bray, Berkshire. From there, he went to Cookham, in the same county, and spent four years at the Odney Club, a hotel owned by John Lewis. Lee and his wife lived on site, but when their two children came along, Lee wanted the sort of work–life balance that is often unobtainable for chefs in professional kitchens.

In 2007, he saw an ad for a development chef at Kerry Foods in Burton on Trent. He went for a job interview. A development chef works on and develops recipes. These days, many great chef-proprietors employ development chefs. They perfect dishes for restaurants and work on recipes that will eventually appear in books. In the case of Kerry, they wanted a chef to develop ready meals.

Lee was told that, as part of the interview process, he would be required to cook three dishes. Although he had considerable experience, he was struggling for inspiration. What would he cook? He looked through his bookcase and came across my *Hot Wok* cookbook. He was inspired. His charm and confidence – and, of course, my dishes – won him the job!

Remember, he had that affection for Asian and Indian food. Working at Kerry would give him the opportunity to develop ranges of Indian and Chinese food. After a couple of years in the job, Lee was well established, and then a new brief came along. What he did not know was that Kerry Foods had approached me about doing a range of ready meals. They wanted it to be authentic, with fantastic oriental flavours. When I agreed, Lee was told about the project. He would be the development chef.

We met at Noon, which was not the time but the name of Kerry's site in London. Lee would later say it was like a meeting with the Chinese Mafia – I arrived wearing a long black overcoat and a black trilby. We spent the day in the kitchen, cooking, testing, tasting. This was the beginning of a process that would continue, on and off, for about fourteen months.

People often ask me about ready meals, so perhaps this is the point to explain how the process works. Kerry had bought the Chinese ingredients that I had recommended, and I would cook up a meal for all of us.

The first four dishes were beef and black beans, sweet and sour chicken, chicken with cashew nuts and chicken with mushrooms. Once I had cooked these dishes, it was a matter of replicating the taste for the ready meals. That was the challenge, and flavour enhancers were not allowed. Stir-frying must be done quickly. If, for instance, you stir-fry a sliced onion, as you might do at home, then it is a fast process and pretty easy. Try stir-frying tons of onions and it is not fast, and the onion does not colour well. The sauces took a long time to perfect, and every few months I would visit to taste and, if happy, sign off. And I couldn't simply say, 'Add a bit more salt.' There are salt restrictions, of course. The dishes were first made in two- or three-kilo vats. Once we were happy with the flavours, they were made in 500-kilo vats, or as a tonne.

Lee and his team worked on the range, developing as they do. Then we would reconvene again, to taste some more, cook and test. Lee was sourcing ingredients and flavours that were new to Kerry; I was keen to make it as authentic as possible. Once my changes were made, Tesco would taste. Between us, we came up with the ideal range of flavours and the correct production method. Following the go-ahead from Tesco, the meals were launched and went onto the shelves. Do not under-estimate the time and energy that goes into ready meals. There are the lead times to think about, the authentic ingredients to source, and then the testing and more testing.

The hard work paid off. The range was a huge success, went on to win awards, and became one of the longest-running ready meal ranges in Tesco or any of the other retailers supplied by Kerry Foods.

One day, Lee and his team of chefs came to London to give a presenta-tion. My schedule was hectic and we arranged to meet at the Dorchester, where I was staying. On this occasion I had been given quite a small room. To confuse the issue, Lee believed that his company had booked another room which would have been large enough for us all to gather and do a tasting. There was no record of the booking.

Anyway, I suggested to Lee that he and his team prepare the food in the hotel's kitchens. There were about fifteen snacks, including prawn crackers, dim sum, spring rolls, wontons and Chinese toast, as well as sweet and sour dipping sauces. When the dishes were prepared, Lee and his team could come up to my room, and the Dorchester's brilliant waiting staff could bring the food up to us. There, we would have a tasting session.

Usually, tasting 'panels' take place in a professional kitchen. Everyone has space and can stand around, dipping into this or that dish. This was the most unusual tasting panel. Six of us crowded into my extremely small room. I perched on a chaise longue. Two members of the team plonked themselves on my bed. Someone else was on a stool, or was it a suitcase? Lee was trying to present fifteen dishes on the trolley.

He turned around to see me on the chaise longue and, in that split second, there was an almighty crash. Somehow he had managed to knock the entire trolley and fifteen dishes of Chinese snacks onto the floor and all over my bed. The room was like Tracey Emin's hymn to a Chinese banquet – sheets splattered with red chilli sauce, pillows dotted with wontons, a carpet of crunchy prawn crackers and crispy spring rolls. We spent ages trying to clean it up and, thankfully, my friends at the Dorchester were very sweet about it.

—

LEE'S ready meal attack at the Dorchester did nothing to destroy our relationship, even if it ruined a carpet. I asked him to join me at Obsession, an annual food extravaganza that takes place at Northcote (formerly Northcote Manor). It is a country house hotel beside the Ribble Valley in Lancashire, where Nigel Howarth is chef-patron and Lisa Goodwin-Allen is executive chef.

The event lasts for a week, and on each night a well-known chef cooks for the guests. I have done this gig twice, both times accompanied by Lee, and it's great fun: we arrive at the hotel a couple of days before the dinner, giving us plenty of time for prep and, yes, luxury.

The 10th anniversary of Obsession was particularly memorable. On the night of our dinner, the restaurant was full: there were about a hundred guests seated in four rooms, and in each room there were television monitors screening the action from the kitchen, enabling the diners to see how we were getting on. This sort of visual entertainment is common in restaurants nowadays, but at the time it was novel and exciting. We were getting on very well. The kitchen was full of activity and energy and, from the comfort of their seats at the tables, the guests could see the dishes coming together in the kitchen.

Lee had done such a brilliant job I thought I would get him a glass of wine. It was a large glass of Rioja. Lee was at the hot plate and his back was to me when I walked up and said, 'Here, Lee, thank you. You know, we're doing well here. There you go…' On hearing my voice, he spun around and happened to be holding a large tray of food. The tray, in turn, knocked the massive glass of Rioja, which flew from the vessel onto my face and my chef's jacket. No ordinary chef's jacket. It was white, with the familiar words 'Ken Hom' skilfully hand-embroidered upon the left breast.

The whole kitchen stopped, froze. Lee was devastated. 'I am so, so sorry.' I burst out laughing. As did the guests in the restaurant, probably, as they watched it on TV. There were attempts to sponge down my chef's jacket, but they weren't successful. Lee describes it as 'one of the worst moments of my life' but it was my fault; I walked up behind him.

I asked Lee to work with me on a few other projects, including a charity event in 2010 for Cherie Blair. The function was held at Tony and Cherie's home in Buckinghamshire, and Cherie invited us to spend the weekend there: arrive on the Friday; Lee and I would cook for the dinner on Saturday night; there would be lunch and a chill-out on the Sunday. The event was set in the diaries for April.

Of course, no one had predicted the full effect of that volcanic eruption in Iceland. The eruption was minor, but it sent volcanic ash into the sky and southwards. There were concerns about aircraft safety, and suddenly flights were cancelled throughout western and northern Europe, affecting travel all around the world for weeks to come. There was pandemonium as everyone tried to find other means of getting from A to B. In my case, the B stood for the Blairs.

Lee did not have any problems. He arrived at the Blairs' house, underwent the security checks and made his way to the kitchen, where he met Cherie Blair and thought, *How surreal is this?* He had no idea how surreal things would become. I was due to arrive on the same day as Lee, but the airborne ash scuppered that, and my flight was cancelled. All flights were cancelled. Meanwhile, Tony was stuck in somewhere or other, unable to beat the ash and make it to the event.

As Lee started to set up, he also began to panic. He was terrified that he would have to cook the dinner on his own, and was simultaneously anxious that only a few people would make it to the event. Cherie was hoping for large donations to her charity, but what if there were no guests and the food went to waste? I arrived a couple of hours before the dinner was meant to be served, to find that Lee was perfectly organised. The dinner was a fantastic success.

Lee and I had been given rooms in a separate cottage on the grounds. The following morning, he was up at seven-ish and started to pack up his car. He remembered that his kitchen equipment – a deep-fat fryer and knives – was in the kitchen of the main house, where we had cooked the meal. So he thought he would dash up to the kitchen to retrieve the equipment. He jogged through the main garden, up some stone steps, and through patio doors and into the kitchen.

He had taken only a few steps into the room when two armed guards in black sprang from nowhere. They were holding automatic weapons, pointed at Lee. One of them shouted, 'POLICE!' Lee put his hands into the air, and his body froze. I mean, he had come to help me out and was only after a deep-fat fryer. Being held at gunpoint wasn't part of the deal.

'GET DOWN ON THE FLOOR!'

Lee knelt down on the floor. He figured this was it; his time had come.

In transpired that one security shift had clocked off and another had clocked on, and the first team had not told the second team that there was a chef in the guest quarters.

One of the guards mumbled into his mouthpiece and, thankfully, Lee was given the all-clear and helped to his feet. With some dexterity, he gathered his deep-fat fryer and knives, and then sprinted at cheetah-speed back to his car. Lee and I had breakfast with Cherie and had a laugh about it, although Lee told me, 'I was shaking in my boots. I've never been so scared.'

———

LEE also helped me out when I was in China a few years ago. I was travelling with Ching-He Huang, and we were making a fascinating TV series for the BBC. Meanwhile, I was also collecting, compiling and writing recipes for the book that would tie in with the series, *Exploring China: A Culinary Adventure.*

As I was in China, I was without a kitchen and needed someone to taste test the recipes. Lee would be the perfect person. It was straightforward enough. I would send him the recipes, he would cook them. He would taste the finished product and give me his critical feedback, thus helping me towards the necessary changes. I also appreciated his view – was something too spicy, for instance? I like very spicy, but heat on the palate is not right for everyone, of course.

Each week I sent him two or three recipes, over a five- or six-week period. I had not accounted for the effect on his domestic life. One day Lee's wife came home and looked into the garden. 'How dare you!' she shouted. Lee had removed the washing from the washing line and shoved it into a laundry basket. On the line, where there had once been sheets, there now hung three Peking ducks, basking in the sunshine.

Another day, when it was snowing, Lee sparked up the barbecue to smoke ducks in green tea. The ducks were phenomenal, but his barbecue melted a nearby snowman built by his daughter. He was rapidly losing popularity at home.

29

Life and Living

LUNCH TODAY WAS Japanese curry. In my small but much-loved kitchen in Paris, I prepared this comforting, one-pot dish in only a minute or two. In a large pan, I browned a few chicken thighs. They came out of the pan and in went the basics of this curry: that is, finely chopped onions, carrots and potatoes (which I had quartered).

I poured in chicken stock, followed by Japanese curry, which is sold in chunky, soft 'blocks', a bit like a large stock cube – break off as much as you want and chuck it into the mix. In keeping with the Japanese palate, it is not too spicy. Anyway, I returned the chicken to the pan and let the whole lot simmer in a slow oven for about an hour, before serving it with a mountain of rice and a bottle of chilli-infused olive oil, in case any of my guests wanted to up the heat.

I buy the cubes not in Japan but in Thailand. Just like Ella Fitzgerald, I love Paris in the springtime, but every year, around about March,

I tend to migrate south to Thailand, where I have a home and enjoy the sunshine.

Aside from stocking up on Japanese curry cubes, I usually have a thorough medical check-up. I stuck to this tradition in March 2010, when I visited my doctor in Thailand shortly after receiving my OBE at the British Embassy.

———

I must digress for a moment, as the OBE deserves a mention.

It all began at Charles de Gaulle airport, as I returned from a trip and switched on my mobile after the plane landed. There was a message from the British Embassy in Paris, asking me to phone. The following conversation took place.

'Hello. This is Ken Hom returning your call.'

'Oh, hello, Mr Hom. We were just checking to see if you are alive.'

At this point, I was getting flashbacks to the Ken Lo moment; the previous time I had been considered dead.

I said, 'I am very much alive.'

'Jolly good,' said the Englishman on the other end of the line. 'Well, in that case, we were just checking to see if you could receive an OBE.'

I almost dropped the phone. You know how special Britain is to me, and I was so moved to be told I would receive the award in the Queen's Birthday Honours. The ceremony would take place in June 2009, but I could not be there as I had planned to visit my mother. She was old and frail and I wanted to see her.

I felt that I had achieved something for my mother. It gave her face and made her feel proud, as if she had done the job well and it had all worked out in the end.

For most of my life she had been unable to understand why I did what I did for a living. Over the years she had said, 'Can't you do something else besides this cooking job? Become a dentist or a real estate agent?' Then one day she saw a photograph of me. I was standing beside the Chinese President inside No. 10 and the photograph appeared in the Chinese newspapers. That's when she phoned and said, 'Maybe you should keep cooking.'

In a peach-sweet twist – and I sense another quick digression – the President, Jiang Zemin, was not as thrilled as my mother. The photograph was taken in October 1999, after I had cooked for him and Tony Blair at the Prime Minister's Downing Street residence. They dined on crab wontons in aromatic broth, stir-fried persillade king prawns, fritto misto of Asian vegetables, and herbal vegetarian fried rice. Dessert was ginger crème brûlée.

Zemin's visit marked the first to Britain by a Chinese head of state. While his Excellency had been briefed about me, he was not expecting to be at my side for the photo-call. In the brilliant blaze of flashbulbs, I took a look in the President's eyes, and could tell he was puzzled and bewildered. He was very gracious and smiled, but I could sense he was saying to himself, 'Why the hell am I being photographed with the cook? We don't do this in China. I mean, he is *the cook*. He's just the guy who makes a meal for us.'

Anyway, as I had a home in Paris, it was agreed that the OBE ceremony would take place in November at the British Embassy in Rue du Faubourg Saint-Honoré, which doubles as the ambassador's spectacular residence. One of my guests was Alain Ducasse, one of the world's finest chefs and a friend for many years, as well as a man with a delicious sense of humour. When I thanked him for coming, he said, 'Don't flatter yourself, Ken. I'd heard about the embassy and just wanted to see it.'

Laughter is so important.

GOING back to the tests at my doctor's in Thailand. One of them is for PSA, prostate-specific antigen. It's a protein produced by the prostate gland, and the level of PSA in the blood is often elevated if there is cancer. My test for PSA showed an anomaly, but when I saw a specialist he explained that this irregularity could be due to a number of reasons, all of them benign and nothing to worry about. 'Come back in two weeks for another test,' he said, and I kept to my diary and went to Hong Kong.

A fortnight later I was back in Bangkok, having a second PSA test. This time the results showed that the PSA had not dropped but was much higher than it had been in the first test. The result was positive – or negative, depending on how you look at it. The doctor recommended a prostate biopsy to determine if cancer was present. Life is funny, isn't it? One moment you can be talking about the moreish succulence of something like Japanese curry; the next you are contemplating your very fate.

I told Ron Batori. He said that the chairman of his company had been diagnosed with prostate cancer and he had undergone an experimental form of treatment that worked for him. The treatment was called 'proton beam therapy'.

It is a type of radiotherapy. While conventional radiotherapy uses high-energy beams of radiation to destroy cancerous cells, surrounding tissue can also be damaged. This can lead to side effects such as nausea, and can sometimes disrupt how some organs function. Proton beam therapy uses beams of protons (sub-atomic particles) to achieve the same effect of killing cells. A 'particle accelerator' speeds up the protons which are beamed into cancerous cells, zapping them dead. Unlike conventional radiotherapy, in proton beam therapy the beam of protons stops once it 'hits' the cancerous cells. This means that proton beam therapy results in much less damage to surrounding tissue.

In 2014, this type of treatment was a point of major discussion in Britain. There was a manhunt when the parents of a five-year-old boy, Ashya King, took him out of Southampton General Hospital without the doctors' consent, and to Prague, where their child could undergo proton beam therapy. Ashya had a brain tumour, but he made a full recovery.

Ron's chairman steered me in the right direction for medical care. This began with Dr Preecha in Thailand. He is renowned around the world for changing men into women and women into men. That's his claim to fame, and he just happened to know the right doctor in Kobe, in the south of Japan.

He said, 'I will send you to Doctor Okuno.' Indeed, Dr Preecha did not just send me to Dr Okuno; he accompanied me to Dr Okuno, and personally introduced us. Dr Okuno did an MRI scan, then took me to the medical centre for further tests and to check that I qualified for the treatment: it does not work for everyone.

As with others who are in a similar situation, I read up about the treatment on the internet. There were contradictory reports, but I decided to go ahead with it, and am pleased that I did so. In a younger man, the cancer cells are more active, and because of my age – I had recently turned sixty – I could have waited and monitored the cancer to see how it developed. Waiting clashed with my psyche. I am the kind of person who thinks, *Let's not wait.*

I was told to return for treatment for a couple of months from the end of June, into August. Over this period, I was to undergo thirty-seven individual treatments, each one involving a zap of the protein beam. Oddly, I was not suffering any symptoms of cancer other than that common symptom, which is … shock. What's more, I would not need chemotherapy, and therefore the potential side effects were minimal. However, the treatment was experimental. This meant that medical insurance would not cover the treatment. I reckoned, *I don't drive a car. Other men spend their money on cars. I would rather spend mine on this treatment.*

—

AND so I went to live in Japan. I had been many times to Japan, but never lived there, which was what the treatment required. Living somewhere is very different to visiting. Being a resident enables you to become immersed in the culture and, of course, to eat Japanese food for every meal of the day over a couple of months. I made the most of it.

I had grown up in a Chinese household, as you know, in which my mother frequently reiterated the horrors that our fellow countrymen had suffered at the hands of the Japanese. Yet here I was with my life being saved by the Japanese. They didn't owe me. I owed them.

I visited Kyoto and Osaka, enjoying travel – everything works in Japan, and the country is truly amazing; I realised then how much I loved it. I went to Hiroshima and asked myself: is there food that is unique to the city? Here is the answer … They do a noodle dish, in which noodles and vegetables are cooked on a smoking-hot plancha – an egg is broken over them, sizzles and foams, and the whole lot is then flipped as it continues to cook rapidly on the grill.

I don't speak Japanese but was learning all the while and, if I could not find a restaurant, I asked for directions and a kind soul would show me to the door. In Tokyo, I met Gwen Robertson, the *Financial Times* editor in Japan, who took me to a vegetarian restaurant at the Golden Temple in Kyoto. I was facing death, but I was discovering something new, and not only novel food experiences. Indeed, the food of Japan enriched and deepened my understanding of the country, and I found it to be a life-enhancing episode. I almost regretted leaving Japan, but something happened which ensured my eventual departure.

———

MY mother fell ill during this time. In July, when I was in the middle of my treatment, her health deteriorated following an operation to remove a tumour. She was in Chicago; I was in Japan, and tried to find a way of catching a flight to the States to see my mother, and, if possible, return in time for the next course of treatment. I was constantly on the phone to my mother's doctor, who reassured me, 'Don't worry, she's not in pain.' Then came the inevitable doctor's questions, such as, 'Would you give permission not to resuscitate her?'

I said, 'No matter what, I don't want her to suffer. Give her painkillers, but don't make her suffer.'

On 15 July, my mother passed away as she slept. I have always felt that she sacrificed so much for me, and I believe that this was the ultimate sacrifice: that she was going so that I could stay. I say that although she died unaware that I, too, had cancer. I did not see the need to tell her. Perhaps instinctively she knew that I was in trouble.

Following her death, I had to carry on with life and the necessity to survive, to live. What else can you do? I had learnt this from my mother. She did not moan or whinge about anything. Instead, she just got on with life. She was never a person who spoke a lot. For instance, I didn't know much about her family until I took her back to China when I was researching my book *The Taste of China*. I wanted to take her back to her roots, and that is when I discovered that she was from a very wealthy family, and that she had grown up with her own maid.

In fact, we met the maid – she had gone into the property business and become a multi-millionaire.

I talked with my relatives in Chicago, and to funeral directors, and we arranged matters so that there was a cremation. Come September, when I had finished my treatment, we would have a memorial service. Once those arrangements were in hand, I continued my treatment, going for beam zaps two or three times a week.

My mother was a good lady. She grew up in a rich family but they lost everything. Constantly aware of her sacrifices, I took care of her, and gave her money. This morning I found myself rummaging through some old correspondence and came across a letter that I had written to her when I was in California in the early '80s. She had kept the note, filed it away, and it reverted back to me after she died. 'My dearest mother,' it read, and then told her that I was enclosing a cheque for $1,000, adding, 'I will send another $1,000 as soon as I have it.' She would have understood the cheque but not the words. I typed the letter using English and knew that she would see her friends at mah-jong; they would be able to translate, and she played mah-jong most days of her life.

I say I gave her cash, but she rarely spent any of the money I sent her. She just put it in a savings account in the bank, which drove me crazy. I would say, 'Mum, that's not what it's for. I am giving you money so that you can spend it.' However, I did not want her to change. As long as she was happy and taken care of; that was what I wanted. She enjoyed eating until her final days. When she turned eighty, I invited 250 guests to a banquet. That was almost the whole of Chinatown.

When I was a child, my mother fed me. When I was an adult, I fed her. The last time we were together was in the spring of 2010, when I treated her to a meal in a Chinese restaurant. My visit to Chicago, my time with my mother, was inadvertently extended.

I was due to leave on a particular day but the cloud of volcanic ash spreading through the air from Iceland meant that flights all over the world were cancelled (and, as you know, that assignment to cook for the Blairs in England was soon to be in jeopardy). Unable to travel, I got to spend a week longer with the woman who had brought me into the world. None of us knows how much time we have on this earth and, through a kind twist of my life story, I was delivered a precious gift from the gods.

WE all deserve one great love affair in our lives and, in that respect, my mother had not been deprived. Hong Jung Hom was born in China on 15 March 1915. As a young man he emigrated to the United States and lived in Arizona. Here, he became Tommy and was not lonely as he had brothers there too. Tommy Hom was my father.

He took a job as a clerk, and then, in the early 1940s, following the outbreak of the Second World War, he went to fight for the American Army and for America. During battle, he was skilled with the machine gun and served in campaigns in central Europe and then, at the end of the war, in Germany.

After the Allied victory, he returned to America in 1946 and, two years later, went from his home in Phoenix to Tucson, where he applied for papers to go to China. He wanted to find himself a wife and was unlikely to find one in Tucson, Arizona.

While he waited for his papers to arrive, he worked for his brother Paul at a grocery store and made money that would help him on his travels. There was talk that Paul gave $1,500 to Tommy. Their brother Teddy, it was said, had also planned to go to China but when he, too, received a gift of the same sum from Paul, he headed instead for Los Angeles, where he squandered the cash.

On arrival in China, Tommy went to his home to visit relatives. Soon after, he was introduced to my mother, and they were married. China was a country in turmoil, and the young couple who would become my parents swiftly embarked on a departure route. They went first to Hong Kong and from there travelled by ship to America, via the Philippines. Once settled, Tommy continued to work for his brother Paul.

After my birth in May of 1949, he enjoyed – I hope – eight months of fatherhood. Then he suffered a fatal heart attack. He vanished from our lives before I was at an age old enough to form ever-lasting memories. To me, he is a man in a few photographs.

My mother, as I have mentioned in earlier chapters, did not talk of my father. Sometimes when she was cross with me, she would say, 'Your father would never do that.' Or, 'Your father would be ashamed of you.' That did the trick; stopped me misbehaving.

A few months after my mother died, I had the task of wading through the scores of boxes that she had left behind. Mum never threw anything away. Among the dusty documents and yellowed papers, I came across a small book which was limited in contents, but those contents meant the world to me.

The book was my father's passport. 'Height: five foot, six inches … Distinguishing features: mole on chin.' There, on its pages were the stamps he had received at each port of visit, and therefore showed his travels. Now, I knew that my parents had married in China and then returned to the States, but I was unsure of the dates.

By following the dates on the stamps, I knew the movements of my parents. They showed that I was conceived in China. So I was made in China.

As my mother did not discuss the past, I was unaware of my parents' marriage. How close were they to one another? I never knew. I never knew until I was in China and went to see an elderly aunt. She poured me tea, and the subject switched from food to my parents, and then my aunt said something that surprised me. It was like the opening of a gift that had been sitting in front of me for decades. 'You know,' she said, 'your mother and father really loved each other. They were very much in love.'

——

WHAT of my surrogate father, my uncle Paul, my first employer (and no relation to my father)? I had not forgotten him. I will never forget him. Many years after leaving Chicago, I found myself back in the city, promoting a newly published book. The King Wah by then was long gone from my uncle's life, but it remained in the family: it was in the hands of his sister-in-law, who was also running a catering company from the kitchen.

Had Uncle Paul not looked after me, perhaps there would never have been a cookbook to promote, and maybe you would not be reading this now. My debt of gratitude to him was substantial. I paid him a visit at his home. When Uncle Paul greeted me, he was as elegant and dapper as I remembered him, smartly dressed in a pristine suit.

'I want to thank you for everything you did for me,' I said.

'No problem, Ken,' he replied. Short and sweet.

——

Stir-Fried Beef with Tomato and Egg

This is a quick and easy dish, which my mother often made using ingredients that were easily available and relatively inexpensive. Here she employed the inventive Chinese technique of combining seemingly disparate ingredients into a delectable blend.

Although I don't know if the recipe is authentically Chinese, it certainly rests today deep in my taste memory. Mother often waited until I returned from school and then would quickly stir-fry the ingredients together: savoury, rich bits of minced beef (which was the only beef we could afford) with soft, ripe tomatoes pulled together with strands of egg in a sauce that will always remind me of her.

Serves 4

225g (½ lb) minced beef

2 teaspoons light soy sauce

1½ teaspoons Shaoxing rice wine or dry sherry

1 teaspoon sesame oil

1 teaspoon cornflour

🥄

4 beaten eggs

2 teaspoons sesame oil

½ teaspoon salt

🥄

1½ tablespoons groundnut or vegetable oil

2 tablespoons finely chopped garlic

1 tablespoon finely chopped ginger

1 tablespoon coarsely chopped fermented black beans

3 tablespoons finely chopped spring onion

1½ tablespoons light soy sauce

1 tablespoon Shaoxing rice wine or dry sherry

2 teaspoons dark soy sauce

1 teaspoon salt

1 teaspoon sugar

½ teaspoon freshly ground black pepper

¼ cup chicken stock, homemade or store bought

3 medium-sized ripe tomatoes (quartered into wedges)

2 teaspoons sesame oil

Put the meat in a medium-size bowl and mix it thoroughly with the soy sauce, rice wine, sesame oil and cornflour. Set it aside and let it marinate for 15 minutes.

In a small bowl, lightly beat the eggs, then mix in the sesame oil and salt, and set aside.

Heat a wok or large frying pan over a high heat until it is hot. Swirl in the oil and when it is very hot and slightly smoking, quickly toss in the garlic, ginger, black beans and spring onion. Stir-fry this mixture for 30 seconds. Mix in the beef and continue to stir-fry, breaking up the meat, for 2 minutes until it begins to lose its raw look. Pour in the soy sauces, rice wine, salt, sugar and pepper. Give the mixture several good stirs and then pour in the chicken stock.

When the mixture comes to a boil, add the tomatoes. When it starts bubbling vigorously, drizzle in the egg mixture and stir it slowly. Once the egg has set, pour in the sesame oil and give the mixture two more stirs.

Ladle the mixture into a bowl and serve at once. 🥣

30

The Turner Point

THERE IS A karaoke machine in my library in Catus. If you really want to appreciate karaoke – and, come to think of it, saké – go live in Japan like I did. As you have read, I enjoy dancing and mastered my moves as a teenager, grooving away to performances of James Brown and co. at the Cheetah in Chicago. Singing is also a form of relaxation and escapism. Cantonese pop songs do the trick; give them a try.

One of those concerts at the Cheetah was unforgettable. Ike and Tina Turner came to town and let it rip. I danced and sang along to the spell-binding Turners, and their tracks have enlivened many a party at the watchtower of Catus.

My friends in this part of France include Alain Dominique Perrin, one of the great entrepreneurs and the man behind the Richemont Group, which has luxury goods brands such as Cartier, Montblanc, Piaget,

Dunhill and Van Cleef & Arpels. Back in 1980, he acquired Château Lagrézette in Cahors. He spent a decade restoring the château, its gardens and vineyard. In 2005, the wine was recognised by *Wine Spectator* as one of the best 100 wines in the world. It's true, the wine is out of this world. Whenever we meet we always eat and drink well. On one occasion, when the Blairs came for lunch, I invited Alain, and they all became good friends.

Alain had a party to celebrate his sixtieth birthday, a spectacular event which was done with all the style and panache I have come to expect of him. The venue was the Musée National de Monuments Français. One of the great institutions of Paris, it is home to plaster casts of French monuments, as well as paintings and sculptures. There were hundreds of guests in this splendid setting, including former prime ministers, government ministers, actors, pop stars and supermodels. The entire French elite were there. Had the roof collapsed, France would have lost its population of VIPs, as well as the nation's beloved heart-throb Alain Delon.

Alain's team had laid on an outstanding and glorious array of food, and downstairs – for the younger crowd – there was a disco with vodka on tap. Word went round that Tina Turner had arrived at the door and, suspecting a scrum, I headed to the back of the room to avoid the crush as people tried to speak to her. Sure enough, a few moments later I could see a mob and imagined the singer was at the centre of it, and I carried on chatting with friends.

Suddenly, Alain's PA dashed to my side. 'Monsieur Perrin would like you to come and meet Tina.' Well, I followed her and noticed that other guests were giving me the once-over as I got closer to Tina. They were a little envious, and thinking, *Who's he?*

Alain introduced me to Tina and, as we sat down together, I said to her, 'You don't know me but I know you. I saw you in 1966 at the

Cheetah. You were performing there with Ike.' And we hit it off immediately, chatting for ages.

Eventually Alain got a word in edgewise. 'Ken is a great and famous chef,' he said to Tina. 'And he has a house near my château and a grand kitchen. I am sure he would be glad to cook for you.'

I said, 'I would be honoured to cook for you.'

Tina said, 'Really? That would be lovely.'

Alain said, 'I will make it happen.'

True to his word, he arranged the date and I was told to make my way to Le Bourget Airport in Paris, where his private jet would fly us down to Cahors. I had been shopping in Chinatown for my ducks and arrived with bags laden with food. These went into the hold and then, as I boarded the aircraft, there was Tina with her husband. The jet had just whizzed them to Paris from Switzerland.

We all flew down to Cahors, and later met for a feast of Peking duck. Tina is a practising Buddhist; she eats meat but little of it. So I made a few interesting vegetarian dishes.

One of these dishes incorporated bitter melon. To the scientist it is a fruit (its seeds are on the inside). But to the cook – and the Chinese – it is known as a vegetable, and an unusual-looking one at that. It is not to everyone's taste and during my travels of China I discovered that even the Chinese must learn to love it.

With a bumpy pale to dark green skin, it has a slightly bitter quinine flavour that has a cooling effect on the mouth. The greener the melon, the more bitter its taste. Many cooks seek out the milder, yellow-green varieties.

To the cooking of this strangely flavoured vegetable. Cut it in half, remove the seeds, discard the membrane and then – to lessen its bitter taste – either blanch or salt it. It is delicious when stir-fried with chillies or braised with fermented bean curd. 🥄

—

'DARLING,' said Tina in her deep voice. 'That bitter melon is delicious.' Most people like to eat, no matter how famous they are. Tina was a keen cook and knew of bitter melon but was one of those detractors. She became a fan that day.

I had a friend, Thierry, who was Tina's most ardent admirer. When I told him of meeting Tina in Paris, he said, 'If ever you do cook for her, you better invite me.' I invited him. Now, Thierry is a big talker but I sat him next to Tina and, for the entire night, his jaw was on the floor. After a magnificent and special evening, Tina departed, clutching a stack of my books, and Thierry danced around the watchtower, waving his hands in the air, exuberant after meeting and eating with the fantastic Ms Turner.

31

... And the Turning Point

MY MOTHER WAS a very giving person. Even though she did not have much, she gave what she had and she shared and, as you have shared my story, you know this much. Even though she was not religious, she believed in karma. One good deed leads to another.

I looked around at what I had, and it took a while because I had too much. I had reached a stage of life when I wanted and needed to downsize. My greatest pleasure in life is travelling, and not much is required for travelling.

Of course, I am fortunate. I have an apartment in Paris, my watchtower in the south-west of France, and when in London my home is the Dorchester Hotel, a grande dame on Park Lane with views over Hyde Park. I had also bought a home in Thailand, which I still have and where I spend a few months of each year. The homes I would keep. I had worked hard for them. Yet sharing was due.

———

I'LL step away from my own story, to return to my friend Ron Batori.

After the Academy, he had moved into the wine trade of Napa Valley. He was a big success, as you can imagine. But one day, we're talking '92, he had had enough of that, too. He kind of needed a change in life, was tired of California, and of America. Ron said to himself, 'I'm leaving. I'm leaving the wine business for good. I'm selling my cellar and I'm selling my house. I'm leaving.'

That is precisely what he did. He had thousands of bottles of great wine. He sold them. He had a beautiful house in the Napa Valley. That went, too. He just got rid of everything.

He applied for a new job, which he had seen in an ad in the *Wall Street Journal*. It was for a post running a school in Bangkok. He got the job. It was not as he had hoped. He arrived at the school only to discover that it was not well run. There were no funds in the school's accounts and, worse, it was offering degrees that weren't really degrees.

It was all a bit hairy. One time he asked the school accountant, 'Why did you pay this bill instead of that bill?'

The response: 'If I don't pay this bill then death to the accountant.'

Ron said, 'I understand.' He found this very stressful, knowing that false dreams and hopes were being sold by the school. He was about to leave Thailand but … but he happened to have a friend back in the wine business of Napa, and this friend bailed him out. He knew a member of Thailand's royal family, and he said to Ron, 'Why don't you run one of my companies?'

He was referring to a company that was in the business of hotels, property development and architecture. So Ron took over a hotel in Phuket. The Boathouse was nothing too large: thirty-five rooms and empty for most of the year. But it was a beautiful little hotel, and right on the water's edge.

Then Ron said to the company owner, 'I have an idea. Why don't we create a wine club? And why don't we make it the best wine list in Thailand? And then I'll call all of my friends that I have in California – Barbara Hansen from the *Los Angeles Times*, Marian Burros from the *New York Times* – and I'll invite them to come over and stay at The Boathouse.'

There was more. 'We'll do Thai cooking classes, as well,' said Ron, madly ambitious and enthusiastic.

So that's what they did. Well, the next thing you know, they've put together a great wine list. Then Ron started something called the Chao Phraya River Wine Club, which was also going on at another of one of their places in Bangkok. Once a month they held a wine event in Phuket and a wine event in Bangkok. Next thing, the PR kicks in and they start getting masses of publicity. Then they won an award from *Wine Spectator* for the Best Wine List: the first place in Thailand to receive a *Wine Spectator* award.

Before you could say 'Cheers!' to their success, the hotel was full. It was still the same hotel it had always been. Its structure had not altered; its location had not shifted. But now people were flocking in for the great food and the fantastic wine. And where they were drinking beer in every other place, people went to The Boathouse to enjoy the delights of its beautiful cellar.

They were doing wine classes, but they were classes with heaps of fun – eight different bottles, each in a brown paper bag, four of them being Australian Shiraz, four being Côtes du Rhône, let everybody taste them. 'OK, which ones are from the Rhône, which ones are from Oz? Now rate them, which ones do you like the best?' It was like a beauty contest ... for wine.

One night, two women came along to the wine beauty contest. At the end of it, they approached Ron and said, 'We're looking for someone to run a wine company in Thailand. Would you be interested?' Remember, he'd quit the wine business and promised never to return.

He said, 'Yes, I would be interested.' The company was called Seagram, the world's largest distillery, and it was separating its wine sector from its spirits division. He was given the job. When friends asked him why he had taken the job when he had promised never to return, he said, 'Wine just followed me. I had no other way.'

He spent eight years at Seagram, took a year off and then took a job with another company. Now, this new company was really small. Along with his colleagues, Ron built it from scratch, from virtually nothing. Early on, they had a staff of three, with one truck delivering bottles of about ten different wines.

Today, the company, Bangkok Beer and Beverages, imports wines, spirits, coffee, mineral waters and other drinks. It supplies more than 600 labels of wine and has 300 people on the payroll. It is, I understand, the biggest company of its kind in Thailand.

There were a few setbacks, including the global economic crisis and a government campaign which tried to deter Thais from buying foreign goods. But, by 2000, the Thais returned to wine. Ron and the company supply hotels and therefore tourists, but the majority of their customer base is Thai.

Long before all this happened, when Ron was still living in California, he had visited Thailand. That first visit was in 1988, and during the trip Ron strolled out of his hotel one day. The life-changing turning point happened right there and then as he stood on the street. Ron said to himself, 'I want to live here.' He still can't quite figure out why. Could have been the heat, the smell, the feel, or that he was living in a moment of not knowing what to do, where to go.

But everything that he saw was exciting and interesting to him. He wanted to be there, in Thailand. Between that trip and 1992, when he went to run the school, he travelled there twenty-five times, sometimes just for a week or so. These days, Ron doesn't have an enormous credit card bill from flying. He lives there.

———

WELL, now you have heard Ron's story. My own turning point took place when I was in my fifties. I'll tell you what happened. My feelings had been formed in Thailand, where the zen-like attitude is marvellously contagious. I started to turn more to Buddhism, which I had known since childhood, but now it became a larger part of me.

Then, when I was in Catus, I felt that, finally, I had achieved the kind of thing you dream about. In this little French village I had a massive house, an incredible wine cellar, a kitchen to die for and with a monster hob – I'm talking about that Maestro Bonnet range, which can reach a heat high enough to make the crispiest-based pizza. I had reached a stage of thinking, *Hold on here, this is too much.*

I mean, I had a whole floor filled with nothing but my clothes. As a child, I did not have any fancy clothes, so when I had money I bought them, often Versace. I had a vast and glittering collection of watches, some of them rare Rolexes. They were all black, as I figured I should specialise in something, so it was expensive black watches. But is that really what life is all about: acquiring a maximum of material possessions?

Shopping therapy was a bad therapy. You think, *I'll buy something and then I'll be happy*. Once you've bought it, you think, *What am I going to do with this now?*

This does not mean that I decided to abandon all of my possessions and wander around like a Buddha without clothes. I don't believe in that approach, either. But I thought that for my soul it would be good to downsize. I am sixty-seven years old and, if I'm lucky, I have ten or twenty years to live. I would like to spend that time unencumbered by *stuff*.

I gave all my clothes to friends. They were all in impeccable condition – the clothes rather than the friends. I suppose I could have had a charity sale, but I reckon that clothes are personal and I had a lot of good friends who were my size. My friends were delighted. Most of the clothes were practically new; ridiculously, I had worn many of the garments only once or twice. The watches were given away or sold.

———

GONE were the watches and clothes. This left me with the wine cellar. Ron Batori had sparked my interest in wine, back in the Berkeley days when I started as a teacher at the Academy. I took Ron's wine class and loved it. I will never forget that taste of 1947 Cheval Blanc, one of the finest wines that has ever passed my lips.

From then, I started to accumulate wine, and with a specific keenness in Bordeaux. I had quite a cellar, with wines dating back to the 1900s. Nine out of ten bottles were clarets.

Wine excited me, particularly when I came across something that I did not expect and which therefore surprised me. For instance, I bought a jeroboam of Mouton Rothschild from 1993. Well, that's an off-year, and others would have told me not to buy it because it was not a good vintage. I bought it because it was cheap, and when I opened the bottle, its contents were superb. (Perhaps, said my friend Jancis Robinson, because it was in a large format, which could have improved the wine's maturing process.)

Jancis, as I have mentioned, had inadvertently inspired me to sell the wine. This was partly because she advised me to drink local wines, which ruled out Bordeaux. But also there were times when she would go into my cellar, with me at her side, and say, 'You need to drink this, you know, Ken.' I thought, *My God, I won't have time to drink all that.* Then there were times when I opened a bottle, hoping for ecstasy, only to be disappointed.

In 1997, I saw for sale a methuselah – holding the equivalent of eight bottles – of Cristal champagne. It was from the 1990 vintage and had been produced specially to be drunk in 2000, so that it could be popped to celebrate the dawn of a new millennium. A friend advised me to buy it, saying, 'You will never see it at this price again.' Its price was $2,000. I paid the money and thought, *New Year's Eve on the eve of the new millennium is going to be one helluva party.*

Well, when the year 2000 rode around, the party was not to be at my house but at someone else's, and with a lot of people I did not know. So I figured I would save it for another occasion. It was 2006, and that bottle was sitting in the cellar, when I read an article about a wine sale in which that very same vintage of Cristal and same sized bottle had sold for $11,000. That's a neat return on the money.

I sought Jancis's advice, telling her that I wanted to share my wine with others in the world. She gave me two options: there were wine agents who would come to see my cellar and give an evaluation, or I could go to Christie's, the established auction house in London. I preferred the latter option, as I had met a man from Christie's when I helped with a charity fundraiser for Action Against Hunger. I figured, *If I am going to sell it, at least I get something out of it.*

The auction was held at Christie's in December 2006, and amounted to 170 lots of hundreds of wines. They included bottles from the châteaux of Pétrus (1966, '78, '82, '86, '88), Mouton Rothschild ('66, '71, '78, '79, '83), and d'Yquem ('71, '88, '91). There was Latour, which included '66 and '70 as well as the complete and faultless 1955. Lafite and Cheval Blanc featured, too. From that great vintage of 1945, there was Haut-Bailly and Branaire-Ducru. But that's enough numbers and châteaux – you get the picture.

The lots included champagnes, including my methuselah of Louis Roederer Cristal Brut. That big bottle raised six times the sum I had paid for it. The auction did not bring me a fortune considering what I had paid for the wine, but my rationale was this: the money paid for my friends and I to drink exceptional wine for about twenty years – at hardly any cost. I had got my money back.

My tastes in wine have changed. There was a time when I had an intellectual approach to wine. Take a bottle of Pétrus '66. You open it, you worship it, you are in awe of it. The brand name is impressive. Today, my tastes have simplified. Now I like young, robust wines. Maybe I like younger because I am older.

And I seem to recall that I was drinking a sparkling champagne on that very cold night in Catus when I discovered Rio. The wind and rainy snow were hammering on my windows and I yearned for somewhere to warm up those early months at the turn of the century, the beginning of the new millennium.

Cashing in air miles could get me to a sunny place. I imagined the globe, hovered over South America, and then zoomed in on Brazil and Rio de Janeiro, which had long intrigued me. For years I had wanted to take myself to that city beside the Atlantic, birthplace of the samba, with its beaches and enchantingly named Sugarloaf Mountain on Guanabara Bay, and home to a seemingly endless and ludicrously hedonistic carnival. Was the bossa nova the soundtrack to my thoughts on that chilly night? Probably, yes.

The very next morning, I made arrangements, booking into the Copacabana Palace – today Belmond Copacabana Palace – without question one of the finest hotels in the world. Since it opened in 1923, the rich and the famous, Hollywood stars and European royalty have luxuriated in its splendour. Barry Manilow stayed here in the 1970s and, over drinks with lyricist Bruce Sussman, wondered why no one had written a song called 'Copacabana'. So they did (along with fellow lyricist Jack Feldman). 'At the Copa' might grate at times but it can start – as well as end – a good party, and has brought fortunes to Barry and his song-writing duo.

And the song is playing in my mind as I sit here now, beside the pool and under an umbrella, shading myself from the thirty-degree heat of January. Should I wish to swim in the sea, the golden-sanded beach is just across the road. Should I crave a visit to the spa, it is just a few steps away, and it has the most wonderful swimming pool – semi-Olympic-sized – as well.

During my first visit, I was fortunate enough to have Claude Troisgros as my guide. Claude is the son of Pierre Troisgros, one of the founders of nouvelle cuisine. Claude left France for Rio, married a Brazilian, opened a restaurant and set up home here. Then he went to New York for a few years and launched another restaurant, which is where I met him in the mid-1980s. Then he returned to Brazil, where he is to this day, and is now a massively successful restaurateur.

Claude's cuisine is French-based, but he has been able to take ingredients from the Amazon and make them into Brazilian cuisine. He's a fun guy, a big TV star, and he loves the country. 'I cried', he told me one day, 'when Brazil lost the World Cup.' 'I'll take you to all the best restaurants,' he said, 'and I'll show you the real Rio.' By the end of the trip I had fallen in love with the city and its people, and returned as often as possible.

For me, a visit always features a big bowl of feijoada, the Brazilian stew of pig – and I mean all of the pig. I like the snout, the ears and the feet, and the crackling. It is an interesting cuisine, which is Portuguese-inspired but eaten, of course, in a tropical climate. The Brazilians are addicted to sweets and pastry, which I am not. However, there are many savoury Brazilian dishes that I love, such as Bolinho de bacalhau (codfish croquettes), Bolinho de aipim com carne seca (fried manioc – or cassava, as it is often known in the Caribbean – with salt-cured beef croquettes) and traditional Picadinho de copa (Brazilian beef casserole served with white rice, sautéed vegetables, toasted manioc, fried egg and fried breaded banana).

In January 2013, there was a fire in a nightclub disco in southern Brazil. It was a great tragedy and a lot of people were trapped in the club because, it was said, there were no emergency exits. The death toll was devastating. About 240 people lost their lives; hundreds more were badly injured in the blaze.

Shortly afterwards, the Copacabana Palace decided to review its own disco and concluded that it would close it down. What would it replace it with? What would fill the space? 'We're thinking of having a tapas bar,' Andréa Natal, the beautiful, elegant general manager told me.

I had an idea, and said, 'Why don't I put together a concept for you?' My proposal was for a pan-Asian restaurant, similar to Yellow River, a very successful British restaurant group for which I had been a figurehead and consultant. The plan took almost a year to be approved, but then it was full steam ahead. A brigade of the hotel's chefs came to Bangkok for ten days, and that is where I trained them, at Maison Chin, a restaurant I was winding down. I devised the menus and continued to work with the team when they were back in Rio.

We called it MEE. That means 'beauty' in Korean. The restaurant has ninety-two covers as well as a sushi bar, and, in January 2014, I was an extremely happy man when we opened its doors and the first guests came to eat. The sushi bar offers slices of tuna, prawn, squid and salmon, as well as horse mackerel, surf clam and geso. We have dishes of truffled quail egg and cucumber with Japanese plum. There is crispy Hong Kong chicken, and stir-fried prawns with crunchy, sweet walnuts. Tonkatsu onsen tamago is a Japanese dish of pork belly, steamed and deep-fried and served with bok choy and slow-cooked egg. For dessert, perhaps mango ravioli filled with yuzu cream and served with a citrus sorbet.

Instantly, it was a huge success. Indeed, so instant was its success that in March the following year I was in Bangkok, and one of the chefs emailed me to say, 'There's a rumour flying around that we are about to win a Michelin star.'

I emailed back, 'You are joking.' He was not, and a star was won, the first ever by the hotel group, which had changed its name to Belmond. I was shocked by the award because MEE had been open less than a year. It was a morale booster for the kitchen, the restaurant and the hotel.

One night, I wandered into the restaurant and spotted a familiar face.

As the maître d', Carlos Eduardo Costa de Silva, whom all know as Cadu, came over to me, I said, 'Correct me if I'm wrong, but isn't that Kate Moss with her son?'

'It's Kate Moss,' he said, before whizzing away, 'but with her boy-friend, not her son.'

When I met the supermodel and her young companion, I said, 'No selfies, please, Kate.' Whenever I come across the world-famous elite, I like to say to them, 'No selfies, please.' It appeals to my sense of humour. Clearly it appealed to Kate's too, because she laughed. We talked (since you ask) about our mutual friend Sir David Tang, founder of the Shanghai Tang fashion chain and creator of one of my favourite restaurants, China Tang, at the Dorchester in London. Inevitably, we also discussed delicious food and cookery books.

—

IN an interview with the *Sunday Times* in 2006, I happened to mention my collection of food and cookery books. There were 3,000 of them, many of them ancient and from all parts of the world, covering numerous types of cuisine and also wine, and written in a wide range of languages. These books lined the shelves of my library in my house in Catus. They had been collected over decades and, wherever I happened to be in the world, I would buy food or cookery books, thus satisfying my compulsion to *have*.

The books included, by the way, the works of that great food writer Elizabeth David, whom I once had the pleasure of meeting. We were introduced by Jenny Lo, who, in between homes, lived briefly with Ms David. One day Jenny said to me, 'Elizabeth would like to meet you.' Well, I was utterly flattered. Her books were some of the first I had bought in Berkeley, and I was inspired by her words and style. She had been the inspiration for Chez Panisse and its philosophy of cooking.

So I went to see Elizabeth, who, though we didn't know it then, was in the last year or so of her life. I was ushered into her bedroom. She was lying in her bed, beside which she had an ice bucket. In it, there was a bottle of Chablis. 'Will you open it?' she said. I obliged. We drank the wine and chatted away – she liked a gossip, too – and then Jenny knocked on the door, trying to point out to me that we were due to go for dinner. The bottle was finished, and I said to Elizabeth, 'You must be very tired.'

'Nonsense!' she said. 'We're having a grand time.' At that point, her hand swept down to the side of the bed out of my sight and when she brought it back up, it was clutching another bottle of Chablis by the neck. She nodded towards the corkscrew, my cue to do the honours. I emerged from her bedroom euphoric. What a star she was.

Anyway, during the interview with the *Sunday Times* I said that I wanted to do something for Britain. The country has been so generous and loving to me. My intention therefore was to give the books to the British public. I just didn't know how to go about it.

Let's cut now to Oxfordshire, and the home of one Donald Sloan, who is pottering around as he prepares the roast and makes the York- shire pudding. His phone rings. It is a friend, Paul, who says, 'Have you seen the *Sunday Times*?' He hadn't, as he was too busy in the kitchen to find time for reading. After lunch he reads my interview, and sees that I am looking to offload my collection of books to a worthy home. He is excited. Donald, you see, heads up the food and hospitality depart- ment of Oxford Brookes University. It is a world-renowned centre of food studies, highly respected by the hotel and restaurant professions.

Donald was well connected and did not have trouble obtaining my email address. He pinged me an email, saying he would like to discuss my collection of books. I never responded. Actually, I did respond but it was three months later, when I was in London and at the Dorchester. I wrote, 'Dear Don, I am in London. Do you fancy lunch tomorrow?' Don dropped everything and the very next day we met in the grand lobby of the Dorchester, and then we ambled around the corner for lunch at Nobu. Indeed, the ever globe-trotting Nobu was in the restaurant – doing a photo shoot rather than eating – and he came over to say hello and have a drink with us. I have known him for years and he's fun company.

The day was also memorable for me, as I got to hear Don's story over good food and a glass, or two, of wine. Don had watched my programmes in the '80s, growing up in a suburb of Glasgow. His father was an academic, often playing host to intellectual visitors from around the world. 'The house was filled with noise, music and food,' Don recalled. 'And it was very normal to be mixing with people from different parts of the world, which was unusual in a suburb of Glasgow in the 1970s.'

Food to young Don was nothing more than an amateur interest, but when he failed to get into the University of St Andrews to read philosophy, he thought he'd have to do something else. So he went instead to Strathclyde University, where he learnt about food and hospitality. Others thought he was mad to take such a course, such was the negative view of the industry in those days. But Don said to me, 'It was the best decision I ever made because it has brought so many opportunities.' Our lunch was one of those opportunities.

After university, Don took a job at an events company. 'I did four days and then realised I had made a terrible mistake. I said to my boss that I was popping out for lunch. I went to the pub, got drunk and never went back.'

He worked at a restaurant in Chiswick, south London, which he enjoyed. Then he took an interesting job, working on a large, funded project that was documenting the market potential for local and seasonal products. That was in 1992, when it was odd to boast that products were British or local. 'My job was to speak to large-scale retailers, to try to find out if there might be a market for seasonal Scottish products.

And there wasn't. They were saying, "What are you talking about? We've built up a huge infrastructure. There's no space for berries from Perthshire."' Supermarkets and food manufacturers were not fussed about local and seasonal. Don's work contributed to a report launched by the agricultural minister of the day.

This job exposed him to the role that food played in society and, after a teaching post in Scotland, he went to Oxford Brookes. He arrived there about twenty years ago, telling himself, 'I'll stay a year or two.' Thank God he stayed longer.

As our grand lunch drew to a close, I was delighted to tell my new friend Don that I would donate my books to Brookes. Jane Grigson had given her collection of books to the university. Pru Leith was about to do the same. I was happy to join the club.

My books, much-cherished over the years (and, in some cases, centuries), would be going to a good home. Donald sent a team to collect the books and when they arrived on my doorstep in Catus, I said to them, 'You've had a long drive. Before you start packing, sit down and I'll cook you a nice lunch.'

The books – for so long my research material – have since been catalogued and fill a large part of the library at Oxford Brookes. Importantly, they are available to the public, and that was the mission.

Often, I go to Oxford to meet and chat with the students. My relationship with Brookes has blossomed. Shortly after handing over my books, the university launched an annual event, the Ken Hom Lecture, at which interesting people come and speak to the students.

Chris Patten gave the inaugural lecture, and Cherie Blair did another one. Jancis Robinson, the famous wine critic, and her husband Nick Lander, the respected restaurant critic, did a duo act one year. Sir David Tang, friend of Ms Moss and me, was as popular as he was controversial.

Sheila Dillon, presenter of *The Food Programme* on Radio 4, was also a speaker, and she arrived dressed flamboyantly in a ballgown. Part of her speech was about Fanny Cradock; hence the ostentatious attire. However, the reference to Fanny did not come until way into Sheila's speech, by which time many members of the audience were confused, thinking, *Perhaps she reckons it's a special occasion.*

So I have divested myself of many possessions and can focus, not on material things, but on the pleasures of cooking and eating and travelling. We all come into this world with nothing – and guess what! – we shall all leave with nothing.

———

LUNCH, in the meantime, can still be enjoyed every day. Which reminds me: I have been back to Nobu with Don. A couple of times, it just so happens. On one of those occasions, as we sat and chopsticked our way through most of the dishes on the menu, another guest in the restaurant – an exquisitely dressed, middle-aged woman – came up to our table. She said, 'Excuse me, I do hope I'm not interrupting.'

'Not at all,' I told her, as she was not.

'I cannot tell you how thrilled I am to meet you,' she said. I was deeply moved, and thanked her. We chatted for a minute or so. Then she bowed her head slightly, put her hands together in praying mode, with palms touching, and added, 'It has been an honour to be in your company. Thank you.' How unbelievably sweet! We shook hands before she turned and went back to her table. Don and I raised our glasses to toast the happy encounter.

Then we heard her say to the others at her table, 'Can you believe that? I've just met the Dalai Lama.'

Acknowledgements

T
HIS BOOK WOULD have never happened if it was not for the perseverance of my good friend and collaborator James Steen. He thought it was a good story about food and wine that was worth telling. We had a wonderful time working on the book together and we drank lots of Chablis. I am eternally grateful for his work on the book and his friendship.

I am, of course, thankful to everyone who appears in the book but there is also a long list of people whose names have not appeared but to whom I owe a great debt as well: Daniel Taurines, Roberto Ceriani, Carol Pogash, Gordon Wing, Heather Holden-Brown, Viv Bowler, Jacques Pépin, Gerry Cavanaugh, Florence Fabricant, Annette Grant, Kendall Oei and Grace Fung, Sian Griffiths, Carole Klein, Lynn Grebstad, my family in Chicago: Joyce, Paul and Betty; Jake Oliver, Claude and Dany Taillardas, Babé Pébeyre, Jacques et Monique Pébeyre, Juliet Pickering, Julian Friedmann and Carole Blake, Jancis Robinson and Nick Lander, Puvadol Saengvichien, Alain-Dominque Perrin, Alain Ducasse, Ann Bramson, Martha Casselman, Barbara Fairchild, Kurt and

Penny Wachtveitl, Denise and Jean-Pierre Moullé, Pierre Hermé and Claude Troisgros.

A huge thank you as well to Jeremy Robson, who decided to publish the book, and to Olivia Beattie, our editor, and to Namkwan Cho and Adrian McLaughlin, who designed the book. I am also extremely grateful to Victoria Gilder, the Robson Press's publicity director.

And how would I have lived without the lovely Luisa Welch, who connects me to everyone and the world! She does it so efficiently and with such class.

I am also indebted to the team in the library and archive at Oxford Brookes University: Daniel Croft, Eleanor Possart, Lisa Hill and Jodi Wilkinson.

There are literally many hundreds of others whose support I am most grateful for over more than four decades of my career. I apologise if I have neglected them on this list but they have my sincere gratitude.

Ken Hom, OBE
Paris, France

Index

Recipes